D0953230

VOICE OF DELIVERANCE

VOICE OF DELIVERANCE

The Language of
Martin Luther King, Jr.
and Its Sources

Keith D. Miller

THE FREE PRESS
A Division of Macmillan, Inc. · *New York*

MAXWELL MACMILLAN CANADA
Toronto

MAXWELL MACMILLAN INTERNATIONAL
New York · *Oxford* · *Singapore* · *Sydney*

The Free Press
A Division of Macmillan, Inc.
866 Third Avenue, New York, N.Y. 10022

Maxwell Macmillan Canada, Inc.
1200 Eglinton Avenue East
Suite 200
Don Mills, Ontario M3C 3N1

Macmillan, Inc. is part of the Maxwell Communication
Group of Companies.

Printed in the United States of America

Designed by REM Studio, Inc.

Frontispiece © Ivan Massar/Black Star

printing number
10   9   8   7   6   5   4   3   2   1

Library of Congress Cataloging-in-Publication-Data

Miller, Keith D.
    Voice of deliverance : the language of Martin Luther King, Jr.,
and its sources / Keith D. Miller.
        p.   cm.
    Includes bibliographical references and index.
    ISBN 0-02-921521-8
    1. King, Martin Luther, Jr., 1929–1968—Oratory.   I. Title.
E185.97.K5M49 1992   91–31277
323'.092—dc20   CIP

The author gratefully acknowledges those who have granted permission to reprint material in this book, specifically:

Passages from "Non-Violence and the Law: The Law Needs Help" by Harris Wofford. *Journal of Religious Thought*, Vol. 15, Autumn-Winter 1957–58. Copyright 1957 by the *Journal of Religious Thought*. Reprinted by permission of the *Journal of Religious Thought*.

Passages from *Horns and Halos in Human Nature* by J. Wallace Hamilton. Copyright 1954 by Fleming Revell. Reprinted by permission of Mrs. J. Wallace (Florence) Hamilton.

Passages from *Ride the Wild Horses!* by J. Wallace Hamilton. Copyright 1952 by Fleming Revell. Reprinted by permission of Mrs. J. Wallace (Florence) Hamilton.

Passages from *The Hope of the World* by Harry Emerson Fosdick. Copyright 1933 by Harper and Brothers, renewed 1951 by Harry Emerson Fosdick. Reprinted by permission of HarperCollins Publishers.

Passages from a letter from Harold Fey to Martin Luther King, Jr. Reprinted by permission of The Christian Century Foundation.

A passage from "Moses at the Red Sea" by C.L. Franklin in *Give Me This Mountain: Life History and Selected Sermons*, edited by Jeff Todd Titon. Copyright 1989 by the Board of Trustees of the University of Illinois. Reprinted by permission of Erma Franklin.

Passages from the recording *Never Grow Old* by C.L. Franklin. Copyright 1984 by Chess Records. Reprinted by permission of Erma Franklin.

A passage from the recording *Nothing Shall Separate Me from the Love of God* by C.L. Franklin (Chess Ch 9154). Copyright by Chess Records. Copyright date unavailable. Reprinted by permission of Erma Franklin.

Passages from "Drum Major Instinct," "Pilgrimage to Nonviolence," "Where Do We Go from Here?," "I Have a Dream," "[How Long?]," and "[I've Been to the Mountaintop]" by Martin Luther King, Jr., in *A Testament of Hope*, edited by James Washington. Copyright © 1986 by Coretta Scott King, Executrix of the Estate of Martin Luther King, Jr. Reprinted by permission of the Joan Daves Agency.

Passages from *Stride Toward Freedom* by Martin Luther King, Jr. Copyright 1958 by Harper and Row. Reprinted by permission of the Joan Daves Agency.

Passages from *Strength to Love* by Martin Luther King, Jr. Copyright 1963 by Harper and Row. Reprinted by permission of the Joan Daves Agency.

Passages from "Prodigal Son" by Martin Luther King, Jr. Copyright 1966 by Martin Luther King, Jr. Reprinted by permission of the Joan Daves Agency.

Passages from the recording *In Search of Freedom* by Martin Luther King, Jr. (Mercury Records, SR 1170). Copyright by Mercury Records. Copyright date unavailable. Reprinted by permission of the Joan Daves Agency.

Passages from the recording *Remaining Awake Through a Great Revolution* by Martin Luther King, Jr. (Creed 3024). Copyright by Creed Records. Copyright date unavailable. Reprinted by permission of the Joan Daves Agency.

Passages from "Letter from Birmingham Jail" in *Why We Can't Wait* by Martin Luther King, Jr. Copyright 1963 by Harper and Row. Reprinted by permission of the Joan Daves Agency.

Dedicated to Ernest Miller,

    Doris Miller,

    Joyce Nettles,

    and the memory of Tom Shaw

CONTENTS

Philosophy is easily simulated. Eloquence is not.

—QUINTILIAN, FIRST CENTURY A.D.

VOICE OF DELIVERANCE

INTRODUCTION

On the first Sunday in February 1968, the fairly small, red brick church on Auburn Avenue looked as ordinary and unassuming as usual. The modest sanctuary was filled with long, smooth, well-varnished pews facing an altar and a choir. Above and behind the choir was the most striking feature of the building—a small, round, stained glass window portraying Christ in the Garden of Gethsemane. When the choir finished belting out the anthem, a preacher stepped into the pulpit wearing his best black robe.

Members of this Atlanta congregation recognized his face instantly, for he looked unmistakably like his father, who had pastored Ebenezer Baptist Church for thirty-seven years. Besides that, they had known M.L. throughout his entire life. He first came to the church while still a baby in his mother's arms. Along with his brother A.D., he attended the Rising Sons class, a Sunday School program for second and third grade boys that was taught by Rev. J.H. Edwards, a postal worker and occasional preacher.[1] Churchgoers remembered that, as a child, M.L. loved to sing "I Want to Be

More and More Like Jesus."[2] Years later Edwards and five other clergy examined and ordained him for the ministry.[3] Everyone in the church had closely followed his career ever since, and they knew they had to arrive early any time M.L. was preaching. He always drew a large crowd.

People came because, while M.L. would always be M.L., he was also Martin Luther King, Jr., a man whose face was instantly recognizable not only at Ebenezer Church, but around the world.

King began his sermon as usual: by calmly stating his title, "Drum Major Instinct," and citing his scriptural text. As was his habit when speaking in African-American churches, he began so slowly, so deliberately that he seemed bored. Then he did what he always did when addressing black listeners: he gradually modulated his rich, baritone voice, picking up speed and emphasis as his hypnotic phrases fell into rolling cadences punctuated by an occasional "Amen!" from his audience. Slowly, the rhythmical baritone grew louder and louder until it reached a thunderous roar when, in the name of God, he condemned the nuclear arms race. The voice swung instantly, dramatically to a whisper before rising quickly in an equal crescendo to denounce American war-making in Vietnam. He ended the sermon by summing up his life and telling his unnamed eulogist what to say at his funeral.

The sermon was thoughtful but strange. Though King was in good health and was only thirty-nine years old, he was talking about his own death and seemed to preach his own eulogy.

Exactly two months later he was assassinated in Memphis. When the funeral occurred at Ebenezer Church, somewhere between sixty and one hundred thousand people tried to elbow their way inside.[4] Initially blocked by the immense crowd, King's father and mother, Martin Luther King, Sr., and Alberta Williams King, could barely navigate their way into the church. The crowd also stymied Rev. Edwards, his wife Susie, and other church loyalists. During the 1920s the Edwards couple relished the sermons of A.D. Williams, who then presided over Ebenezer Church. They knew Williams's daughter, Alberta, back when she and King, Sr., were still courting. And they devoted many evenings and weekends to serving on essential church committees. But on this day, unable to fight their way into their beloved church, they gave up and drove home. Edwards missed the funeral of the best third grade pupil in the Rising Sons class.[5]

Many of the nation's leading celebrities and politicians, however, managed to squeeze through the small doors of the church.
Some of them—including Richard Nixon—had never supported
King. But other Americans truly cared: on television an estimated
one hundred twenty million people watched the pomp and ceremony.[6]

Because the conclusion of King's "Drum Major Instinct"
seemed tragically appropriate, his family now played a tape of his
instructions to his eulogist. The nation could join the Ebenezer
congregation in hearing how he wished to be remembered: as
someone who tried to subordinate his innately selfish desire, his
"drum major instinct," to a stronger wish to serve humanity.

Students of King have never understood this eulogy or the
magnificent sermon that it concludes. They have failed because no
one has noticed a popular preacher in Florida named J. Wallace
Hamilton. In 1949 Hamilton delivered a sermon called "Drum-
Major Instincts," which his church printed that year and which he
revised for national publication three years later.[7] Although King
did not acknowledge his source and never publicly mentioned
Hamilton's name, he borrowed most of "Drum Major Instinct"
from Hamilton.

Hamilton focuses on the last verses of Mark 10, which tell of
James's and John's request to sit near Jesus in His glory. King bases
his sermon on the same text.[8] Hamilton and King interpret the
request as selfish and attribute the selfishness to a universal desire
to feel important, to be a drum major at the head of a parade. Both
preachers organize their sermons around the powerful—albeit
mixed—metaphor of the drum major instinct. Both recall Alfred
Adler's postulate that the longing for recognition serves as the
strongest impulse of human personality. King's account of this
desire mirrors Hamilton's:

HAMILTON: We begin early to ask life to put us first. Our first cry as a baby
    was a bid for attention. . . . All through childhood the drum-major
    instinct is a major obsession; unashamedly, children ask life to grant
    them first place; they are little bundles of ego. . . .[9]
        In adult life we still have it; we never quite grow out of it. . . . We
    like to do something good, and we like to be praised for it. . . . The
    warm glow we feel when we hear ourselves applauded, when we see
    our names in print, is vitamin A to our ego. Praise has never made

anybody unhappy; we like it even when we know we don't deserve it. We like it when we don't believe it and . . . we dislike it only when we hear it bestowed too much on others.[10]

KING: And you know we begin early to ask life to put us first. Our first cry as a baby was a bid for attention. And all through childhood the drum major impulse or instinct is a major obsession. Children ask life to grant them first place. They are a little bundle of ego. . . . Now in adult life, we still have it, and we really never get by it. We like to do something good. And you know we like to be praised for it. . . . And somehow this warm glow we feel when we are praised, or when our name is in print, is something of the vitamin A to our ego. Nobody is unhappy when they are praised, even if they know they don't deserve it, and even if they don't believe it. The only unhappy people about praise is when praise is going too much toward somebody else.[11]

King also repeats Hamilton's notion that the quest for attention pushes people to join too many groups and to succumb to the glibness of advertisers.[12] Like Hamilton, King views racism as a result of the selfish desire for superiority.[13] Like Hamilton, he observes the same egocentrism in world affairs. Whereas Hamilton detects the impulse in Mussolini, King observes it in the nuclear arms race, the "bitter, colossal contest for supremacy" that threatens worldwide conflagration.[14] King argues that, like individuals, ". . . nations are caught up with the drum major instinct." Updating Hamilton, King cites the United States as a chief offender for its "senseless, unjust war" in Vietnam.[15] Quietly merging his voice with the Psalmist, King reports God's ability to stop war by commanding, "Be still and know that I'm God."[16]

Echoing Hamilton, King returns to the Gospel of Mark by examining Jesus's response to the request of James and John.[17] Instead of rebuking his followers, Jesus urges them to be first in goodness and morality; or, as King restates Jesus's principle, ". . . he who is greatest among you shall be your servant."[18] King reinforces this notion by explaining, ". . . everybody can be great because everybody can serve."[19] Describing Jesus, King spotlights his lowly origins and lack of worldly accomplishments. Extending for three paragraphs, this account corresponds to a quotation in a work by Harold Bosley:[20]

BOSLEY: Here is a man who was born in an obscure village, the child of a peasant woman. He grew up in another obscure village. He worked in a carpenter shop until He was thirty, and then for three years He was an itinerant preacher. He never wrote a book. He never held an office. He never owned a home. He never traveled two hundred miles from the place where He was born. He had no credentials but Himself.[21]

KING: He was born in an obscure village, the child of a poor peasant woman. And then he grew up in still another obscure village, where he worked as a carpenter until he was thirty years old. Then for three years . . . he was an itinerant preacher. . . . He never wrote a book. He never held an office. . . . He never owned a house. . . . He never went two hundred miles from where he was born. . . . He had no credentials but himself.[22]

Again King fails to acknowledge his source.

He concludes his sermon by elaborating, embroidering, and personalizing Hamilton's metaphor of the drum major. King tells his eulogist not to rattle off his glittering triumphs, which one would certainly expect to hear at a funeral for a Nobel Peace Prize winner. Instead, wanting someone to note his attempt to be a servant, he seamlessly incorporates a command from Jesus, urging his eulogist to apply Jesus's words to him:

I want you to be able to say that day
    That I did try to feed the hungry.
I want you to be able to say that day
    That I did try . . . to clothe those who were naked.
I want you to say on that day
    That I did try . . . to visit those who were in prison.[23]

King also weaves into his closing the first verse, third verse, and chorus of "If I Can Help Somebody," a popular gospel song by Alma Androzzo.[24]

Although most of "Drum Major Instinct" comes from Hamilton's text, virtually every sentence of King's sermon embodies a system of knowledge and persuasion created by generations of black folk preachers, including his father and grandfather. This system of voice merging enabled King to borrow sermons and skillfully intertwine his language and his identity with those of his sources.

Here King's voice merging involves a process of self-subordination that seems to enact the theme of self-effacement and servanthood that Jesus proclaims. By orchestrating the words of Hamilton, Bosley, the Psalmist, Jesus, and a gospel song, King subordinates himself to the religious language sanctified by Protestant communities. Black preachers, of course, had practiced a similar kind of self-subordination for many generations in their humble and often anonymous sermonizing. They paradoxically subordinated themselves to established religious language in order to create expansive and recognizable personas. Synthesizing the words of his sources, King generated a similarly humble self when he proclaimed "Drum Major Instinct."

For King, this process was not unusual. In literally scores of previous sermons, he borrowed extensively and without acknowledgment from the sermons of Hamilton and other preachers.

In addition to his sermons, King's speeches, essays, and books incorporate material from unacknowledged sources. For example, his "Nobel Prize Lecture" includes several passages from Hamilton.[25] One of them offers an analogy about Ulysses and Orpheus; another describes in detail how nations can eliminate world hunger.[26] Yet another relates Hamilton's extended metaphor of a world house. Compare:

HAMILTON: I read somewhere that after a famous novelist died, they found among his papers a list of suggested story plots, ideas for possible future stories, of which he had underscored this one: "A widely separated family inherits a house in which they have to live together." Too bad that someone can't write a story on that, and tell us how to do it, for it is the great new problem of mankind! We have inherited a house, a great "world-house" in which we have to live together—Gentiles and Jews, black and whites, strong and weak, a family widely separated in ideas, culture, interests—who, because we can never again live without each other, must learn, somehow, in one world, to live together.[27]

KING: Some years ago a famous novelist died. Among his papers was found a list of suggested story plots for future stories, the most prominently underscored being this one: "A widely separated family inherits a house in which they have to live together." This is the great new problem of mankind. We have inherited a big house, a world house in which we have to live together—black and white, Easterners and Westerners, Gentiles and Jews, Catholics and Protestants, Moslem and Hindu—a family unduly separated in ideas, culture, and interests who, because we can never again live without each other must learn somehow in this one big world to live with each other.[28]

Far from being peripheral, Hamilton's ideas and phrases are pivotal to King's "Nobel Prize Lecture."

Yet, despite the enormous importance of Hamilton and other preachers to King, no articles, columns, essays, dissertations, and books about King mention Hamilton, Bosley, or other preachers whose sermons King borrowed throughout his entire public career. The King literature also fails to note the origins of the folk pulpit during slavery and says little about how that pulpit nurtured him throughout his entire life.

Instead, many scholars focus on King's years in white graduate schools, where he read prestigious European philosophers— notably Plato, Spinoza, Kant, Locke, Nietzsche, Hegel, and Marx— and distinguished American theologians—especially Walter Rauschenbusch, Reinhold Niebuhr, and Paul Tillich. Researchers make the well-entrenched claim that King's ideas stemmed from his reading of Euro-American thinkers enshrined by the academy.[29] One scholar, who seems to speak for many, claims that for King the distance between his hometown and Boston University was "measurable in intellectual light years."[30]

But, as others suggest, King's magnificent rhetorical triumphs do *not* reflect his tutelage from white professors.[31] *Nor* does his persuasiveness result from his study of any of the Great White Thinkers whose works he examined in graduate school. Instead, King succeeded largely because he resisted numerous ideas proffered by his professors and the Great White Thinkers and instead drew on two powerful and popular rhetorical traditions. The first is a veritable torrent of sermons delivered and published by Harry Emerson Fosdick, Hamilton, Bosley, and other prominent (and mainly white) preachers. The second, underlying, and more significant influence was the black folk pulpit of King's grandfather, father, Rev. Edwards, and several generations of anonymous, often illiterate folk preachers. Although slave religion and the folk pulpit have been systematically patronized, distorted, obscured, scorned, ignored, and dismissed by many King scholars and most other students of religion, these decidedly humble black traditions served as King's major rhetorical and intellectual resources. Providing the means of shaping King's magnificent oratory, black folk Christianity contributed in a singular way to changes wrought by the 1960s struggle for racial justice.

There are several reasons for the failure of journalists, biographers, and the public to understand how King's language worked. Researchers have mistakenly taken at face value King's own account of his ideas and language. They ignore his sources because he failed to acknowledge his borrowing and rarely spoke of preaching traditions, white or black. Instead, in his youthful essay "Pilgrimage to Nonviolence," he claimed that his intellectual development resulted primarily from reading accomplished philosophers and theologians. Scholars have failed to notice that King borrowed large segments of this essay from less prestigious writers whose names he did not mention. In fact, he used borrowed passages to explain what he claimed to have learned from famous philosophers.

Another reason for our unfamiliarity with King's sources is the inherent difficulty in examining folk sermons from past decades. The pulpit orations of King's grandfather are unavailable for study, as are almost all the sermons of his father and most other folk homilists. Indeed only a small handful of black folk sermons have ever appeared in print. Though commercial records of famous folk sermons sold briskly in years past, these albums are now very difficult to locate.[32] Moreover, only a few people have ever seriously attempted to study the folk pulpit. Their studies are often patronizing or otherwise flawed.[33] In short, scholars' lack of knowledge about folk preaching repeats and reflects our culture's general indifference to—and sometimes disdain for—African-American folk religion.

As for Fosdick, Hamilton, and other white preachers important to King, our cultural amnesia has dissolved them from memory. Though their sermons were broadcast over both local and coast-to-coast radio pulpits and collected in literally hundreds of popular volumes, most Americans either have never known or have entirely forgotten these preachers. The niche their sermons occupied has now been filled by self-help books. Instead of seeking divine guidance, Americans now want secular wizards to inform them about proper diet, exercise, sex, and well-being.[34] Though college students continue to scrutinize texts by famous theologians, only a dwindling number of ministers and seminarians still open the pages of dusty sermons.

Moreover, though we usually make the false equation between creativity and complete originality, King never did. Like folk preachers who preceded him, he expertly blended others' voices with his own; in his public discourse, no matter how much he borrowed, he invariably sounded exactly like himself. And he seemed—and was—absolutely sincere. People have overlooked King's borrowing mainly because his training in the folk pulpit enabled him to borrow in an incredibly skillful, unselfconscious way.

King negotiated between the universe of black folk culture contained within the sanctuary of Ebenezer Church and the universe of print exemplified by libraries, bookstores, and publishers. Not only was this negotiation important to King, it was absolutely crucial to the triumph of the civil rights movement.

While in hindsight we consider King's status as *the* civil rights leader to be "natural," something we take for granted, many civil rights activists did not. Most protestors belonged to other organizations—the NAACP, and, especially, the Congress of Racial Equality (CORE) and the Student Nonviolent Coordinating Committee (SNCC)—not to King's numerically smaller Southern Christian Leadership Conference (SCLC). As president of the NAACP, Roy Wilkins considered himself—not King—the "natural" leader of black America and bristled at suggestions to the contrary. Wilkins was plainly chagrined by King's ascendency and jealous of his fame. Along with other members of the NAACP hierarchy, Wilkins believed that legal efforts and lobbying by the NAACP— not King's mass marches and civil disobedience—would achieve integration. For that reason, he and other NAACP officials regarded their work as far more important than King's protests, which they privately castigated as media shows.[35]

While grassroots SNCC activists were far more militant than Wilkins, many of them also resented the attention that King received, sometimes mocking him as "De Lawd." They reasoned that, although SNCC and CORE did most of the work of registering voters and organizing sit-ins, King wrongly received most of the credit. For their own efforts, they were rewarded with shootings and beatings that journalists, the FBI, and the Kennedys frequently ignored.

King's unique status was not self-evident to many who breathed the movement, slept the movement, suffered the movement, and sometimes died the movement. He was a minister, but so were many other agitators, including most of his lieutenants. He mastered Gandhian nonviolence; but so did dozens of others, including James Farmer more than a decade earlier. He volunteered for jail duty, but so did Farmer and hundreds of others. He headed a major political organization, but so did Farmer, Wilkins, John Lewis, and James Forman. He choreographed dramatic confrontations with Southern sheriffs, but so did Farmer, Lewis, Hosea Williams, and others. He exhibited statesmanlike abilities to listen, deflect hostile criticism, and lead despite deadly opposition; but so did Farmer, Lewis, Diane Nash, Fannie Lou Hamer, and many others.[36] He proved an expert political strategist and organizer, but so did Farmer, Lewis, Nash, Ella Baker, Bayard Rustin, and many others. He risked his life, but so did Farmer, Medgar Evers, James Meredith, and literally hundreds of others. He survived attempted assassination, but so did Farmer, Meredith, all the Freedom Riders, and others. He was martyred for the cause of black rights, but so were Evers, Malcolm X, and many more. Serving as a minister, practicing nonviolence, and dying for a cause are all admirable and uncommon qualities. But *none* of these qualities alone or in combination made King unique, for he shared them with Farmer and their colleagues.

However, unlike them, King became a media magnet and a superstar. His crusades in Birmingham and Selma attracted international acclaim while the media yawned in unison when, between those campaigns, Farmer and CORE staged a strikingly similar protest in Louisiana.[37] Together, dozens of journalists and the public bestowed on King a spiritually resonant, almost magical name that was not the name on his birth certificate. In the eyes of the press and most of America, King emerged as a uniquely powerful leader. But how did this process occur? What made King a superstar?

The answer to this question can be stated in a single word: language. King's unmatched words galvanized blacks and changed the minds of moderate and uncommitted whites. Others could embrace nonviolence, get arrested, and accept martyrdom. But only King could convince middle-of-the-road whites about the meaning of the revolutionary events they were witnessing on their television screens. His persuasiveness did more than surpass that of his colleagues. It enabled him to accomplish what Frederick Douglass, Sojourner Truth, W.E.B. DuBois, and his own models and mentors had failed to achieve. By persuading whites to accept the principle of racial equality, he made a monumental contribution to solving the nation's most horrific problem—racial injustice.

King did so by translating the message of the folk pulpit into the idiom of Hamilton and Fosdick—an idiom most suited to persuade white listeners. As Ralph Abernathy's widow, Juanita Abernathy, observes, ". . . religious principles are instilled in you early." She emphasizes the importance of King's training in the black church, insisting

> You can't just say that one person did it. There's no such thing. Totally impossible. . . . For Martin Luther King to be the Martin Luther King he was, there had to be a whole lot of little folk, a whole lot of unsung heroes . . . to give him the impetus, to give him the stamina. And they made their contributions. They were just not heard as loudly.[38]

These people included black preachers whom King heard as a young man, including L.M. Tobin and William Holmes Borders, who "laid the groundwork" for the freedom struggle. Also contributing were King's father and grandfather, who preached a gospel of redemption similar to the "progressive and social gospel" that Mrs. Abernathy heard as a child in rural Alabama.[39]

Although some stress the emotional nature of folk preaching, it actually offered far, far more than vocal pyrotechnics and formulaic phrases. To understand King, one must explore folk homilists' rich and expansive cosmos, their highly imaginative system of knowledge, and their enduring theme of hope. Folk preachers' sturdy and compelling worldview underlies both King's language and the "street rhetoric" of his protests, marches, and arrests.

Kept alive in the folk pulpit, the same religion that equipped slaves to withstand whips, auction blocks, and bloodhounds swayed a nation to accept the precept of racial equality. By informing and undergirding King's language, slave religion helped set aside the greatest burden this nation had ever shouldered—the burden of racial injustice. Generations of anonymous, often illiterate slaves and folk preachers deserve credit for their worldview and their message, which King brought to consummate expression in "Drum Major Instinct" and many other sermons and speeches.

If we comprehend King's use of black and white homiletics, we can begin to understand how his language worked. We can begin to see why liberal Northern Protestants opened their wallets for his cause. We can start to grasp his amazing power to move previously apathetic white audiences. Then we can analyze how social change —not simply social protest, but social change itself—actually occurs.

We can do so by examining King's distinctive ability to synthesize two sermonic traditions and use them to propel and interpret a vast social upheaval. More than any other ability of any other person, this specific talent helped foster the permanent, sublime achievements of the civil rights movement. Instead of mistakenly crediting renowned philosophers and theologians, we should finally recognize those who actually fueled King's incandescent oratory. We need to notice and applaud each of these people—especially the preachers and churchgoers in and around the red brick walls of Ebenezer Church. It is time to give credit where credit is due.[40]

ONE

EXODUS

I n May 1956 Martin Luther King, Jr., stepped into the pulpit of the Cathedral of St. John the Divine. From one end of the spacious, vaulted nave, King gazed at members of this white congregation who had crowded into their large Gothic building. He also scanned the faces of blacks who had come from Harlem to hear a newly prominent African-American leader. Undoubtedly he expected a friendly reception, for the New York cathedral served as a bastion of Episcopalian liberalism.

For their part, churchgoers wondered about this twenty-seven year old preacher with an eloquence reportedly far beyond his years. They sympathized with his leadership of a six-month old bus boycott in Montgomery, Alabama—an effort to turn Christian love into a nonviolent political campaign. To many he must have seemed an appropriate choice as the guest preacher for a service celebrating the second anniversary of the landmark Supreme Court decision to end segregation in American schools. But at least a few others must have wondered whether the pastor of the church, Rev. James Pike, should have invited a preacher recently convicted of violating an antiboycott law.

While listeners perused their bulletins for the title of the sermon, "Death of Evil on the Seashore," King began by reciting Exodus 14:30 ("And Israel saw the Egyptians dead upon the seashore"). He reflected on the harshness and frequency of evil and mentioned the New Testament image of tares interfering with the growth of wheat. Surveying major world religions, he weighed their various attempts to interpret the strife between good and evil—the major drama of human existence. Next he asserted the Christian view of the final victory of goodness and quoted declarations by William Cullen Bryant ("Truth crushed to earth will rise again") and Thomas Carlyle ("No lie can live forever").

After this introduction, King recalled the noble adventure of the Exodus. He recounted the dehumanizing slavery inflicted upon the Hebrews and sketched their dramatic, providential escape from the cruel Egyptians. Following the Israelites' miraculous passage through the Red Sea, the Egyptian army drowned as it attempted to recapture the Chosen People. This event, he argued, illustrates the underlying goodness of the universe—a point he underscored through a glowing affirmation of James Russell Lowell—

> Truth forever on the scaffold, Wrong forever on the
>   throne,—
> Yet that scaffold sways the future, and, behind the
>   dim unknown,
> Standeth God within the shadow keeping watch above
>   His own.

King then interpreted the overthrow of European imperialism as a series of events recapitulating the Exodus. He explained the Exodus as nothing less than God's repeating liberatory act, an archetypal event spiralling through history. During this century God has continually recycled the drama of the Exodus—in India, Pakistan, China, Indonesia, and Africa. Throughout Asia and Africa, he noted, oppressed people "won their freedom from the Egypt of colonialism." They can now "move toward the promised land." The Exodus also recurs in the lives of American blacks, who experienced an American "Egypt of segregation" until exactly two years earlier when the Supreme Court divided the Red Sea in the case of *Brown v. Topeka.*

King closed by merging his own half-sentence with a half-sentence and a repeated exclamation from Handel's *Messiah:* ". . . the kingdoms of this world shall become the kingdoms of our Lord and His Christ, and He shall reign forever and ever. Hallelujah! Hallelujah!"[1]

The sermon King rang off the stony walls of the cathedral served as a harbinger of literally thousands of addresses to come. Through his explication of Biblical Exodus and contemporary Exodus, he sounded the theme of deliverance that became the dominant and overarching message of the entire civil rights movement. Like King's theme, the sources of ideas for "Death of Evil" proved useful on hundreds of occasions, as did his method of composition.

Without acknowledging Phillips Brooks, King based his pulpit oration on Brooks's sermon "Egyptians Dead Upon the Seashore." A much-admired abolitionist preacher from Boston, Brooks based "Egyptians Dead" on Exodus 14:30. Seizing this unprepossessing verse, Brooks interpreted the Egyptian corpses as a powerful symbol of God's ability to thwart evil. His view of the drowning incident especially appealed to King. Compare:

BROOKS: The parted waves had swept back upon the [Egyptians]. . . . all that the escaped people saw was here and there a poor drowned body beaten upon the bank, where they stood with the great flood between them and the land of their long captivity and oppression. It meant everything to the Israelites. . . . It was the end of a frightful period in their history . . . the Egyptian captivity was at an end.[2]

KING: But as soon as the Egyptians got into the Red Sea the parted waves swept back upon them. . . . As the Israelites looked back all they could see was here and there a poor drowned body beaten upon the seashore. For the Israelites, this was a great moment. It was the end of a frightful period in their history. It was a joyous daybreak that had come to end the long night of their captivity.[3]

King also wove several other unacknowledged sources into his sermon. His brief mention of tares and wheat distills an analysis from George Buttrick's *Parables of Jesus.*[4] His account of various global religions mirrors a sermonic discussion by Harry Emerson Fosdick, a famous radio preacher from New York City. Compare a segment from Fosdick to one from "Death of Evil":

FOSDICK: All the great religions have so pictured life in terms of conflict. Hinduism called it a conflict between reality and illusion; Zoroastrianism a conflict between light and darkness; Platonism a conflict between spirit and matter; traditional Judaism and Christianity a conflict between God and Satan.[5]

KING: All the great religions have seen this tension at the center of life. Hinduism called it a conflict between illusion and reality; Zoroastrianism looked upon it as a tension between the god of light and the god of darkness; Platonism called it a conflict between spirit and matter; traditional Judaism and Christianity called it a conflict between God and Satan.[6]

King discovered his Carlyle quotation in Fosdick's *On Being Fit to Live With*.[7] His citations from Bryant and Lowell could have come from many sources, for the citations amounted to homiletic commonplaces.[8] The line from Bryant attracted ministers' attention at least as early as 1898, when the president of the black National Baptist Convention used it to embellish a sermon.[9] Fosdick called it a "saying."[10] King's own professor of homiletics, Robert Keighton, treated Bryant's statement as though it were a proverb.[11]

Lowell's lines were, if anything, even more popular than Bryant's. A renowned black pastor quoted them before the turn of the century.[12] Fosdick fit it into two sermons that King read and in a third volume of homilies as well. Lowell's poem resurfaced in another book that King read and in published homilies of at least five other preachers.[13]

In a later, expanded version of "Death of Evil," King enlarged the analysis of tares and wheat that came from Buttrick; he also added a good-over-evil litany from Fosdick's *On Being Fit*.[14] He included further lines from Lowell ("Though the cause of Evil prosper,/'Tis Truth alone that's strong") that enhanced two sermons by Fosdick and a book of meditations.[15] He also selected a passage from Shakespeare ("There's a divinity that shapes our ends . . .") that had appeared in *On Being Fit* and in works by three other prominent preachers.[16]

King's later "Death of Evil" also includes a chestnut from

Matthew Arnold that Fosdick and others had seized and four
lessons from the historian Charles Beard.[17] Fosdick and several
others taught Beard's metaphorical lessons, which one homiletician
described as well-known generalizations.[18] William Holmes Borders, a pastor King heard as a child and adolescent, repeated one of
them as well.[19]

While published sermons are important wellsprings for the
ideas of "Death of Evil," King's pivotal source was not Brooks's
"Egyptians Dead Upon the Seashore," Buttrick's *Parables of Jesus,*
sermons by Fosdick, or any other printed text. The main source for
King's theme of deliverance from oppression—which he propounded in virtually every sermon, speech, essay, interview, column, and book of his entire career—was the folk religion of
American slaves. His equation of black America and the Hebrew
people revived and updated the slaves' powerful identification with
the Israelites suffering under the yoke of the Pharaoh. And his
interpretation of the Exodus as an archetypal event expressed the
distinctive worldview of those who longed for a new Moses to
emancipate them from an American Egypt.

King learned about slave religion from his father, a folk
preacher, and adopted its vision of deliverance as the foundation of
his thought and oratory. Indeed, the worldview of slaves proved far
more important for King than anything he learned at Morehouse
College, where he earned an AB degree; Crozer Theological
Seminary, where he obtained a Bachelor of Divinity; and Boston
University, where he received a PhD.

On the assumption that King's mind was almost a *tabula rasa* by
the time he enrolled at seminary, researchers have persistently
claimed that his ideas grew from his reading of famous Euro-
American philosophers and theologians. By attributing King's
thought and language to his encounters with philosophers, scholars
have crafted a highly distorted image of King. An accurate understanding of King's ideas and language requires an examination of
his intellectual evolution beginning not with his first years in
seminary but at the beginning. Beginning, that is, with the slaves.

Over long decades slaves exercised their religion under extremely difficult circumstances. Laws usually prohibited them from
learning to read and write, leaving most unable to read the Bible.
Sermons thus served not only as an important means of religious
instruction but, for many blacks, the *only* means of instruction apart

from music. Like their fellow slaves, most preachers had no recourse but to imbibe religion from other preachers—not from the Bible or other texts.

Ignoring print culture, folk preachers nurtured and polished their highly oral form of religious art, which they perfected despite the harshness of slavery. White observers often noted the awesome oratorical skills of popular slave preachers.[20] Electrifying sermons ensured not only the propagation of Christianity but possibly the continued existence of African-American people. Eugene Genovese argues convincingly that without slave preachers' affirmation of hope amid immense hardship, slaves might not have endured at all:

> The religion practiced in the quarters gave the slaves the one thing they absolutely had to have if they were to resist being transformed into the Sambos they had been programmed to become. It fired them with a sense of their own worth before God and man. It enabled them to prove . . . that no man's will can become that of another unless he himself wills it—that the ideal of slavery cannot be realized, no matter how badly the body is broken and the spirit tormented.[21]

Slave religion promised salvation in both this world and the next. Frederick Douglass and others remarked the double meaning of spirituals, which pointed to both earthly freedom and heavenly redemption.[22] Indeed, as various historians explain, the theology of slaves featured both this-worldly and otherworldly salvation blended to form what is aptly described as "a pervasive theme of deliverance."[23] In recounting their religious experiences, some ex-slaves emphasized their conversion epiphanies, which involved a repudiation of sin and an ecstatic acceptance of Jesus Christ as Savior.[24] Proclaiming otherworldly deliverance based on such conversions, slave preachers sometimes exulted in the rewards of the afterlife.

They also offered hope for this life. One clear manifestation of slaves' this-worldly religion was an intense and widespread identification with Old Testament figures. Slaves sympathized profoundly with the struggles of Mary, Daniel, Noah, Ezekiel, Joshua, Jonah, and Moses—most of whom participated in social upheavals and each of whom figures prominently in spirituals.[25] Along with Jesus, the Old Testament heroes favored by slaves faced terrible hardships and difficult odds before achieving resplendent victories. Slaves saw these hardships as parallel to their own oppression and viewed Biblical success stories as a harbinger of their own eventual Biblical-style liberation. In the words of one interpreter, ". . . blacks reasoned that if God could lock the lion's jaw for Daniel . . . then he could certainly deliver black people from slavery."[26]

Expressing a particular fascination with Moses, African Americans pervasively identified with the Chosen People held captive in Egypt—an identification evident in many spirituals about Moses, the Pharaoh, the Red Sea, the wilderness, and/or the Promised Land: "Didn't Ole Pharaoh Get Lost [in the Red Sea]," "O Mary Don't You Weep [. . . Cause Pharaoh's Army Got Drownded]," "Turn Back Pharaoh's Army," "I Am Bound for the Promised Land," "Way Down in Egypt Land," "O Walk Together Children," "Joshua Fit De Battle of Jericho," "Go Down, Moses," and others.[27]

In 1808 eminent African-American preacher Absalom Jones interpreted a national law banning the slave trade as an act of providence equivalent to the Exodus. Just as God *"came down to deliver"* the Israelites from the Egyptians, Jones declared, He *"came down* into the British Parliament" when it outlawed slave ships and *"came down* into the Congress of the United States" when it approved a comparable ban.[28] Like Jones, Richard Allen, founder of the African Methodist Episcopal Church, and David Walker, the nineteenth-century radical, did not hesitate to equate slaves with the Hebrews suffering under the Egyptians. Anonymous folk preachers offered the same identification. "The Eagle Stirs Her Nest," a folk sermon delivered at least as early as the 1860s, compares God's love for the Hebrews in the wilderness to an eagle's care for her young. By explaining the revival of the Israelites enslaved in Babylon, the slave sermon "Dry Bones in the Valley" relates a variation of the Exodus theme of deliverance from captivity.

African Americans composed songs, preached sermons, and wrote tracts about the Exodus because no other story proved more sublimely expressive of the theme of deliverance. The overwhelming significance of the Exodus to black Americans led one slave historian to observe, ". . . the name Moses grew as important in Africans' minds as the person had been in Israel's eyes, and dominated the future of blacks as Moses had dominated the history of Jews."[29]

By identifying with the Hebrews in Egypt and with other
Biblical heroes, slaves telescoped history, replacing chronological
time with a form of sacred time. This substitution enabled Old
Testament characters to become slaves' immediate predecessors
and contemporaries as they freely mingled their own experiences
with those of Daniel, Ezekiel, Jonah, Joshua, and Moses. Slaves
could vividly project Old Testament figures into the present because
their expansive universe encompassed both heaven and earth and
merged the Biblical past with the present.[30] For example, in a
popular spiritual they extended the Old Testament by raising a
question:

> He delivered Daniel from de lion's den,
> Jonah from de belly of de whale,
> And de Hebrew children from de fiery furnace,
> And why not every man?

In these lyrics Daniel, Jonah, the Hebrew children, and the narrator
of the spiritual live contemporaneously. A similar extension is
evident in the ring shout, when slaves went into the forest and
became transformed into the Hebrews, marching through the
wilderness and following Joshua around the walls of Jericho.[31]
When liberation finally occurred, some blacks regarded Abraham
Lincoln, Harriet Tubman, or the Union army as Moses.[32]

As they leapfrogged geography and chronology, slaves often
collapsed Moses and Jesus into a single, mighty figure able to
shatter the manacles of slavery.[33] Uniting Moses and Jesus, they
could search for a new Moses in Mississippi and Alabama. The
conflation of Moses and Jesus occurred, for example, in the
imaginative lyrics of a spiritual:

> Jesus Christ, He died for me.
>   Way down in Egypt Land.
> Jesus Christ, He set me free,
>   Way down in Egypt Land.[34]

Here the composer transcends time and distance to locate both
Jesus Christ and the narrator in Egypt and to enlist Christ as Moses.
The composer locates a self by consulting Biblical models, freeing
those models from any constraints imposed by their historical

contexts, and entirely ignoring all barriers separating past and present events.

Because their God-ruled universe of sacred time was reliable and ultimately just, it bolstered slaves' confidence that the deity who liberated the Hebrews would eventually free Southern blacks. Slave theology and slaves' invocation of sacred time served as exceedingly astute and imaginative responses to their situation. Genovese explains the wisdom of African-American theology, especially its tendency to merge Moses and Jesus:

> For black slaves who were determined to resist the powers that be and yet powerless to defy them openly, who looked longingly toward delivery from bondage and yet had little thirst or opportunity for vengeance, who sought spiritual redemption in Heaven and yet could not ignore their need for bodily redemption in this world, the assimilation of Moses to Jesus provided the way to reconcile all contradictions.[35]

One method of expressing sacred time is to treat Old Testament characters as prototypes of New Testament figures. This practice is called typology. Thus, as an example of typology, Adam by the tree in the Garden of Eden became perfected in the person of Jesus crucified on a wooden cross. Thus, Moses the deliverer prefigures Christ, the perfect deliverer. Archbishop Desmond Tutu of South Africa provides a striking example of typological Christian thought:

> Jesus is but the Greek form of Joshua who led the Israelites across the Jordan River into the Promised Land. . . .
>
> What was not fully realized in the Old Testament would find complete fulfillment in the New. Matthew sees Jesus as a second but greater Moses. . . . Luke, describing the transfiguration, tells us that the subject of the conversation between Jesus, Moses, and Elijah had to do with the destiny He was about to accomplish in Jerusalem. And Luke uses the Greek word *Exodus* to describe that event. It can't have been merely coincidental.[36]

Typology can also apply to the present, for Christians may treat Biblical figures and events as types recurring throughout human existence, up to the present moment. Thus, typology patterns history according to knowable and repeatable forms of experience.

It does not merely present a system of symbols, for believers view typological events as literally true. Nor does typology entail analogy, for, unlike analogy, typology introduces and sustains an entire and coherent worldview, fitting human experience into a system of interpretation both sturdy and flexible.

While typology is a theological system, it also serves as a method of self-recognition. One discovers one's self within a set of knowable types of people and events that continually recycle throughout the morality play of human existence. The advantage of typology lies in its ability to organize all experience and provide direct access to the meaning of life.[37] In a typological universe Christians' task is simply to understand how new circumstances fit into a set of Biblical coordinates. Typology enables speakers to create extremely powerful arguments because it serves not only as a system of persuasion, but as a system of knowledge provided by God. Typology turns the universe into a clean, well-lighted place where people can recognize and understand themselves.[38]

Though its worship services were often derided as nothing more than emotional circuses, black folk religion continued to transmit its theme of deliverance long after emancipation. Like slave religion, subsequent black Protestantism combined this-worldly and otherworldly salvation. A distinguished preacher and longtime friend of the King family, Gardner Taylor, observes that the sermonizing he heard as a boy presented a "blurring" of social and personal redemption and "an indistinguishable mixture" of earthly and heavenly liberation.[39]

In folk sermons the otherworldly and this-worldly forms of liberation did not work in conflict, but rather confirmed and reinforced each other. As far as black Baptists were concerned, anyone could experience salvation by renouncing sin and accepting Jesus Christ as Lord. Salvation guaranteed a heavenly afterlife, and separate heavens did not exist for blacks and whites. Because folk preachers viewed all people—black and white—as candidates for heaven, they proclaimed a theology at odds with segregation. Simply by teaching that a heavenly reward results from faithful service to God—not from white skin—preachers implicitly questioned whether an entire social system should revolve around skin color. If God viewed black people as equal to whites and placed both groups in the same heaven, then one could easily ask why whites would practice segregation.

Preachers' expertise about heaven and hell enhanced their persuasiveness about daily concerns as well. The centrality of the church in the lives of black people gave it the ability to speak with authority about every issue, including white oppression.[40]

Just as the this-worldly and otherworldly strands of slave theology continued long after emancipation, so did the slaves' sense of sacred time.[41] Throughout the decades of segregation, folk preachers continued to project Biblical figures into the present, using them to understand and define the present circumstances of their congregations.[42]

Some preachers invoked sacred time by transporting themselves into the Biblical past. During this century one observer marvelled at a black preacher's ability to talk "to his congregation about Moses and Daniel at mid-day as though he had eaten breakfast with them."[43] Another explains, "One of the best-known beginnings of a Bible story in the whole Black preaching tradition is, 'I saw John, down on the Isle of Patmos, early one Lord's Day morning.' "[44] Yet another preacher leapt into the New Testament by confiding, "I hear Paul saying one day . . ."[45]

Other ministers projected their listeners into Biblical settings. In 1942 a Tennessee preacher equated contemporaries with a valley of human skeletons addressed by Ezekiel; he declared, "The Christians make themselves dry bones." Implying that some of his listeners might be dead, he added, "You'll find dry bones in the church."[46] A Texas preacher identified some of his congregation with a wayward Biblical character, "We still got ahr progicul [prodigal] sons with us. Yes, we has. Dey's plenty of progicul sons right heah today."[47]

And just as slave preachers and the composers of spirituals related Exodus to African-American experience, so did black ministers after slavery. For example, five decades after the Emancipation Proclamation, L.J. Coppin updated the typology of Exodus: "Fifty years brings us to the border of the Promised Land. The Canaan of our citizenship is just before us and is infested with enemies who deny our right to enter."[48] In 1926 J.M. Gates incorporated the lyrics of "Go Down Moses" into his recorded sermon "Moses in the Wilderness." Writing of his childhood, one observer recalls, ". . . our ministers held forth about Moses using the rod to part the waters of the Red Seas. More than once the minister would go on to suggest that there were some 'Black Moseses' in the making."[49]

Sacred time and typology underlie some of the most famous sermons by C.L. Franklin, the dominant folk preacher of the 1950s and 1960s. Inasmuch as the sermons of King's grandfather, his father, and many other folk preachers are not available for study, Franklin's recorded and transcribed sermons provide a valuable window for understanding the tradition that King absorbed as a child.[50]

Franklin's credentials are impressive. Pastor of the huge New Bethel Baptist Church in Detroit, he regularly packed auditoriums around the country, sometimes receiving several thousand dollars a night for his preaching. He recorded scores of sermons that sold widely on blues record labels and, during the 1960s, allied himself with King and opposed black nationalism.[51] Like everyone else, King, Jr., admired Franklin.[52]

In the mid-1950s, aware that blacks still suffered from the semi-slavery of segregation, Franklin based his sermon "Moses at the Red Sea" on their continuing identification with Israelites enslaved in Egypt. He interprets the story of Moses in a straightforward typological fashion:

> In every crisis God raises up a Moses. His name may not be Moses but the character of the role that he plays is always the same. His name may be Moses or his name may be Joshua or his name may be David, or his name, you understand, may be Abraham Lincoln or Frederick Douglass or George Washington Carver, but in every crisis God raises up a Moses, especially where the destiny of his people is concerned.[53]

Franklin then explicates God's ability to help everyone threatened by Pharaoh's army while backed up against a Red Sea.

In his mid-1950s sermon "Dry Bones," Franklin elaborates and applies Ezekiel's vision of human bones rattling together as they miraculously reassemble. The Book of Ezekiel equates this revival with the renewal of the Chosen People held as slaves in Babylon. Franklin subtly identifies black Americans with the bones Ezekiel rejuvenates and with the revitalized Hebrews, as blacks struggle in "a valley of slavery and oppression, a valley of sorrow."[54] Like "Moses at the Red Sea," "Dry Bones" intertwines Hebrews' experience of slavery with blacks' experience of segregation.

In his early-1970s rendition of the traditional sermon "The

Eagle Stirs Her Nest," Franklin equates God's care for the Hebrews to an eagle's concern for her young. God tends to the Chosen People like a mother eagle stirring her eaglets out of the nest, causing them to make their initial, faltering attempts at flight, and then soaring down to rescue them as they plummet to the earth. Like the eagle, God prevents His children from living smugly and encourages them to flap their own wings. The famous folk preacher recalls instances of God stirring the nest of the lazy and swooping down to save the needy, who sometimes find themselves lost in the wilderness. For example, God stirred the nest of America when blacks migrated from the South to the North. He stirred the nest of Detroit's auto makers when workers went on strike. And He stirred the nest of race relations when he anointed King and the civil rights movement to disrupt segregation. All these events recapitulate the eagle's experience with her young and God's ministrations to the Hebrews wandering in the wilderness.

Franklin assumes the mantle of an authoritative interpreter of God's Word when he defines contemporary dramas as sequels to the Exodus, to the story of Ezekiel's miraculous preaching, and to the Deuteronomic account of the eagle stirring her nest. Franklin creates himself through his magisterial ability to transmit the theme of deliverance and explain contemporary struggles through Biblical archetypes. In all three sermons, God's deliverance of the Chosen People foretells His eventual liberation of black America.

Seeing themselves as vessels for the voice of God, folk preachers freely borrow each other's sermons—a practice their listeners appreciated. "Eagle" and "Dry Bones" have reappeared in the folk pulpit ever since they were first delivered in the 1860s.[55] In 1961 a folk preacher brought fits of religious joy to churchgoers in Birmingham who heard his "Dry Bones" at a civil rights meeting sponsored by the local leader of King's 1963 Birmingham crusade.[56] At Jesse Jackson's ordination service in 1968, Franklin preached "Dry Bones." Jackson later rendered his variation of the same pulpit address.[57]

In their quest for homiletic material, folk preachers quarry not only each other's sermons but other sources as well, including hymns and spirituals.[58] Formulaic passages and lyrics float from minister to minister and are easily adjusted to fit the needs of a particular occasion.

Of necessity, the language of black oral culture is highly

repetitive. Reiteration ensures that knowledge, which cannot be transcribed, will be remembered by both speakers and audiences. In the absence of print, people rarely develop a sense of words as a species of private property. Folk preachers borrow partly because their culture fails to define the word as a commodity and instead assumes that everyone creates language and no one owns it.[59] As Henry Mitchell explains, black folk preaching is "by its very nature oblivious of the rules and requirements of the majority culture."[60]

By ignoring white rules and following their own penchant for borrowing, preachers gain many advantages. Repetition enables congregations to participate fully in a service. Able to anticipate what comes next, churchgoers can more easily shout, sing, clap, or dance.[61] Borrowing also enhances a preacher's status with an audience that demands authority, not originality; appropriateness, not personal expression, the gospel of Jesus Christ, not the views of an individual speaker. Pastors validate themselves by adopting the legitimated persona of those who have preached "Eagle," "Dry Bones," and other legendary sermons. A minister can develop authority by embracing well-loved discourse, creating a voice by melding it with those of earlier, sanctified bearers of the Word. Moreover, borrowing gives preachers another means of invoking sacred time and transporting the living past into the present. Familiar sermons do not reenact the past as strictly as does the act of celebrating the Last Supper. But they do plunge congregations into ritualistic repetitions of previous worship experiences.

Originality, on the other hand, precludes reenactment and thus can easily spell failure to deliver the Word, which is known, shared, confirmed, and reconfirmed by a large historical community. A speaker's uniqueness is not problematic; after all, no two human beings are identical. But a speaker's worthiness to represent a sacred tradition *is* problematic. When preachers merge their voices with earlier spiritual leaders, they practice a form of self-making that resembles, supplements, and reinforces their system of Biblical typology.

Preachers recirculated specific, legendary sermons because the time-honored theme of blacks/Hebrews struggling against slavery never lost its usefulness. The old message of oppression and deliverance remained continually relevant. How could preachers ignore Biblical stories about slavery when blacks still experienced the semi-slavery of segregation? Preachers were not about to abandon their effective gospel of hope despite hardship, a gospel that had sustained black people for many decades. "Moses at the Red Sea," "Eagle," and "Dry Bones" enabled pastors and their listeners to continue their identification with their slave forebears and with the Hebrews who escaped the Pharaoh and wandered in the wilderness only to be re-enslaved in Babylon. If God's followers in the Bible overcame slavery in both Egypt and Babylon, then His African-American disciples would eventually achieve a glorious triumph as well. No boundaries of miles and centuries could hamper the reemergence of Biblical hope.

This hope was not embalmed in detached, lifeless sermons. Rather, preachers initiated a powerful electrical charge that surged back and forth between pulpit and pew. In contrast to the listlessness of many white preachers, ordinary black homilists routinely and visibly aroused churchgoers from their lethargy, drained their anguish, and revitalized their spirits with the intoxicating elixir of the gospel. For many decades the black pulpit served indisputably as a weekly power station transmitting strength and endurance to an exploited people.

The African-American church also provided a haven of refuge. Because the church was the only large institution that blacks operated entirely by themselves, it served as the institutional center of black life.[62] Between services that sometimes lasted for hours, churches functioned as music schools, concert halls, recreation clubs, educational centers, and sites for political debates and town meetings.[63] Whenever whites stripped blacks of their humanity, the church offered dignity. A black woman might work as a maid her entire life, but she could maintain her self-respect by coordinating a youth program or teaching Sunday School. Congregations also served as extended families. Churches cared for members bereaved and widowed, and churchmen served as father figures for boys growing up without a father.

Not only did folk preachers organize their all-important institutions, they also provided civic leadership. As W.E.B. DuBois explains in his celebrated *The Souls of Black Folk:*

> The Preacher is the most unique personality developed by the Negro on American soil. A leader, a politician, and orator, a "boss," an intriguer, an idealist—all these he is, and ever, too, the centre of a group of men, now twenty, now a thousand in number. The

combination of a certain adroitness with deep-seated earnestness, of
tact with consummate ability, gave him his preeminence, and helps
him maintain it.[64]

Even whites recognized the status of African-American preachers.
In a small Southern town, if whites decided to pave a few streets,
the mayor would often sit down with a respected preacher to decide
which streets to pave in the black community.

Two such preachers were King's grandfather and father. Indeed, literally hundreds of folk sermons by Martin Luther King, Sr.,
shaped the vision and language of Martin Luther King, Jr. Like
other messages in the folk pulpit, King, Sr.'s sermons extended the
communal spiritual tradition begun by slaves.

And so did "Death of Evil." There the slaves' protest became
King's protest, their worldview his worldview, and their cry for
deliverance his cry. Their vision of the Exodus as a constantly
recurring event became his interpretation of the 1954 Supreme
Court decision as the parting of an American Red Sea. Folk
preachers' methods of voice merging and self-making also served
him well in "Death of Evil." Instead of reviving "Eagle," "Dry
Bones," or other traditional folk sermons—none of which appealed
to white listeners—he modified and synthesized printed texts by
Brooks, Fosdick, and others. Adapting their sermons meant translating blacks' traditional theme of Exodus into an idiom that white
people would finally understand.

TWO

THEY CAN'T OUTTALK HISTORY

K ing absorbed the slaves' worldview at Ebenezer Church, which his father pastored for forty-four years. Mesmerized by his graduate training, King scholars have often overlooked the earliest and most significant influence on his language—the religion of Ebenezer Church. Older members of that church, however, have realized for years that the scholars were wrong. Like others in the Ebenezer congregation, Rev. Edwards emphasizes the importance of understanding King's boyhood experiences. Well-acquainted with King's parents during their entire adult lives, Edwards also knew King, Jr., throughout his life. He criticizes journalists, scholars, and members of the public who ignore King's childhood:

> They never said anything about his early years. They go back to Morehouse [College]. . . . Dr. Mays and others got praise for having shaped the life of Martin Luther King, Jr. I just let them go on and talk.

Then, holding up his 1938 Sunday School rollbook that recorded the attendance record of M.L. King, Jr., he continues:

> But this [rollbook] speaks louder than anything I have to say. Like I told you, this is really history here; and whatever they say, they can't outtalk history. They must come back to this. [Laughs] So I just sit quietly by and let 'em talk and let 'em do. But if they ever have to refer to his early training, I'm going to have to produce this and say, "How do you account for this? At nine years of age!"[1]

King's conditioning in the black church, however, began long before he was nine years old. In January, 1929, Michael King, Jr., was born into what he later described as "a very congenial home situation"—specifically, the Atlanta home of his grandfather and grandmother, Rev. A.D. Williams and Jennie Williams.[2] Living in the Williams home were his parents, Rev. Michael King, Sr., and Alberta Williams King. A preacher in a small Baptist Church, Michael King, Sr., was also an older student at Morehouse College. A few years later he changed his name to Martin Luther King, Sr., and his older son became Martin Luther King, Jr.[3] Family members knew the child as "M.L.," while friends preferred his earlier nickname, "Mike."

The son of an alcoholic sharecropper in rural Georgia, King, Sr., grew up in appalling poverty, feeding his parents' pigs and chickens and currying the family mule. He experienced racism firsthand; indeed, his autobiography is little more than the chronicle of a lifetime struggle against segregation. As a young child he witnessed a white mob barbarically murder a black man. While quite small, he himself was brutally beaten by a white millowner. When his mother discovered what had happened, she personally confronted the attacker, pummelling him in front of his employees. Humiliated by a woman, he did not dare strike back. Delia King's revenge was rare, however, for whites almost always triumphed over blacks. In another incident the young King, Sr., boldly disobeyed his father by reminding a white boss of the cottonseed money owed to his father. Though the boss grudgingly paid the money, he retaliated by firing James King, by preventing him from finding other work, and by throwing the King family out of their home.[4]

Like his mother and many other African Americans, King, Sr., found solace and recognition in the church, where people enjoyed his singing for hours on end. When he tired of currying the mule and following a plow, he became a preacher and moved to Atlanta in hopes of finding a congregation.

In those days, King, Sr., reports, he had "an educational background so poor that [his] reading level was barely beyond a rank beginner's" and he "could hardly write at all."[5] He found English "so puzzling" that it resembled "some foreign tongue." Discovering within himself "no natural talent for study," he nevertheless determined to gain an education, attending school for several years in order to prepare himself for Morehouse College.[6] Even after years of poring over books, however, his progress was so meager that the registrar at Morehouse refused his request to matriculate. Upset by this decision, he burst into the president's office and pleaded for admission, which the surprised president granted. After failing freshman English twice, he persevered until he finally graduated from Morehouse in 1930 at the age of thirty-one.[7]

This hard-working student with rough, country ways also began courting Alberta Williams, daughter of A.D. Williams and a student at Spelman College, a women's school adjacent to Morehouse. In Williams, the prominent minister of Ebenezer Church, King located an outstanding mentor whom he and others regarded as a "man of firm determination, strong self-reliance, and broad vision."[8] Also hailing from rural Georgia, Williams developed his following at Ebenezer Church partly through what King, Sr., terms a "powerful, thundering style" in the pulpit—a style that included the whooping and moaning popular among folk preachers.[9]

In 1898 Williams earned a degree from Morehouse, which, like Spelman, was built on land donated by John D. Rockefeller.[10] A skillful organizer of church and community functions, Williams served as president of the Atlanta Baptist Ministers' Union and treasurer of the National Baptist Convention, the most formidable ecclesiastical organization in black America. Under his direction Ebenezer Church offered food, clothing, and medicine to the needy of his city.[11]

Williams emerged as an important city leader after the Atlanta race riot of 1906—a horrific affair involving white attacks on innocent blacks, fifty of whom lost their lives. Responding to the riot and to Southern racism in general, Williams joined the NAACP, one of whose founders, W.E.B. DuBois, then taught at Atlanta University. Exceptional organizational skills helped Williams become the chief NAACP fundraiser in the city.[12] He also sponsored a boycott that put a white racist newspaper out of business and defeated a city bond proposal that ignored black schools. The first black high school in Atlanta, which King, Jr., attended, was built partly through Williams's exertions.[13] In recognition of his many achievements, he received an honorary doctorate from Morehouse in 1914.[14]

After six years of courtship, Williams's daughter Alberta married Michael King in 1926; the couple moved into the Williams home, where they continued to live after their three children were born.

When Williams died unexpectedly in 1931, the elder King faced a daunting challenge as he assumed the Ebenezer pastorate. His father-in-law's final years coincided with the onset of the Great Depression, a decline in church membership, and a resultant loss of revenue. As King, Sr., tells the story, the moment he accepted the call to the Ebenezer pulpit, a local bank was padlocking the church's doors. Only his skillful negotiations with bankers enabled the Ebenezer trustees to reopen their institution.[15] That success portended others. His booming folk preaching, resolute fundraising, and unusual organizational skills enabled his flock to grow despite the debilitating effects of segregation and the Depression. Like Williams, this "giant of a man" became a leader of black Atlanta and served as a trustee of Morehouse College, the school that had not wanted to admit him.[16]

King's pastoral responsibilities included counseling church members through family crises and personally vouching for the credit of those facing unfriendly bankers about to foreclose on their homes. Again like Williams, King made sure his face was instantly recognizable at the local jail, where he bailed out wayward members (and their kinfolk) who were involved in scrapes with the law. As one church loyalist recalls, "He would give you a lecture about being in jail, but he would bail you out, too."[17] Despite his sometimes gruff and authoritarian demeanor, churchgoers grew to respect and love their resourceful pastor. Indeed, some of the older, regular members of Ebenezer Church can hardly talk about the kindness and concern of "Daddy" King, as he was affectionately known, without having tears come to their eyes.[18]

King's wife and mother-in-law also proved essential to the Ebenezer community. After the death of her husband, Jennie Williams convinced the congregation to anoint King, Sr., as his successor. Living in the home of her daughter, son-in-law, and their children, she shared the responsibility of raising her grandchildren. For her part, the widely respected Alberta Williams King organized a choir at Ebenezer Church and later served as organist for the church and for the Women's Auxiliary of the National Baptist Convention.[19]

King, Jr., obviously felt a very strong affinity with all the members of his family. In an autobiographical essay written around the age of twenty, he records his admiration for his stern, demanding father, who "always put his family first."[20] He explains his family life as an "intimate" one where "love was central" and hails his grandmother as "saintly," noting that she took a special interest in her grandchildren, especially himself.[21] Speaking of his closeness with his brother and sister, he declares, "to this day there still exists that intimate relationship [among my siblings and myself] which existed between us in childhood."[22]

He also identified profoundly with Ebenezer Church. For him, family was church and church was family. Anxious to please his parents, he reports that at age five he joined the church in imitation of his sister's example.[23] A close family life, King, Jr., explains, accounts both for his acceptance of the Christian faith and his loyalty to the church. A happy childhood in a loving home, he notes, enabled him to "lean more to optimism than pessimism."[24]

But racist incidents invaded this charmed family circle. When the elder King took his six-year-old son M.L. to buy a pair of shoes, a clerk asked them to leave the white section of the store and join other black customers at the rear. After King, Sr., politely demurred, the clerk became insistent. Refusing to accept this form of segregation, the proud minister led his son out of the store and groped fruitlessly for an explanation of the store's policy. On another occasion a policeman pulled over the elder King's car, demanding "Boy, show me your license." Rev. King pointed to M.L., Jr., who sat next to him, and bravely informed the officer, "He's a boy. I'm a man."[25]

Racism also cost the younger King a close childhood friend when his white companion's father forbade his son to associate with black children. The incident led King's parents to inform him about racial discrimination. Instead of hating whites, his father and mother repeatedly insisted, ". . . it was [his] duty as a Christian to love [them]."[26] Although unable to overcome his "anti-white feeling" until he went to college and worked with interracial groups of students, from that point he obeyed his parents' injunction of rejecting racism while accepting white people as human beings.[27]

This experience mirrored an earlier one of his father. When his mother was dying on the farm, King, Sr., returned from Atlanta to care for her. After he explained his intense hatred of white people, she made him promise not to hate. "Hatred," she insisted, "makes nothin' but more hatred, Michael. Don't you do it."[28] Just as the elder King struggled to follow his mother's dying wish, the younger King struggled to obey his parents' admonition to hate segregation while loving those who practiced it.[29] This attitude served him well every day of his adult life.

At Ebenezer Church, King, Jr., also learned about preaching. As children, he and his siblings had no choice but to hear their father sermonize at countless church services. Guest preachers sometimes filled the Ebenezer pulpit and occasionally delivered such traditional folk sermons as "The Eagle Stirs Her Nest" and "Dry Bones in the Valley."[30] As a child and teenager, King, Jr., also heard William Holmes Borders, a promising minister located one block from Ebenezer Church.[31] In addition he may have heard live or recorded sermons by Rev. J.M. Gates of Atlanta, a legend in the folk pulpit during the 1920s and 1930s.[32] Later he may have heard C.L. Franklin, who was accurately dubbed "the most famous preacher in the gospel circuit" and whose commercially recorded sermons sold by the thousands.[33] Packing a large auditorium in Atlanta, Franklin thrilled crowds that included several pillars of the Ebenezer congregation. And he once preached from the Ebenezer pulpit.[34]

Like Gates and Franklin, King, Sr., exemplified a folk pulpit tradition begun during slavery.[35] Licensed to preach at age fifteen, he began his pulpit career in a small, rural church at a time when, according to his own testimony, he could scarcely read and write. He was not alone, for the church deacons who heard him did not know the alphabet.[36] Blessed with a good memory, he listened carefully to apparently illiterate "old-time preachers"—possibly former slaves—who "provided [him] with a great sense of the gestures, the cadences, the deeply emotive quality of their styles of ministry." He recalls copying their example: "And when I was alone, I would try to duplicate the things I heard them do."[37]

From this beginning the self-taught young preacher went on to master the idiom, drama, and rhetorical fireworks of African-American folk preaching—and its dual theme of this-worldly and otherworldly deliverance. Throughout his life King, Sr., remained comfortable with the highly oral religious culture that nurtured him as a child. Having "no natural talent for study" did not interfere with his successful ministry in a thriving church.[38] According to one report, when his children were young, King, Sr., "walked the benches" by preaching joyously as he ambled up and down the pews of the church while church members swooned.[39] His sermons also featured two unmistakable hallmarks of the black folk pulpit: call-and-response exchanges with listeners, whose outbursts punctuated his rhythmical phrases, and a calm-to-storm delivery. The calm-to-storm pattern involves a slow, placid beginning; a middle that gradually becomes more rhythmical; and a climax tumultuous and rapturous enough to rock the walls of a sanctuary. Buoyed by his success in his church, he retained the vocal pyrotechnics of folk preaching throughout his long career, bringing them to his prayer at the Democratic National Convention of 1976.

Like other folk preachers, King, Sr., almost certainly borrowed sermons. In separate interviews, King, Sr., and his friend Benjamin Mays described the practice of borrowing as "very common" among the preachers they knew. When the elder King began his career, he could by his own admission neither read nor write. Therefore, he had little choice but to continue doing what he began as a child, that is, to "duplicate" the sermons of the preachers he heard. How else could he have composed a sermon, particularly in a tradition that endorsed the practice of borrowing sermons? He almost certainly duplicated not only orthodox black Baptist theology and a roof-lifting delivery, but also Biblical texts that served as cornerstones for sermons; broad frameworks and the major points of those sermons; and standard oral formulas that floated freely among preachers and fit into almost any sermon.[40] Like others, the senior King undoubtedly created distinctively individual variations within the architectonic structure of familiar sermons.

Like their fellow folk preachers, Williams and King, Sr., affirmed slave theology by blending earthly and heavenly salvation. Merging religion and political agitation, they explicitly denounced racism from the Ebenezer pulpit.[41] King, Sr., also expounded the Exodus narrative and thus reiterated the this-worldly side of slave theology.[42]

Again like Williams and many other black clergy, King, Sr., not only proclaimed racial equality, he also did something about it. In 1935 he led roughly a thousand demonstrators to Atlanta's City Hall, where they demanded the right to vote. The next year, he supported the protest of black teachers who wanted pay comparable to that of their white counterparts. He also provided leadership for the Atlanta Voters League.[43] In the late 1940s he entered the City Hall of Atlanta and used elevators marked with signs reading "Whites Only." Soon the signs came down.[44] For good reason, he became known as a "chronic complainer" about segregation.[45]

As a matter of religious and political principle, King, Sr., strongly urged his congregation to vote. Atlanta's black ministers expressed their faith "that voting was powerful as an agent of change."[46] His own expression included campaigning for successful mayoral candidate William Hartsfield, a racial moderate. As one parishioner tells the story, while extolling Hartsfield's virtues, the elder King once pounded his fist down on a lectern so hard that he shattered his watch. When white campaign aides offered to pay for the timepiece, the self-reliant minister respectfully replied, "No, thank you. I can buy my own watch."[47]

One block from Ebenezer Church, William Holmes Borders was expanding his congregation and constructing a large edifice known as Wheat Street Baptist Church. Educated at Morehouse and at Garrett Seminary of Northwestern University, Borders offered brief sermons on a radio program called "Seven Minutes at the 'Mike.'" Through his broadcast pulpit he advocated comparable expenditures for black and white education, urged blacks to help fight World War II, and branded black disfranchisement a form of "taxation without representation."[48] Beginning in 1943, when King was fourteen, locally printed, paperback collections of Borders's sermons began to appear. In one of them, Borders observed, ". . . the rugged fact that 'All Blood Is Red' blows asunder the position of racial or national superiority."[49] Indeed, he lambasted racism more openly and more often than any other preacher in

Atlanta.[50] During the 1940s or 1950s, he joined King, Sr., in preaching about the Exodus—in his case an entire series of sermons applying the Biblical lesson of Moses to the lives of African Americans.[51] He also encouraged economic development, raised money to bury victims of lynching, promoted voter registration, and eventually built a multimillion dollar, low-income housing project adjacent to his church.[52]

Treating religion and race as inseparable, Borders joined Williams and King, Sr., in intertwining the personal gospel and the social gospel. For all three men, the soul-saving dimension of their broad theology was at least as important as the theme of deliverance from segregation. By affirming a loving, personal God who sent His Son to redeem sinners, they sought as many converts as possible. Emphasizing their view of God as a loving father who sustains His children, they also stressed sin and damnation. Indeed one listener notes that Williams "did not hesitate to place certain people in hell who he felt deserved to be there. He would name names."[53]

Like Williams, King, Sr., proclaimed his belief in a literal heaven and hell. An older member of the Ebenezer flock jokingly noted that on cold Sunday mornings the fire visible in the church's wood-burning furnace reminded everyone of what hell was like.[54] Sermons about hellfire expressed Williams's and King, Sr.'s deep conviction that evil and sin abound in human life. They held that human beings err by rejecting God. Not simply misguided, such rebellion represents a futile attempt to elevate human personality above divine law. Furthermore, sin reflects an innate inclination toward evil that each person has at birth. This tendency is coupled with a corresponding desire to acknowledge the fatherhood of God and to obey his will. Their sermons proclaimed the conflict between good and evil as the basic drama of every human life—a theme that abounds in King, Jr.'s "Death of Evil" and in many of his other sermons as well.

In the hands of Williams, King, Sr., and Borders, the personal gospel and social gospel complemented and reinforced each other. By adhering to the principle that, in the elder King's words, "In the act of faith, every minister becomes an advocate for justice," the three ministers reflected the traditional tendency of black clergy to interpret all reality as "interconnected, interwoven, and interlocked."[55] Like slave preachers before them, in their efforts to save souls, the Ebenezer and Wheat Street pastors implicitly questioned racial inequity by affirming that black souls would enter the same heaven as white souls.

King, Sr.'s attempts to win converts led a Pulitzer-Prize winner and others to mistakenly portray him as a narrow-minded fundamentalist.[56] Yet, instead of espousing anti-intellectual dogma, the patriarch of Ebenezer Church embraced an open and capacious religion. His broad-mindedness probably began as early as his years at Morehouse College, which had no fundamentalist professors.[57] And, quite unlike most people, whose thinking narrows as they age, he grew more open-minded as the years and decades went by. For example, he put into practice his faith in the compatibility of folk religion and modern theology, ushering into his church a diversity of theological conceptions and pulpit styles. He invited Franklin and other whooping folk preachers whose jolting delivery rattled the stained glass windows of his church. With equal enthusiasm he welcomed urbane intellectuals who had studied in some of the best graduate schools in the nation. These figures included Mordecai Johnson, president of Howard University, and Benjamin Mays, president of Morehouse College.[58]

The elder King's broad-mindedness is particularly evident in his close and abiding friendship with Mays, who held a PhD from the University of Chicago. Often appearing at his friend's church, the reflective Mays appointed King, Sr., to the Morehouse Board of Trustees. Although scholars often write as though the folk preacher King and the academic Mays had little or nothing in common, such a bond existed that a long-time secretary of the church describes the two men as being "like brothers."[59]

But, again like Williams, the elder King clearly expressed conservative views about personal habits, disapproving of drinking, smoking, dancing, and playing pool. For this reason, the younger King's home was strict as well as loving. He and his brother A.D. had to cope with the tightly enforced rules and stern personality of his father, who spanked his sons into their teenage years.

The early experiences of young M.L. and A.D. King fit a pattern described by James Farmer, another minister's son. As Farmer explains, to live as a black preacher's kid—or "PK"—is to be "exposed to merciless scrutiny, spared no censure, even denied most of the childhood mischief indispensable to growing up." He continues, "Every part of the PK's life is colored by the fact that he is a preacher's child. He breathes it in the air, suckles it from his mother's breast." This environment is "an oven, firing to white heat any incipient abilities put there."[60] Typically a "PK" will either rebel or conform.[61]

Young M.L. and A.D. King did both. Certainly they rebelled. Flouting King, Sr.'s admonitions, his teenage sons began dancing, drinking, smoking, and playing pool.[62] They repeatedly tested their father's willingness to impose discipline.

A.D. continued to defy his parents. Even after entering adulthood, he sparred regularly with his father, unable either to win a father/son argument or walk away from one. After starting as a student at Morehouse, he dropped out, married early, drank heavily, and became insecure and troubled.[63] But A.D. also conformed. Having taken a long detour, he finally entered the ministry, strongly supported civil rights, and did little publicly to detract from his brother. A.D.'s rebellious conformity was most evident when he preached inspired sermons while drunk.[64]

His brother also rebelled. As a young man, in addition to dancing and playing pool, M.L., Jr., developed exceedingly liberal religious views. Characterizing most of his Sunday School teachers as "unlettered" and all of them as believers in the literal truth of the entire Bible, he tells how, at age thirteen, he "shocked [his] Sunday School class by denying the bodily resurrection of Jesus."[65] In later years, he conducted an ongoing dispute with his father, countering his father's precepts with more progressive views.[66] Rejecting his father's advice, he refused to marry the woman King, Sr., preferred and, when his schooling was over, turned down King, Sr.'s offer to co-pastor Ebenezer Church.

But M.L., Jr., also conformed—much more than A.D. M.L.'s religious doubts began at age thirteen and developed while he attended Morehouse, which was an extension of his church and family. After all, Morehouse was his father's alma mater, the source of his grandfather's honorary PhD, the college his parents had selected for him, and the institution his father would later serve as a trustee. His doubts mushroomed only until he discerned "profound truths" underlying scriptural "legends and myths"—truths more important than his discovery that the Bible was not always historically accurate.[67]

Reconciling this perspective with that of his parents was not terribly difficult. When King, Jr., faced his examination to be ordained as a minister, the committee asked him about the Virgin Birth. He denied that Jesus was born of a virgin. Edwards, King, Sr., and other members of the committee disagreed with the younger King's refusal to accept the entire Bible as literally true. But, despite this difference, they had no trouble ordaining him as a minister.[68] They did so because, unlike fundamentalists, they did not regard Biblical literalism as a litmus test of true Christianity.

While King, Jr., did rebel against the more conservative notions of his evangelical boyhood church, he clung tightly to its most important teachings, especially its dual theme of deliverance. Cut "from the same mighty oak" as his father, he sought earthly redemption, devoting his life to a crusade against racism.[69] He also embraced the doctrine of heavenly salvation. As his autobiographical essay indicates, his grandmother's death when he was nine years old led his parents to explain heavenly afterlife. Her death and his family's response to that loss, he notes, "is why today I am such a strong believer in personal immortality."[70] He never swerved from this belief, which he expressed in eulogies for civil rights martyrs.

By accepting the Christian precept of a heavenly salvation and the need to struggle against segregation, King as a young man affirmed the two chief strands of slave religion and the black folk pulpit. His faith in otherworldly and this-worldly redemption sustained him throughout his life. In its essentials his message of deliverance repeated the appeal and the hope that multitudes of slaves and anonymous folk preachers had proclaimed both explicitly and implicitly—but always loudly—for well over a hundred years. What remained was for King to learn what no black person had ever discovered before—how to persuade whites to accommodate the black demand for deliverance from injustice.

THREE

THE BIGGEST PROBLEM
FACING THE WORLD

Bracing himself against the back of a hard, wooden pew was a familiar experience for the teenage M.L. King, Jr. So was listening to a sermon against segregation. But the calm, dignified speaker he heard every week at the chapel of Morehouse College eschewed his father's oratorical pyrotechnics. Moreover, this professorial gentleman did not promulgate the dogma of the complete infallibility of scripture. Although he was already a friend of M.L. King, Sr., who became a Morehouse trustee, he favored a less emotional, more intellectual approach to religion. This approach captivated M.L. King, Jr., who found the speaker's points "especially alive and intense."[1] When the service was over, the adolescent King sometimes followed the smooth orator to his office where they would chat about his just-completed sermon.[2] The preacher was Benjamin Mays, president of Morehouse College.[3]

In the early 1940s Morehouse experienced serious financial hardship. While black colleges were often strapped for funds, World War II compounded the problem by draining many students from the all-male institution and, of course, their tuition payments as well. Acting as president, Mays enlarged the student body by granting early admission to better-than-average high school pupils. So in 1944 Morehouse admitted a number of such students, including the fifteen-year-old King, Jr.

The campus was already familiar to this young student. As a seventh grader he attended Atlanta University Laboratory School, which was located near the buildings of Morehouse. And he already knew Benjamin Mays. On a number of occasions King's parents brought their children to concerts and other events at Morehouse, where they sometimes hobnobbed with Mays.[4]

Though Professor George Kelsey and others at Morehouse stimulated King's development, none was more important than Mays himself, whom King later described as "one of the great influences in my life."[5] Together Mays and Kelsey provided their students with a more scholarly version of Christianity than that proffered at Ebenezer Church. The bond between Mays and King grew strong and lasted throughout the rest of King's life. Mays mediated between King and his father during the Montgomery bus boycott, offered the benediction at the historic 1963 March on Washington, defended King's opposition to the Vietnam War, and delivered the graveside eulogy following his assassination.

Undoubtedly, however, Mays mattered most to King during his years at Morehouse. There he performed the invaluable function of introducing the undergraduate King to the universe of liberal, white Protestantism—a large network of pulpits, congregations, journals, and publishers who would offer him rhetorical, political, and financial support of a kind that no other black American received before or since.

The son of illiterate sharecroppers in South Carolina, Mays grew up in a world where whites accorded blacks the same status as dogs and rabbits.[6] Escaping the same climate of rural poverty and oppression that King, Sr., had resisted, Mays relentlessly pursued his intellectual interests. Realizing that an intelligent black man would probably be killed in the South, he went North to obtain a higher education, graduating from Bates College in Maine and earning a PhD at the prestigious University of Chicago. There he observed Robert Maynard Hutchins, the most distinguished college president of this century. Mays could not possibly have found a better model for learning how to act as a college president. While at the University of Chicago, he also took formal instruction from noted Protestant theologian Henry Nelson Wieman.[7]

Before coming to Morehouse, Mays discovered his gifts as an administrator, rising to the deanship of the School of Religion at Howard University. Described by Kelsey as a man of the "highest integrity," the stately Mays contributed scholarship about the history of African-American religion and often delivered speeches and sermons.[8] With some regularity he travelled to international Christian conclaves, reporting on those meetings for W.E.B. DuBois's journal *Crisis*. Paul Tillich and Reinhold Niebuhr, America's premier theologians, included him in a small circle of outstanding scholars and theologians who, over a certain period, met twice a year to debate pressing religious issues.[9]

Like DuBois, A.D. Williams, King, Sr., and William Holmes Borders, Mays opposed racism. Writing in *Crisis* in 1939, he prophetically declared: ". . . I am convinced more than ever before that the biggest problem facing the world today is the problem of race. If the gospel of Jesus Christ cannot solve the race problem, Christianity is doomed."[10] Nine years later he joined other black leaders in supporting national civil rights legislation.[11] In 1952, while addressing the Divinity School of Yale University, he argued that segregation was "the greatest scandal within the Church" and "the greatest curse that can be imposed upon any one." He added, "We cannot escape the use of pressure or coercion of some kind . . ." in the struggle against racial injustice.[12]

Not only did Mays forcefully decry segregation through essays in *Crisis* and speeches at Yale, he also made his views known on his own campus. In 1943, a year before King entered Morehouse, he conferred an honorary doctorate on Paul Robeson, the world-famous champion of racial equality. On that occasion Robeson delivered the Morehouse commencement address, decrying racial prejudice as "an ugly shadow" on the ideals for which American soldiers were fighting in the war against Hitler.[13] Delivering sermons that King heard, Mays personally attacked segregation from the pulpit of Morehouse Chapel.[14]

Combined with the influence of his family, the instruction of Mays, Kelsey, and other Morehouse personalities prompted King to announce his call to the ministry during his junior year.

An able scholar, orator, journalist, teacher, administrator, and advocate for racial justice, Mays served as a pivotal role model for many Morehouse students, including King. King later undertook the same kind of multifaceted leadership that Mays had exerted. What Mays had been to liberal black (and to a lesser degree white) religious and academic circles King—with the benefit of a huge political movement and television—would be to America.[15]

With their eyes on the ministry, King and his friend Larry Williams sampled various appeals from exemplary pulpits and traveling preachers. They savored respectable sermons by L.M. Tobin, a prominent minister in Atlanta, and scholarly presentations by Mays and Vernon Johns, a highly outspoken, extremely well-educated preacher. Often Larry Williams and King turned their radio to weekly national broadcasts of sermons by Harry Emerson Fosdick and Ralph Sockman. Down the street from Ebenezer Church, which Williams had also attended, the teenage friends heard the popular Borders. Williams liked Borders so much that he became his assistant. Despite the scholarly training and the polish of several of these ministers, they never entirely suppressed the tradition of the folk pulpit, which always came "bleeding through" in one way or another.[16]

Concluding his last year at Morehouse, King imitated Borders's example by studying at a reputable Northern seminary. He secured letters of recommendation from Mays and other Morehouse mentors and was admitted to Crozer Theological Seminary, a white school near Philadelphia. Helping King make a transition from his black culture in Atlanta to life on a white campus was Rev. J. Pius Barbour. A friend of King's father, the colorful Barbour often invited King and other black seminarians to his home, where they ate, laughed, and engaged in "bull sessions" about religious topics.

After graduating from Crozer, King followed Mays's example by entering a PhD program at a recognized Northern university, in his case Boston University. In his last year at Boston, he met Howard Thurman, Mays's former student at Morehouse and the new dean of Marsh Chapel at Boston University. Through his lectures and sermons, the mystical Thurman enraptured white audiences.

While at Crozer and Boston, King explored the philosophy of Plato, Locke, Spinoza, Nietzsche, Kierkegaard, Hegel, Marx, Gandhi, and others. And he contemplated the musings of reputable American theologians. He read Walter Rauschenbusch's *Christianity and the Social Crisis* and Reinhold Niebuhr's *Moral Man and Immoral*

Society—two works frequently alleged to have shaped his thought and politics. He almost certainly perused C.C. Morrison's journal, *Christian Century;* years later, he published in its pages his essay "Pilgrimage to Nonviolence" and the famous "Letter from Birmingham Jail."

Despite the scholarly attention to King's years at Crozer and Boston, his important work there *by far* has been the least noticed— his careful scrutiny of sermons by Harry Emerson Fosdick, George Buttrick, J. Wallace Hamilton, and other important, liberal white preachers. King later borrowed and adapted many of their sermons.

To understand King's experiences in graduate school, we must examine them within the context of Protestant history—a milieu in which Rauschenbusch, Niebuhr, and Fosdick figured prominently. King scholars and the public have badly misunderstood this milieu. Vastly exaggerating King's debt to philosophers and theologians, scholars have failed to comprehend the importance of sermons to King and the crucial relationships among preachers and theologians. In addition, researchers have ignored the dramatic impact that World War I, the Depression, and World War II exerted on Protestantism by the time King entered seminary.

Before World War I the social gospel of Washington Gladden and Walter Rauschenbusch exerted a hypnotic appeal on tens of thousands of liberals. Decades later, the same magnet continued to attract many of the professors and students King knew at Crozer and Boston.

Drawing on the heritage of the abolitionist movement, the social gospel initially served as a response to the brutalities of laissez-faire capitalism. In 1876 Gladden declared: "Now that slavery is out of the way, the questions that concern . . . our free laborers are coming forward; and no intelligent man needs to be admonished of their urgency."[17] Gladden and other social prophets crusaded for the labor movement. While they concentrated on the rights of workers, they also championed women's suffrage and other reforms.

A chorus of like-minded leaders extended Gladden's message into the twentieth century. In 1906 Charles Reynolds Brown delivered a series of lectures published as *The Social Message of the Modern Pulpit.* Echoing Gladden's support of labor, this volume equates workers with Hebrews enslaved in the Egypt of cutthroat capitalism. The following year Rauschenbusch published his best-selling *Christianity and the Social Crisis* and assumed Gladden's mantle as the most persuasive exponent of the social gospel.

While Gladden, Brown, and Rauschenbusch joined fundamentalists in advocating unvarnished Biblical religion, they also criticized conservatives for ignoring the full dimensions of the gospel. Agreeing that believers should evangelize for Jesus Christ, social gospellers also worked to eliminate civic ills. Progressives rebelled against the fundamentalist tendency to privatize religion by reducing it to spiritual fire insurance protecting the faithful from the flames of everlasting hell. Christianity is both personal and social, they insisted, and places demands on business and political affairs that followers must obey. In their refusal to restrict religion to personal redemption, adherents of the social gospel took inspiration from the Bible, especially from the Exodus, the Hebrew prophets, and the love ethic of Jesus.

Believing that Christian principles apply to every corner of life, social gospelers attempted to Christianize their families, schools, businesses, and government. Gladden and Rauschenbusch buoyantly announced that institutions could actually exemplify the Kingdom of God on earth—a purpose expressed in the title of Rauschenbusch's book, *Christianizing the Social Order.* Saluting "the immense latent perfectibility in human nature," Rauschenbusch regarded the goal of baptizing the entire social order as quite practical.[18] (He did not, however, wish to enshrine Christianity as the legal religion of the state.)

Despite their insistence that Christian ethics should permeate American life, Gladden, Rauschenbusch, and most other liberal white Protestants reserved their impassioned rhetoric to espouse workers' rights—not racial justice. During the decades that segregation became the dominant and official pattern of Southern life, white Protestants did not interfere significantly with the novel institution of Jim Crow. Nor did they prevent Southern racists from stripping blacks of their newly acquired right to vote. Like others of their race, white religious liberals often celebrated the politically inoffensive program of Booker T. Washington. They frequently displayed what one church historian aptly characterizes as "sentimental paternalism" toward blacks.[19]

For example, at the beginning of the new century Gladden advocated black accommodation to the laws and mores of segregation and naively promised blacks that their good character would lead to full citizenship "as sure as tomorrow's sun shining."[20] Although Rauschenbusch was someone who generally stood "for the man down under," he almost never mentioned race and essentially overlooked the suffering of African Americans.[21] A few white Protestants did object to segregation, disfranchisement, and violence against blacks. However, Gladden, Rauschenbusch, and most of their fellow white Christians failed to notice that their grandly inclusive social gospel ignored the worsening condition of their fellow black Protestants.[22]

By contrast, prominent African-American church leaders strongly protested the humiliation of segregation and the loss of the vote. In 1898, five years prior to Gladden's blithe prediction of certain progress, Francis Grimke, a well-known black churchman, denounced the ineffectuality of the Fourteenth and Fifteenth Amendments and lashed white ministers for their silence about racial hatred and violence. For their faint-hearted refusal to decry the murder of blacks, Grimke blasted white clergy as "dumb dogs that cannot bark," "hypocrites in the pulpit," and "whited sepulchres."[23] Two years before Gladden's promise of full citizenship, another esteemed black pastor declared, "Class and race antipathy has been carried so far in this great Christian country of ours, that it has almost destroyed the feeling of that common brotherhood. . . ."[24]

During the late nineteenth and early twentieth centuries, Frederick Douglass, W.E.B. DuBois, Paul Robeson, and a host of other secular black advocates joined Grimke and other black clergy in roundly and repeatedly condemning racial violence and injustice. But white Protestants ignored the eloquence of those who loudly deplored the exploitation of African Americans.

Unlike the deteriorating condition of blacks, the chaos of war did disturb the heady optimism of white religious liberals. Recoiling from World War I, progressives groped for nonviolent alternatives to the conflagration of that war. Many morally earnest Europeans and Americans embraced pacifism, which they regarded as the only reasonable response to the boundless devastation of modern warfare. The Fellowship of Reconciliation (FOR), an organization of Christian pacifists, sprang up as one expression of a profound, widespread desire to abolish war. Rauschenbusch and like-minded leaders eagerly joined the FOR. Early in the century, the ardent pacifist C.C. Morrison founded the interdenominational journal

Christian Century, which became a weekly bellwether of liberal Protestantism. The articulate Morrison enlisted distinguished religious writers to contribute to *Christian Century* and its sister journal *Pulpit,* which he also edited. Many of these authors routinely advocated nonviolence and railed against war.

One of the most frequent contributors to *Christian Century* was a remarkable social gospeler named Harry Emerson Fosdick. After World War I and an abrasive confrontation with fundamentalists, Fosdick assumed a New York City pastorate. He did so only after convincing John D. Rockefeller, Jr., and other members of the church to move their institution to a less wealthy neighborhood. From his new pulpit at Riverside Church, Fosdick espoused nonviolence; lambasted nationalism; and, despite Pearl Harbor, kept his vow never to endorse another war. For nineteen years he delivered the message of progressive Protestantism every Sunday over an NBC national radio pulpit. Although his former student Ralph Sockman also commanded the airwaves of national radio, Fosdick presided as the undisputed dean of liberal preachers. On a given Sunday he enjoyed a national and international congregation of well over two million listeners, including Larry Williams and the teenage M.L. King, Jr. At times a couple in, say, Iowa would make a once-in-a-lifetime trip to New York City to see Babe Ruth or Joe DiMaggio swat a home run and hear their beloved radio minister in person.

The cheerful and productive Fosdick authored over fifty books, many of them collections of sermons. Through such homilies as "Christianity's Stake in the Social Situation," which appeared in his 1933 volume *Hope of the World,* he enthusiastically expounded a more realistic and less utopian version of the social gospel. With sermons like "Through the Social Gospel into Personal Religion," he balanced economic and international concerns with calls for individual devotion and faith.[25]

After World War I the New York pacifist led a host of mainly younger, often eloquent preachers who joined him in reviling war—which Fosdick deemed "suicidal"—from one platform to another.[26] They looked to the love ethic of Jesus (and sometimes to Gandhi) for alternatives to brute force. These pacifists included Halford Luccock, a witty and prolific writer who later penned a regular column for *Christian Century;* Leslie Weatherhead, Britain's most famous preacher; E. Stanley Jones, a missionary to India; C.C.

Morrison; and George Buttrick.[27] While in Chicago, Mays heard Fosdick preach pacifism and then, in Mays's words, "read everything Fosdick ever wrote."[28] Together with his former Morehouse student and friend Howard Thurman, Mays joined the cavalcade of preachers who explicitly repudiated all forms of war.[29]

Together, these articulate pacifists promoted the doctrine of turning-the-other-cheek so successfully that after World War I pacifism became almost *de rigeur* in many Protestant circles.

But the extent of the European catastrophe and the reality of power politics dashed the idealism of Reinhold Niebuhr, the dominant American theologian of the era. Embracing socialism and pacifism early in his career, Niebuhr wrote regularly for *Christian Century* and at one point headed the FOR. But in the early 1930s he resigned from the anti-war organization to launch a lengthy career as the leading religious critic of pacifism, which he labeled "parasitic."[30] He assailed all other forms of utopianism as well. Dismissing perfectionist hopes as illusory, he displayed a splendid eloquence in becoming what his biographer correctly terms "the liberal crusader against liberalism."[31] Indefatigable before his stroke in 1952, Niebuhr fulfilled this polemical role brilliantly through countless sermons, lectures, essays, articles, and books. He helped reshape Protestant thought into a form closer to his own conception, which is often dubbed "neo-orthodoxy" or "Christian realism."

In his important 1932 volume, *Moral Man and Immoral Society*, Niebuhr argues that individuals behave more ethically than groups and that nations by their very nature operate mainly from self-interest, not goodwill. He maintains that the paradoxically egocentric and impersonal quality of global political and economic life may necessitate the use of coercion and force. Minimizing the ethical distinction between violence and nonviolence, *Moral Man* accuses Gandhi of refusing to admit the coercive nature of his nonviolent tactics. When it appeared, the book caused a furor, stimulating both thought and counterattack and straining Niebuhr's relationship with his socialist and pacifist friends. Unabashed by the controversy, Niebuhr extended his argument in subsequent books.

Along with a group of academic colleagues, Niebuhr helped Paul Tillich leave Germany in 1933 and assume a professorship at Union Theological Seminary in New York City, where Fosdick, Niebuhr, and Tillich all taught for many years (and where Buttrick taught more briefly). In contrast to Niebuhr, Tillich constructed an abstract, amorphous theology that ignored the ambiguities of politics and the failure of reform. Despite his ability to attract a considerable American following, Tillich clearly failed to influence Fosdick and other preachers, including King.[32]

Unlike Tillich's metaphysics, Niebuhr's thorough critique of liberalism exerted a great impact on Protestant homiletics. His criticism of secular and religious idealism offered preachers a theological corrective both troubling and valuable in a world alternately besieged by monstrous wars and a global depression. As late as 1925 a young Halford Luccock could echo Rauschenbusch's call for "the actual Christianization of the entire social order" and brand as "a fatal heresy" the refusal to accept such an ambitious plan.[33] However, cries for the unsullied Kingdom of God to come to earth subsided rapidly during the 1930s as the once-promising new century revealed one horror and tragedy after another. By the end of the 1930s the Nazis seemed destined to prove Niebuhr's lament that ". . . the universal aspects of European culture are being completely destroyed."[34]

When Germany invaded Poland, Protestants agonized over a possible response. After observing Nazi war-making from London, Leslie Weatherhead disavowed total nonviolence and voiced support for the Allied cause.[35] Across the Atlantic, George Buttrick corresponded with Franklin Roosevelt in a futile effort to prevent America's entry into the war.[36] C.C. Morrison and *Christian Century* opposed Roosevelt's Lend-Lease policy and counseled a high-minded isolationism—a position vigorously rejected by Niebuhr, who strongly endorsed FDR's assistance to the Allies. Although Morrison and Fosdick never abandoned their pacifist convictions, Pearl Harbor erased the lingering doubts of many others, who joined Weatherhead and Niebuhr in accepting the grim necessity of war.

Despite the collision between the expected Kingdom of God and the blitzkrieg of Adolf Hitler, the faith of Fosdick and other liberal stalwarts flourished during the 1930s, 1940s, and 1950s. In fact this period was "a heyday for the Protestant pulpit."[37] Literally millions of people heard and read ordinary and famous liberal preachers. Far fewer people bothered to become acquainted with the work of Tillich, Niebuhr, and other theologians. In fact, many more people absorbed the sermons of a single preacher—Fosdick

—than heard and read the work of Tillich, Niebuhr, and all other theologians combined.

Locating their faith between the utopianism of Rauschenbusch and the anti-utopianism of Niebuhr, Fosdick and other preachers advocated a middle position of optimism despite tragedy. They abandoned the sunny perfectionism of the early social gospel, but nonetheless yearned for a world without Hitlers and, possibly, without war. By adding a recognition of sin to the social gospel, Fosdick, Hamilton, and other popular preachers created a new, moderated religious optimism that appealed to tens of millions of Americans. Hamilton expressed sentiments typical of many midcentury preachers when he acknowledged the virtue of Niebuhr's realism while branding war as both cause and result of a "chain reaction of evil" that "must be broken."[38]

Although Niebuhr's prestigious ideas impinged on Fosdick, Hamilton, and other homilists, one outstanding quality of their preaching is its general independence from contemporaneous theology. Despite a common view that homiletics derives from theology, thousands of liberal sermons preached between 1920 and 1968 (the year of King's death) resemble each other far, far more than they do the work of Niebuhr, Tillich, or any other theologian. Struggling with Niebuhr's challenge to liberal dreams, preachers substantially moderated Niebuhr's thought. Moreover, one searches in vain for theological antecedents for literally thousands of sermons about popular homiletic topics. Preferring their own, more accessible ideas, preachers made almost no attempt to transmit theologians' ideas directly to the masses. For that reason, when King and other seminarians examined sermons, they scrutinized a sturdy, distinctive homiletic tradition—not a watered-down version of theology by Rauschenbusch, Niebuhr, Tillich, or anyone else.

Some of these sermons addressed the subject of race. During the era of Fosdick and Niebuhr, white Protestants began to show glimmerings of awareness about the status of blacks. Unlike Gladden and Rauschenbusch, outspoken white pastors during the 1930s and 1940s occasionally decried racial oppression. In *Moral Man* Niebuhr displayed remarkable foresight by claiming that blacks could employ Gandhian methods to combat segregation.[39] Fosdick lamented the "social problem" of "racial prejudice" at least as early as 1933.[40] E. Stanley Jones protested racial inequities in

1936, and Hamilton of Florida—virtually the only celebrated liberal to hold a Southern pulpit—joined the protest by 1946.[41] During World War II Fosdick flatly announced, "Race prejudice is as thorough a denial of the Christian God as atheism and it is a much more common form of apostasy."[42] With increasing frequency, mainline denominations and the Federal Council of Churches (later the National Council of Churches) passed resolutions against racism.[43]

Another sign of improving racial attitudes was white liberals' willingness to listen occasionally to well-educated black academics and pastors. Just as the pulpit circuit enabled a corps of white preachers to develop a national following, it also helped launch black intellectuals into the Protestant firmament and later offered important platforms for King.

Appearing frequently on the pulpit circuit, King's models— Benjamin Mays, Mordecai Johnson, and Howard Thurman—and other black pulpit legends addressed the Chicago Sunday Evening Club and similar forums.[44] Churchgoers attending the Detroit Lenten Series—another important stop on the route—heard Buttrick; Sockman; Mays; H.H. Crane, the leading Methodist minister in Detroit; and Gardner Taylor, a titan of the black pulpit and friend of the King family.[45] Mordecai Johnson sermonized Fosdick's congregation at Riverside Church.[46] When Buttrick and Thurman ministered at Harvard University and Boston University respectively, they swapped pulpits at least once a year.[47]

As white Protestants added black speakers to their pulpit circuit, they also integrated the lists of contributors and editors of their journals and books. Mays, Thurman, and Taylor wrote for *Christian Century, Pulpit,* or both. Mays also edited a selection of Rauschenbusch's writings and, during the late 1950s, joined Buttrick as an editorial associate for *Pulpit.* Masterminding the twelve-volume *Interpreter's Bible,* Buttrick invited Thurman to collaborate with himself, Luccock, Sockman, Gerald Kennedy, and others in creating an extensively detailed Biblical commentary that still serves as a landmark of Protestant scholarship. Johnson, Mays, and Taylor also contributed homilies to a compendium of *Best Sermons*—a nearly annual series featuring pulpit orations by Fosdick, Buttrick, Weatherhead, Niebuhr, Tillich, Luccock, Kennedy, Sockman, Robert McCracken, and virtually all other outstanding liberal preachers.[48] Some white Protestants also wrote for and read the *Journal of Religious Thought*, edited by Mays's friend, black academic William Stuart Nelson.[49]

But despite white liberals' increasing attention to the estate of African Americans and increasing respect for African-American intellectuals, race never emerged as a dominant religious issue for whites prior to the Montgomery bus boycott. Throughout the 1940s Fosdick—the main torchbearer for the social gospel—decried segregation in strong terms but did so only occasionally. Though numerous other preachers intermittently criticized Jim Crow, literally hundreds of liberal homiletic collections between the 1920s and the middle 1950s mention racial topics with great brevity or not at all. And despite Niebuhr's prescience about the potential of Gandhian strategy to aid blacks, Niebuhr's *Moral Man* contains only a small handful of pages that analyze black/white relations, which he treats briefly in his other books as well.[50]

In contrast to their white counterparts, many African-American professors and preachers treated racism as an extremely pressing concern. While Niebuhr analyzed Gandhi from the comfortable confines of his office at Union Seminary, members of the black religious intelligentsia ventured to India to absorb the principles of nonviolence directly from the Mahatma himself. These leaders included Thurman, Johnson, Mays, and Nelson. In a conversation with Thurman in 1935, Gandhi confidently predicted that American blacks would perfect the philosophy of nonviolence in their struggle for racial equality.[51]

Upon their return to the United States, Johnson, Nelson, and Thurman elucidated Gandhian ethics in churches, colleges, and small discussion groups. Mays's comparison of India's untouchables and America's blacks caught the attention of Fosdick, who quoted it approvingly in 1944.[52] Nelson wrote academic essays explaining nonviolence and taught the first course on nonviolence ever offered at an American university.[53] As early as the 1930s, George Kelsey listened to conversations at Morehouse about the use of Gandhian methods.[54] Walter McCall, King's closest friend at Morehouse, remembers that similar discussions attracted King's attention during their undergraduate years a decade later.[55]

However, despite Morehouse students' interest in things Gandhian, the first class in nonviolence could have originated nowhere but Howard University, for during the 1940s Howard had no rivals as the North American center of Gandhian thought. Even one of

Howard's students, Harris Wofford, journeyed to India and developed a passion for nonviolence before becoming the first white male to enter Howard Law School.

Of course, the Gandhian faculty at Howard sparked an interest in nonviolence among other students as well, including James Farmer. Mays and Nelson taught Farmer, and Thurman directed Farmer's master's thesis. Describing his relationship with the mystical Thurman as one of "great rapport," Farmer grew captivated by the social concern that Thurman added to his intoxicating brew of poetry and mysticism. He followed Thurman in becoming a pacifist and a Gandhian.[56] Branching off from his employer, the FOR, Farmer founded the Congress of Racial Equality (CORE). In 1942, after Thurman helped Farmer organize the first cadre of CORE members, CORE became the first civil rights group to apply Gandhian tactics against segregation.[57]

Remembering this large historical backdrop, we can reconsider King's graduate studies and the sources of his eloquence.

Following the Montgomery bus boycott of 1955–1956, King wrote "Pilgrimage to Nonviolence," an essay focusing on his intellectual development during his stay at Crozer and Boston. Any serious attempt to understand King's experiences in graduate school must begin with a careful exploration of "Pilgrimage." According to "Pilgrimage," as a seminarian and doctoral candidate King grappled with the thought of Hegel, Marx, Nietzsche, Rauschenbusch, Niebuhr, and other intellectual giants as his professors coached him from the corner. "Pilgrimage" concentrates on five major topics that occupied King's studies—the social gospel of Rauschenbusch, Communism, Gandhi and nonviolence, Niebuhr's neo-orthodoxy, and love. The essay notes three minor themes that King also encountered—Hegel's dialectic, Personalism, and interrelatedness. A later version of "Pilgrimage" mentions his scrutiny of Tillich.[58] According to both renditions of the essay, King's ability to synthesize diverse strands of formal Western thought and Gandhian ideas prepared him to guide the Montgomery bus boycott.[59]

King scholars often repeat and expand the interpretation that King expresses in "Pilgrimage." But, though "Pilgrimage" has long been taken at face value, it is not what it appears to be. King's earlier autobiographical essay is reliable, but "Pilgrimage" most definitely is not. It is undependable because *none* of the sources King mentions for his eight sets of ideas is the original, pivotal source of his thinking.

King explains four major themes through his unacknowledged use of eight passages by seven writers whose names do not appear in the essay. He borrows passages from Fosdick to explain what he claims to have learned from Rauschenbusch. He replays lines from Robert McCracken, Fosdick's successor at Riverside Church, to explicate his response to Marx and other Communists. He incorporates language from William Stuart Nelson, Harris Wofford, and another writer to delineate his interpretation of Gandhi and nonviolence. And he adapts texts by Fosdick, Nelson, George Kelsey, and an ethicist to explicate the nature of love. The intertextual pattern is plain: King uses lines from lesser-known writers to account for his responses to famous philosophers, theologians, and Gandhi.

Unaware of King's use of sources, scholars often extract language King borrowed from the seven less prestigious writers to "prove" what King learned from "big name" authors whose names dominate "Pilgrimage" and accounts of King's intellectual maturation.[60] This approach fails to explain King's education. Given the problematic nature of "Pilgrimage," all the ideas in the essay should be seen afresh.

Despite what he wrote in "Pilgrimage," King arrived at seminary with his most important ideas already intact. Although the African-American church does not appear in "Pilgrimage," it provided him with the foundation for virtually all the ideas of the essay. In addition, the black folk pulpit supplied him with the rhetorical assumption that language is common treasure—not private property—and with a well-established practice of borrowing and voice merging that he adapted to print. This tradition enabled him to create language that was tapestry instead of patchwork. In the case of "Pilgrimage," it equipped him to unite parts of eight texts by seven writers, to place his distinctive imprimatur on the resulting intertext, and thereby to create a coherent and highly convincing self. The white-educated PhD that emerges in "Pilgrimage" constitutes a substantial portion of King's entire philosophical persona—an identity that spurred the spectacular success of the civil rights movement and that the nation now enshrines in a federal holiday.

This persona begins with the claim that King embraced the social gospel because he read Rauschenbusch. However, King uses words from Fosdick's *Hope of the World* to describe what he says he learned from Rauschenbusch. Compare:

FOSDICK: Any church that pretends to care for the souls of people but is not interested in the slums that damn them, the city government that corrupts them, the economic order that cripples them . . . would hear again the Master's withering words: "Scribes and Pharisees, hypocrites!"[61]

 . . . "If religion ends with the individual, it ends."[62]

KING: I spent a great deal of time [in seminary] reading the works of the great social philosophers. I came early to Walter Rauschenbusch's *Christianity and the Social Crisis*, which left an indelible imprint on my thinking. . . . It has been my conviction ever since reading Rauschenbusch that any religion which professes to be concerned about the souls of men and is not concerned about the social and economic conditions that scar the soul, is a spiritually moribund religion. . . . It has well been said: "A religion that ends with the individual, ends."[63]

In a later version of "Pilgrimage," King's formulation of the social gospel mirrors Fosdick's expression even more closely:

KING: Rauschenbusch gave to American Protestantism a sense of social responsibility that it should never lose. The gospel at its best deals with the whole man. . . . Any religion that professes to be concerned about the souls of men and is not concerned about the slums that damn them, the economic conditions that strangle them and the social conditions that cripple them is a spiritually moribund religion. . . .[64]

Clearly King did not advocate the social gospel because he read Rauschenbusch. Instead King clearly reiterates Fosdick's declaration of the basic tenet of the social gospel.

King's reliance on Fosdick instead of Rauschenbusch should surprise no one. Even though Fosdick remained a pacifist, he was a chastened pacifist whose religion—like that of Mays and other antiwar preachers—reflected little of what King terms the "false optimism" of the early social gospel.[65] By advocating optimism despite tragedy, Fosdick and other preachers steered the ship of

Protestantism between the shoals of an overly simple perfectionism and the reefs of a world-weary "realism." Fosdick appealed to King because Fosdick was more current and less utopian than Rauschenbusch. Also, from the moment that King was ordained as a minister (before he left home for seminary) until the end of his life, he was at heart primarily a preacher—not a formal theologian or an academic. It was only natural that he—along with thousands of other ministers—would study sermons by the most brilliant white preacher of the day.

Furthermore, while Rauschenbusch popularized the social gospel, Fosdick and other preachers saved it from a theological dustbin—not only by placing bounds on its hopefulness, but also by applying it to segregation. In marked contrast to Rauschenbusch, Fosdick opposed racial injustice and did not mind saying so. Although Fosdick did display a measure of paternalism toward blacks, especially in the early years of his long career, he protested racism with some regularity from the mid-1930s until he retired in the mid-1940s.[66] During that retirement, he ardently supported the civil rights movement, firing off a telegram to President Kennedy endorsing King's Birmingham crusade. Quite unlike Rauschenbusch, Fosdick embraced a social gospel that recognized the debilitating effects of racial prejudice.

Inasmuch as King criticized segregation and discrimination virtually every time he produced a speech, sermon, essay, column, or book, it is far more reasonable to believe that he learned about the social applications of Christianity from Fosdick, who denounced segregation, rather than from Rauschenbusch, who ignored it. King's social gospel bore a much stronger resemblance to Fosdick's views than to those of Rauschenbusch or Niebuhr. He used Fosdick's language because he strongly identified with Fosdick's thought and believed that Fosdick's words would elucidate the social gospel better than those of anyone else.

One might, I suppose, explain King's development simply by adding Fosdick to King's ledger of intellectual debts. One might argue that reading Fosdick in addition to—or instead of—Rauschenbusch converted King to the social gospel. Clearly Fosdick and the other sources for "Pilgrimage" deserve recognition in relation to King, especially since King's readers responded to their words—not those of Rauschenbusch. But merely listing Fosdick on the roll call of influences would not provide a satisfactory interpretation of King's social Christianity.

Indeed, King's awareness of the social gospel did not stem primarily from reading Fosdick or Rauschenbusch or anyone else. Nor did it develop from his professors' tutelage. Plainly his initial and most pivotal instruction in the social gospel occurred at Ebenezer Church. There he heard his father's sermonic exhortations about the Exodus, voting rights, and equal pay for black teachers; there he learned of his father's leadership of a voting rights march in 1935, when he was six years old. There he undoubtedly reflected on his grandfather A.D. Williams's successful boycott of a racist newspaper; on Williams's work to defeat a school bond proposal that bypassed black schools; and on Williams's success in prompting the construction of the first black high school in Atlanta, which King himself attended. Along with Larry Williams, King the teenager received advanced lessons in the social gospel from the likes of Borders, Mays, and Vernon Johns—each of whom was a master of the black pulpit.

Moreover, all these ministerial figures—A.D. Williams, King, Sr., Borders, Mays, and Johns—interpreted poverty and race as profound religious issues that Christians necessarily confronted and that the institutional church necessarily tackled. In marked contrast to Gladden and Rauschenbusch, all these black ministers placed segregation on their list of social evils that God viewed with contempt. And, unlike Fosdick, all of them frequently decried racism. Given the political struggles and triumphs of A.D. Williams, King, Sr., Borders, Mays, and Johns, no one should take seriously the repeated claim that King had to wait until seminary before learning the social gospel. Fosdick and other white preachers reinforced, clarified, and elaborated the black social gospel that King had absorbed as a child—the this-worldly strand of deliverance devised by slaves and reiterated by A.D. Williams, King, Sr., and other folk preachers.[67]

King's experience as a black person shaped his ideas in many other respects as well. "Pilgrimage" explains that, after becoming familiar with Rauschenbusch, King read Niebuhr's *Moral Man.* He notes that Niebuhr's rejection of pacifism left him initially confused. He reports being challenged by Niebuhr's refutation of "the false optimism characteristic of a great segment of Protestant liberalism."[68] He also observes that Niebuhr prompted him to accept "the glaring reality of collective evil."[69]

However, by the time King matriculated at seminary in 1948, he hardly needed to resolve the conflicting insights of Rauschenbusch and Niebuhr. Their theological disagreement was already settled. Although Niebuhr's prose illuminated the tragedies of World War II and the Holocaust, those unimaginable tragedies themselves had already convinced every sane person of "the glaring reality of collective evil." Like Fosdick, Niebuhr here reinforced what King had already absorbed.

In the later version of "Pilgrimage" King states that he was "raised in a rather strict fundamentalistic tradition."[70] If King, Sr., even remotely approached being a fundamentalist, then King, Jr., must have heard a great deal about the pervasiveness of sin. Fundamentalists stress little else but the abundance of sin and the need for grace. Like King's maternal grandfather, his father preached hellfire as God's punishment for unrepentant sinners. Listening to his father's fervent preaching, King had little choice but to develop a well-ingrained sense of sin as a deep, pervasive reality.

Had he lacked the benefit of his father's sermonizing, he would hardly have needed to read Niebuhr to grasp the immense potential of human evil. As a child, all he needed to do was glance at the system of segregation. Where could one find a better example of the pervasiveness of sin and "the glaring reality of collective evil"? King did not need the prodding of Niebuhr to awaken from a state of fatuous optimism because he never suffered from such a state. Under segregation blacks in the South confronted collective evil every single day. They did not enjoy the luxury of naïve optimism.

King's understanding of love also came from the black church, not a white theologian. Despite the claim that King was influenced by Anders Nygren's *Agape and Eros*, Nygren's dense, erudite prose never appealed to King. Ignoring Nygren, King anatomizes love by incorporating passages from William Stuart Nelson, George Kelsey, and an ethicist King studied at Crozer.[71] Moreover a number of King's sentences derive from Fosdick's *On Being Fit to Live With:*

FOSDICK: Love in the New Testament is not a sentimental and affectionate emotion. . . . There are three words in Greek for love . . . *Eros* . . . that is one. . . . in Platonic philosophy it means the yearning of the soul for the realm of the gods. . . . *Philia*—that is another Greek

word. It meant intimate personal affectionateness and friendship. . . .
agape . . . means understanding, redeeming, creative good will. . . .
"Love your enemies"—it is nonsense to command that, if it means
feeling affection for our foes; but if it means . . . extending even to
them an understanding, saving, creative good will . . . that makes
sense.[72]

KING: In speaking of love at this point, we are not referring to some
sentimental or affectionate emotion. It would be nonsense to urge
men to love their oppressors in an affectionate sense. Love in this
connection means understanding, redemptive good will. . . . There
are three words for love in the Greek New Testament. First, there is
eros. In Platonic philosophy *eros* means the yearning of the soul for
the realm of the divine. . . . Second, there is *philia* which means
intimate affection between personal friends. . . . *Agape* means understanding, redeeming good will for all men.[73]

Undoubtedly, Fosdick and the three other writers helped refine
King's conception of love.

Fosdick's linguistic analysis of the three Greek words for love
was certainly not unusual. Indeed, during the 1940s and 1950s
other preachers explicated the same distinctions between *eros,
philia,* and *agape*.[74]

But King's first lessons about love came earlier. As he attests in
his "Autobiography of Religious Development," he initially learned
about love from his family and from his early exposure to the
Christian gospel, which strongly emphasizes the principle of *agape*.
To become a Christian, one must accept Christ as the ultimate
revelation of God's love. And one must learn to "Love the Lord thy
God with all thy heart, with all thy soul, and with all thy mind" and
to "Love thy neighbor as thyself," for these two commandments
form the cornerstones of the faith. Without question the theme of
redemptive love pervaded the Sunday School lessons, prayers,
hymns, and sermons of Ebenezer Church, just as it did in other
churches.

In "Pilgrimage" King implies that he chose Boston University
to study Personalism, which is often called Boston Personalism.
This implication is accurate, for a favorite professor at Crozer,
George Washington Davis, pointed him toward Boston, where his
mentors included Edgar Brightman, L. Harold DeWolf, and other
Personalists.

As King remarks in "Pilgrimage," Personalism holds "that the clue to the meaning of ultimate reality is found in personality."[75] Personalist theologians concentrated on the most basic and orthodox affirmation of Christianity—that God takes a fatherly, personal interest in all human beings. In their formal, academic idiom Brightman, DeWolf, and other Personalists elaborated that belief.

Although these discussions attracted interest during the first half of the century, Personalism proved a highly unsatisfactory theology. It certainly failed to enlist the kind of enduring attention that Tillich's and Niebuhr's work continue to receive. Personalism lost its appeal because, instead of resolving conundrums and challenging old doctrines, as Tillich and Niebuhr were doing, Personalists repackaged familiar precepts. A notably thin body of thought, Personalism lacked both novelty and the depth and complexity of Niebuhr's competing theology. A major weakness of Personalism is its naïve retention of the perfectionism of the early social gospel, which other theologians and preachers jettisoned during the 1940s and 1950s. Affirming undaunted hopes, Personalists failed to weigh seriously the monstrous evil of Adolf Hitler. As sentimental optimists, they wildly underestimated the philosophical entanglements and ethical ambiguities of the post-Darwinian, post-Freudian age. One critic of the period explains that, through Personalism, "the dead moon of the [utopian] social gospel" continued to hang over Boston University throughout King's years there.[76]

Despite these enormous problems, Personalism attracted King. Clearly reflecting the inclinations of his Personalist mentors, his dissertation comprises part of the larger Personalist project of creating a metaphysics on the principle of personality. As such, his dissertation completely avoids politics, economics, race, and all other social issues. Its central purpose is to criticize Tillich and Henry Nelson Wieman for conceiving of God as an abstract and impersonal being remote from the human lifeworld. Instead of constituting an impalpable Ground of Being or abstract creative process, King contends, God is personal and personality provides the best clue to the meaning of life. Couched in the highly stilted, self-conscious diction of the religious academy, King's book-length student essay amounts to an extremely orthodox response to Tillich and Wieman.

King's recondite dissertation never received much attention

until, in the fall of 1990, scholars at Stanford University announced that he had plagiarized substantial portions of it.[77] This plagiarism offers still further evidence that his professors' ivory-tower theological formalism failed to deeply engage his mind. In addition, he stubbornly resisted their most sacrosanct assumptions about language. Refusing to take their rules seriously, he adhered instead to folk preachers' assumption that language is always shared and never owned.

Of course, a plagiarized dissertation is a failed academic project. But King's dissertation failed long before anyone discovered his plagiarism. It forms part of what Protestantism has rightly judged an unsuccessful Personalist effort to construct an interesting alternative to the formulations of Tillich, Niebuhr, and other noteworthy theologians. Today almost no one prizes, studies, or even remembers Personalism for itself; instead, we value Personalism because it played a role in King's life. None of the Personalists anticipated this state of affairs during the years they taught King.

Despite the weakness of Personalism, during the early 1950s King embraced it to such an extent that, when writing "Pilgrimage," he named it his "basic philosophical position."[78] He observes, ". . . [Personalism] gave [him] metaphysical and philosophical grounding for the idea of a personal God."[79] But Personalism proved attractive to King not because its ideas were stimulating and provocative, but for the opposite reason. He appreciated Personalist ideas because they were reassuringly familiar. His gravitation to Personalism is unsurprising inasmuch as the Personalists emphasize the same fatherly, personal God he heard praised in every sermon, hymn, and prayer offered at Ebenezer Church during his childhood and adolescence.

By celebrating a God as a mighty, loving Father able to assist His suffering children, Personalists rebutted Tillich's impersonal deity. They supplied an academic justification for ordinary Christians' belief in the Fatherhood (i.e., Personhood) of God. Of course, the Fatherhood of God serves as the core conviction of African-American folk religion and the rest of Judeo-Christianity. Like Fosdick and Niebuhr, Personalists upheld and vindicated part of the religion of King's parents, grandparents, and King himself. Not only did folk religion sustain blacks through dreary decades of slavery and segregation, its concept of God withstood the scrutiny of white theologians and professors at prestigious Northern universities.

Fortunately, unlike Personalism, the faith of King's parents and grandparents combined reliance on a personal God with a serious conviction about human sin. Unlike Personalists, slaves and folk preachers regarded the struggle against oppression as *the* central theological issue. For that reason, despite King's statement to the contrary, slave religion—not Personalism—was always his "basic philosophical position."

Another portion of the persona that emerges in "Pilgrimage" comes from King's invocation of Hegel as the stimulus for his understanding that "growth comes through struggle."[80] Hegel's theory holds that history proceeds through conflict as a thesis meets its antithesis and produces a synthesis. Thus, in Hegel's view, historical progress entails tension and never occurs painlessly. This theory of history supposedly prompted King to realize that rational negotiation would never overturn segregation without political pressure. In reality, like other thinkers, Hegel reinforced King's earlier instruction in dissent. Through his successful protests, A.D. Williams taught his son-in-law, King, Sr., that progress comes only as the fruit of political struggle.

Even if the elder King had somehow failed to pass on that lesson, King, Jr., was not required to read Hegel to learn that social change comes from struggle. The lesson was everywhere. Abolitionist rhetoric had not eliminated slavery; only a mammoth civil war could expunge the peculiar institution. Later Frederick Douglass promised that further progress would result only from protest. Early in the new century, without citing Hegel, the founders of the NAACP built their organization on the premise that struggle—not Booker T. Washington-style accommodationism—would lead to justice. In addition, the Bible relates several dozen tales of God's hand-picked heroes fighting against overwhelming odds to fulfill the divine will. The favorite figures of black folk religion—Moses, Daniel, Jonah, Noah, Joshua, Mary, and Jesus—all fit this pattern.

These lessons about tension and agitation were not lost on civil rights protestors. Unschooled in Hegel, Rosa Parks accepted the necessity for struggle before refusing to yield her seat on a bus in Montgomery. Several thousand blacks who appeared at the first meeting of the Montgomery bus boycott had never heard King and had never perused Hegel's tomes. Yet their attendance at the rally demonstrated their sense that racial gains would come only as a result of struggle. Having accommodated to segregation for decades, they realized that, accommodationism had failed miserably. Had they lacked such a realization, they never would have boycotted the buses of Montgomery, thereby risking both their livelihoods and their lives.

Like other blacks in Montgomery, King accepted the need for struggle chiefly because black American frustration had reached its limits and because the Bible depicted and sanctioned struggle. Hegel provided King a formal, Euro-American validation for what he had learned and would continue to learn from black history and black Christianity.

Yet another motif in "Pilgrimage" also comes from the black church. King declares, ". . . *agape* means a recognition of the fact that all life is interrelated."[81] He concludes his essay by adding, "[God] works to bring the disconnected aspects of reality into a harmonious whole."[82] King's theme of interrelatedness expresses the traditional tendency of black clergy to see all reality as "interconnected, interwoven, and interlocked."[83]

In sum, the most important intellectual influence on King does not appear in "Pilgrimage" and rarely makes more than a cameo appearance in accounts of King's worldview. This person provided King an example of a preacher who was also an activist; he proudly sent King to three universities, connected King with Mays and thus with a large Protestant network, and enthusiastically welcomed King as his co-pastor during the last eight years of King's life, despite the allegedly foreign ideas King had acquired in supposedly alien graduate programs. This person—Martin Luther King, Sr.— deserves recognition.

Nurturing their son throughout his entire life was the project of both King, Sr., and his wife Alberta Williams King. Not only was she an able parent and dedicated Christian, she also served as a church organist who communicated her love of music to her children, making sure that King, Jr., took piano lessons as a child. Years later King often spoke following performances by such stellar gospel singers as Mahalia Jackson and Cleo Kennedy. He encouraged group singing during protest rallies and called songs "the soul of the movement."[84] Like folk preachers before him, including his father, he incorporated the lyrics of spirituals, hymns, gospel songs, and patriotic standards into his discourse. Plainly his mother encouraged his affinity for music and, along with her husband, helped foster the close relationship between the rhythms and content of King's oratory and the cadences and lyrics of religious songs. The metrical, rolling lines that make King's oratory memorable (e.g., "I have a dream," "Let freedom ring," "How long?") exemplify the forms of parallelism abounding in folk sermons. They also reflect the repeated refrains of spirituals, gospel standards, and hymns. The musical qualities of King's phrases are unmistakable.

Given King's obvious and enormous debt to his parents, the black church, and the black community, one could easily wonder why he wrote "Pilgrimage" as he did. He may have actually believed that some, most, or all of the essay truly represented the growth of his ideas. That is, writing in his late twenties, fresh out of graduate school, he may have felt that several or all of his important conceptions came from the "big names" whose tomes he had just finished perusing. Possibly he thought that his ideas came from philosophers, even if his words did not. After all, most newly minted PhDs believe that they learned much from their prolonged studies. King may have thought as much himself. And he may have temporarily accepted his professors' dismissal of the black community, which they signalled by assigning white works entirely devoid of African and African-American thought.

While King may have believed his words in "Pilgrimage," I maintain that he wrote mainly or entirely of necessity, not conviction. Had he credited his father and his community for nurturing his ideas and leadership, white readers of "Pilgrimage" would never have admired him or have granted him a philosophical persona. They would have regarded him as merely another black preacher objecting to segregation. King placed a philosophical patina on his oratory and himself in order to persuade whites who ignored appeals from other eloquent blacks. Mining sources for his essay meant merging his voice and his identity with a highly prestigious tradition of the white majority. Establishing his credentials as a careful student of Hegel and Marx aided him in making his central and overriding argument for this-worldly liberation from oppression. Citing Rauschenbusch, Niebuhr, and Tillich meant marshalling a nearly unassailable argument from authority. He essentially told whites that the stellar thinkers of modern Protestantism and all Western philosophy joined him in demanding the repeal of segregation. This message proved extremely formidable, especially when combined with his argument that the Bible and the Declaration of Independence likewise demanded racial equality.

The magisterial public persona crafted in "Pilgrimage" helped define King's dedication to civil rights as the noblest possible involvement of a rigorous mind—an intellect that had spent years contemplating sanctified traditions of Euro-American thought. The persona created by "Pilgrimage" lent King a uniquely authoritative aura, entitling him to enormous admiration that no other civil rights leader ever received. This aura proved invaluable in convincing whites to dismantle legalized segregation and thereby implement the time-honored, yet radical black demand for this-worldly deliverance.

FOUR

DUST AND DIVINITY

T hroughout his public career King constantly barn-
stormed the nation to crusade for civil rights, delivering
two or three hundred addresses per year. Flying to
distant states, he routinely interrupted each of his civil
rights operations—including those in Montgomery, Birmingham,
and Memphis—to greet large audiences in person. In his eagerness
to address far-flung crowds, he even paused from hiking the famous
fifty-mile march from Selma to Montgomery. His pressure-filled
marathon lasted year after bruising year throughout almost the
entire twelve years and three months of his public life. His speaking
schedule virtually never flagged—despite assassination attempts,
death threats, jail sentences, and the weight of making life-and-
death decisions while scrutinized by the entire world.

This arduous speech-making continued a grand, nineteenth-
century tradition that Gladden, Rauschenbusch, Fosdick, and other
masters of the Protestant pulpit had extended well into the twentieth century. Aiding King's herculean effort was a formidable
rhetorical network that was developed by Fosdick and other famous
preachers.

King cultivated a massive white audience by fully exploiting a well-established pulpit circuit, packing auditoriums and churches in Chicago, Detroit, New York, and other popular stops. The pulpit route had served as an unparalleled resource for several generations of American Protestants. Long before King emerged as a national figure, the circuit routinely enabled notable figures to crisscross the country as they sermonized one gathering after another. It also gave tens of thousands of churchgoers (especially those in the Northeast and near the Great Lakes) a chance to hear Fosdick, Hamilton, Buttrick, Howard Thurman, and others in person. During certain times of the year, local churches released Hamilton and other silver-tongued orators to circulate on this well-beaten rhetorical path. Tillich, Niebuhr, and other theologians and academics also relished opportunities to preach. For years Niebuhr used most of his weekends to rally listeners to his species of Christian realism. On some of the same weekends and during the summer, Halford Luccock and other professors of homiletics occasionally joined the popular procession.

Renowned ministers honored invitations to address annual state, regional, national, and international conventions for each of the mainline Protestant denominations. They also ventured to Detroit, where H.H. Crane and his colleagues sponsored the Detroit Lenten Series. There a cavalcade of beloved homilists spoke during most days of the entire Lenten season.

The most important stop on the circuit, however, was the Chicago Sunday Evening Club. Founded in 1907, the venerable religious club featured a glittering, interdenominational cast of homiletic stars, including Rauschenbusch, Niebuhr, Fosdick, Hamilton, Buttrick, Mays, Thurman, Luccock, Crane, Sockman, Bosley, Robert McCracken, Gerald Kennedy, Mordecai Johnson, E. Stanley Jones, and Leslie Weatherhead.[1] Filling the club's rostrum were such additional luminaries as Booker T. Washington, Jane Addams, William Jennings Bryan, William Howard Taft, Franklin D. Roosevelt, and Ralph Bunche.[2] What preacher would not have coveted an invitation to join the rhetorical parade at the august Chicago Sunday Evening Club and other forums on the circuit?

King eagerly and regularly followed the entire homiletic tour. Appearing on slates of speakers with Mays, Buttrick, and other headliners, he participated in the Detroit Lenten Series for seven years between 1958 and 1968. He sermonized Crane's large Central Methodist Church of Detroit on at least six different occasions, sometimes repeating a sermon on the same day.[3] He also spoke at the Chicago Sunday Evening Club during each of the six years between 1958 and 1963.[4] And, at McCracken's behest, he preached at Fosdick's Riverside Church in 1961, 1962, and 1964.[5] In 1967 he chose the Riverside sanctuary as the site for his first well-publicized, full-scale denunciation of American war-making in Vietnam.

King did so while writing (and supervising ghostwriters for) scores of columns and essays and several books. He aimed this material primarily at the same audiences who heard him in Chicago, Detroit, Riverside Church, and elsewhere on the circuit. Like Fosdick, Niebuhr, Mays, and many others, he favored the journals C.C. Morrison founded—*Christian Century* and *Pulpit*. He published two sermons in *Pulpit* and six essays in *Christian Century*. He also served as editor-at-large for *Christian Century* from October 1958 to November 1964—an important gesture to progressives and an indisputable expression of his general compatibility with views of the journal.

The people who heard King's sermons and read *Christian Century* also bought works issued by the Harper company.[6] A general trade press, Harper also served as one of the two or three leading sources of liberal Protestant books. It published the brightest lights of Protestantism, who together authored hundreds of volumes advertised in *Christian Century* and *Pulpit*. While the Harper list falls into several genres, collections of sermons were far more numerous than works of any other category. Between 1926 and 1968 (the year King died), Harper released nineteen works by Fosdick and dozens by Buttrick, Thurman, Luccock, McCracken, Kennedy, Bosley, Morrison, Rauschenbusch, Niebuhr, Tillich, Charles Reynolds Brown, and John Sutherland Bonnell.[7] The company also issued two anthologies of sermons delivered at the Chicago Sunday Evening Club.[8] In 1944, Harper published Gunnar Myrdal's *An American Dilemma*, a seemingly comprehensive and definitive study of American race relations. The company also printed religious volumes attacking segregation, including *The Christian Way in Race Relations*, which William Stuart Nelson edited in 1948.[9]

Not surprisingly, King chose Harper as the publisher for all five of his books: *Stride Toward Freedom, Strength to Love, Why We Can't Wait, Trumpet of Conscience,* and *Where Do We Go from Here?* Like the pulpit circuit and *Christian Century,* Harper afforded him yet another means of cultivating a large group of liberal Northern supporters. By responding enthusiastically to his message, this core white constituency offered him a powerful political base in the white community—a base that no other black leader has enjoyed before or since.

King developed white support not only by retracing the oratorical itinerary of Fosdick, Hamilton, and Buttrick, but also by modelling his sermons after theirs. Despite the claim that his language germinated from his formal study of philosophy and theology, his discourse thoroughly and consistently rebuffs such a view. Instead of being miniature theological essays, his sermons strongly resemble those of preachers who illuminated the circuit and whose writing shone on the pages of *Christian Century, Pulpit,* and books issued by Harper and other presses. His sermons and most of his successful discourse—including such speeches as "I Have a Dream" and "I've Been to the Mountaintop"—are decidedly homiletic, not philosophical or theological.

The clearest reason to view King as a preacher instead of a philosopher is his pervasive but unacknowledged use of homiletic sources. Indeed, a huge number of his published and unpublished sermons—including every homily in his 1963 collection *Strength to Love*—contain substantial amounts of borrowed material. Many of his strategies of argumentation and Biblical cornerstones for sermons came directly from texts by Fosdick, Hamilton, Buttrick, and other well-known preachers. So did his system of knowledge, themes, structures, analogies, metaphors, illustrations, aphorisms, quotations, and whole paragraphs of exposition.[10] He sometimes selected non-homiletic sources as well, most notably Buttrick's *Parables of Jesus* and Thurman's *Deep River.* But he almost never chose works of philosophy or theology.

King also used unacknowledged sources in "I Have a Dream," "Letter from Birmingham Jail," "Mountaintop," and most of his other speeches, essays, and books.[11]

He and other black ministers were hardly the only clergy who traded sermons. Not only did workaday white pastors take material from famous preachers, so did the famous preachers themselves.

While they embodied a sturdy, autonomous tradition and remained largely independent of contemporaneous theology, hundreds of their published sermons strongly resemble other published sermons. From their colleagues' texts, homilists garnered assumptions about knowledge, homiletic structure, and modes of argument. They also swapped subjects, themes, analogies, quotations, illustrations, and Biblical foundations for sermons.

Among the most useful of these Biblical texts were the parables of Jesus, especially those about the prodigal son, the good Samaritan, and the wealthy fool. For example, Hamilton's 1954 homiletic collection *Horns and Halos in Human Nature* revolves almost entirely around the prodigal son. More Protestant sermons about the exploits of the prodigal and the compassion of the Samaritan may have appeared between 1900 and 1960 than in any comparable period of Protestant history.

Like most of his white models, King frequently sermonized on the parables. Seeking thoughts on these stories and many other subjects, he often turned to *Horns and Halos* and other works by the gifted preacher J. Wallace Hamilton.

Born in Canada, Hamilton ministered to Pasadena Community Church in St. Petersburg, Florida for almost forty years. Nearly every year he hopscotched the nation to address the Methodist Annual Convention and many other audiences, including Fosdick's Riverside Church.[12] In St. Petersburg, his magnetic preaching attracted thirty-five hundred souls—so many that the pews could not hold them. Taking a cue from drive-in theaters, church leaders handled the overflow by paving a large parking lot beside the sanctuary. Members and visitors drove into the lot and, while seated in their cars, listened to the service through outdoor loudspeakers mounted on their windows. In *Horns and Halos* the popular pastor of the "drive-in" church used the tale of the prodigal son as the basis for wide-ranging reflections about the mixture of good and evil, the horns and halos that everyone wears.[13]

Hamilton's musings stirred King's thoughts when, in January 1958, King walked into the auditorium of the Chicago Sunday Evening Club and received a standing ovation. Though members of this group often heard highly distinguished orators, this reception was an honor they rarely bestowed. When the sermon ended, the hall resounded with more applause for what the organizer of the club termed a "magnificent address" that served as "an inspiration to all."[14] In this presentation—"What Is Man?"—King interpreted humanity as a mixture of good and evil, body and spirit. He offered three possible responses to the question raised by his title: a mere body—"little more than an animal"; a beautiful, almost heavenly spirit; and a combination of the two.[15] He identified Christianity with the third response. After noting the first two views, he discussed Psalms 8:4–5 ("What is man . . . ? Thou hast made him a little lower than the angels."), then divided the sermon into three sections: humanity as body, humanity as spirit, humanity as sinfulness. He argued that, having both bodies and souls, we need God's forgiveness to redeem us from sin.

Much of "What Is Man?" came from Hamilton's *Horns and Halos*. Psalms 8:4–5 serves as a Biblical cornerstone for a sermon in that volume. From that text, "Remember Who You Are," King borrowed large portions of the arrangements and ideas for "What Is Man?"[16]

King's discussion of the body—material reality—included Fosdick's distillation of the social gospel—a passage that King also employed in "Pilgrimage" and elsewhere.[17] Discussing the body, he answered the challenge of empiricism, which denies the divinity side of the human equation. Ridiculing this view, he reduced it to the claim that the human body is worth a total of ninety-eight cents. The illustration could have come from a different volume by Fosdick; Gerald Kennedy's collection of homiletic illustrations; or another published sermon. It became such a cliché that readers of *Christian Century* grew tired of it and nominated it for extinction.[18] Avowing that atoms behaving accidentally could not produce Shakespeare, Beethoven, Raphael, and Jesus, renowned preacher Charles Reynolds Brown anticipated King's claim that materialism cannot explain the glories of Shakespeare, Beethoven, Michelangelo, and Jesus.[19] At least two other eminent preachers provided similar arguments.[20]

Like his remarks on materialism, King's literary quotations were not new. To illustrate pessimism, King borrowed a misanthrope's definition of the human race ("a disease on this planet").[21] To illustrate skepticism, he borrowed from Fosdick an empirical thinker's definition of life ("a physiological process with a physiological meaning").[22]

King's quotation from *Hamlet* ("What a piece of work is man!") served as a counterweight to cynicism. Not only did Hamilton anticipate the quotation in *Horns and Halos*, so did Bosley, Mays, the author of a pamphlet that King owned, and several others. Like King, each of these writers ignored Shakespeare's irony, employing Hamlet's exultant declaration as a simple expression of excessive optimism.[23] For the conclusion of "What Is Man?" King recited an anonymous, ten-line poem that graced two sermons by Allan Knight Chalmers, a professor at Boston University whom King knew.[24]

Five years after delivering "What Is Man?" in Chicago, King revised it for *Strength*, including much of what he borrowed earlier from Hamilton plus two other passages from *Horns and Halos*.[25]

King's text had numerous other, longstanding antecedents in the history of Protestant homiletics. In the early eighteenth century John Wesley, founder of the Methodist Church, presented two sermons titled "What Is Man?" Both address Psalms 8:4 and proffer a standard, dualistic view of humanity as a combination of body and soul. In 1889 an African-American preacher based another version of "What Is Man?" on Psalms 8:4, describing humanity's physical structure, intellectual ability, and sinful behavior.[26] In a 1924 volume called *What Is Man?*, another religious liberal provided a similar perspective.[27] Expounding on Psalms 8:4, prominent Midwest pacifist E. F. Tittle proposed his version of "What Is Man?" in 1928. Five years later, in a sermon about Psalms 8:4, Tittle defined humanity as a dualistic blend of matter and spirit or "dust and divinity."[28] In 1939 a Yale professor of religion advanced a similar position in another book titled *What Is Man?*[29] Publishing his variation of "What Is Man?" four years later, William Holmes Borders affirmed every human being as simultaneously a "creature of dust" and a "creature of divinity."[30] In 1949, using Psalms 8:4 as his Biblical cornerstone, yet another progressive minister presented yet another version of "What Is Man?"[31]

Hamilton founded two sermons on Psalms 8:4.[32] Tillich also spun a sermon around this appealing scripture, as did Bosley and at least four other ministers whose work got into print, including the author of King's pamphlet.[33] Gardner Taylor quoted Psalms 8:4 as well, as did Leslie Weatherhead.[34]

The enduring popularity of the dust-and-divinity theme

helped ensure that members of the Chicago Sunday Evening Club would receive King's sermon enthusiastically. And they did. However, despite King's enormous debt to Fosdick, Hamilton, and other white preachers and despite his extremely significant involvement in their network, he always remembered the dual theme of physical and spiritual deliverance trumpeted in the black pulpit. Like "Pilgrimage" and most of his other discourse, "What Is Man?" translates traditional African-American theology into an idiom that white Protestants could easily assimilate. In other words, King's sermon is a traditional black homily dressed up for white listeners.

To argue that humans are both physical and spiritual—dust and divinity—is to supply the metaphysical basis for the slaves' dual theme of deliverance. King contends that humans are physical beings, implying their eligibility for this-worldly liberation from earthly oppression. He also maintains that humans are spiritual beings, implying their eligibility for otherworldly salvation. Most of his sermon elaborates the metaphysical basis for the two forms of redemption.

Moreover, King not only implies the dual theme of liberation, he encapsulates it in an easily digestible form. He indicates that, because he is a pastor, he should "not only be concerned about mansions in the sky" but also about "thousands of people who go to bed hungry at night."[35] Then he incorporates Fosdick's claim that true religion must attack poverty.[36]

In effect, King argues, Christians must address pressing social issues because humans are physical beings with physical needs. Their material deprivation should be relieved because it prevents their deliverance in this world. Elsewhere in the sermon, he notes harsh deprivation occasioned by racism, war, colonialism, and imperialism.[37] Of course, the expoitation of one group by another through racism, colonialism, and imperialism strongly parallels the exploitation that slaves protested when they yearned for a new Moses. And, as King explains in "Death of Evil," a new Exodus can and will overcome exploitation caused by racism, colonialism, and imperialism.

By mentioning "mansions in the sky" and "streets flowing with milk and honey," King reinforces the traditional concern of slaves and other Christians about going to heaven.[38] While he does not emphasize this point, it nonetheless upholds the second part of the dual theme—the belief in heavenly salvation. In effect, he announces that, while he affirms the otherworldly strand of the dual theme, he emphasizes the demand for deliverance here and now. Borrowing Fosdick's message about the social gospel meant adapting for white listeners his father's and grandfather's demand for redemption in heaven and on earth.

As preached by Wesley, Tittle, Borders, Hamilton, and King, the motif of dust-and-divinity proved palatable not only because it had become highly familiar, but also because body-and-soul dualism was and is an extremely orthodox Christian position.

On many other occasions as well, King chose topics that were not only well-tested, but also unassailably orthodox. Consider two other sermons in *Strength*—"Three Dimensions of a Complete Life" and "A Tough Mind and a Tender Heart." Both articulate the need to avoid extremes in achieving a balanced Christian life.

Based on an unprepossessing passage from Revelations ("The length and the breadth and the height of it are equal"), "Three Dimensions" was one of King's favorite pulpit orations.[39] It served as the first sermon his bride-to-be Coretta Scott heard him preach and as his trial sermon at Dexter Avenue Baptist Church in Montgomery.[40] He also offered it in Alabama, New Orleans, upstate New York, Chicago (twice), at Ebenezer Church, and at St. Paul's Cathedral in London.[41]

The main source for all versions of "Three Dimensions" is Phillips Brooks's homily "The Symmetry of Life."[42] Brooks and King begin by portraying John's vision of the new Jerusalem, a city symmetrical and complete, and build their entire sermons on the comparison between an ideal city and an ideal humanity. The two preachers arrange their sermons in three major sections—the first devoted to length, the second to width, and the third to height. For both homilists, the commanding metaphors are the same: length designates self-development, width indicates concern for others, and height denotes relationship with God. Both Brooks and King celebrate self-fulfillment and achievement while warning of the dangers of self-absorption. Both declare that living without God is existing "without a sky."[43] And both conclude by recapitulating the importance of developing symmetrically the three dimensions of a healthy life—love of self, love for others, and love for God.

King also explains that the Biblical Naaman was a great man

except for his leprosy; then he lists others whose greatness was belied by a single shortcoming. This "Great, but" passage echoes a portion of Fosdick's *On Being Fit*.[44]

Unlike Fosdick, however, King compares America to Naaman and locates America's dramatic flaw in its practice of slavery. In the *Strength* version of "Three Dimensions," King replaces Brooks's discussion of proper white-collar careers with a litany of black achievers parallel to one that Mays celebrated in 1957.[45] Through these alterations of his sources, King emphasizes black oppression and the possibility of black redemption.

Encased in an exceedingly orthodox sermon about balanced Christian living, King's argument about black America becomes almost irrefutable because his larger, framing argument is as balanced theologically as it is geometrically. By wrapping his racial protest in what amounts to theologically indisputable discourse, King comes as close as possible to foolproofing his protest.

The civil rights leader followed a similar process when he preached on a familiar passage from Matthew ("Be ye therefore wise as serpents and harmless as doves").[46] King modelled "A Tough Mind and a Tender Heart" on "The Mind and the Heart" by Gerald Kennedy, the Methodist bishop of Los Angeles.[47] Detailing the need for a tough mind and a tender heart, Kennedy uses four categories to organize the four sections of his sermon: soft mind, tough mind, hard heart, tender heart. King divides his text into three sections: the need for a tough mind, not a soft mind; the need for a tender heart, not a hard heart; and the need to recognize God as the ideal embodiment of toughmindedness and tenderheartedness.

Both Kennedy and King note that Jesus expects Christians to combine the paradoxical qualities of the serpent and the dove. Both preachers note the difficulty of achieving such a synthesis. Both define the tough mind as sharp and penetrating and celebrate the toughmindedness of science. They interpret intellectual lapses as expressions of softmindedness. Finally, they describe the hard heart of someone unable to love and laud the tender heart as the source of compassion.

Departing from Kennedy's text, King identifies softmindedness as a cause of racism and devotes nine sentences to analyzing and condemning the softmindedness underlying segregation.[48] Again, for white listeners and readers, the undeniable orthodoxy of King's

general theme—and almost every other feature of this sermon—
helped legitimize his urgent cry to abolish segregation.

King also promulgates stock themes in his sermons about
Jesus's parables of Dives and Lazarus, the rich fool, the good
Samaritan, and the prodigal son. Several of these homilies stemmed
from Buttrick's *Parables of Jesus* of 1928—a work that other preachers also quarried for their published sermons.[49] *Parables* provides in
lapidary prose a masterful and comprehensive treatment of its
subject combined with thoughtful applications to current American
life. Ministers often consulted this work because, for several decades, no one else wrote about the parables in such a rigorously
authoritative, yet accessible manner.

In this volume and many others, Buttrick displayed his Biblical
expertise with the skills of a popularizer, making the best scholarship available to educated, general readers.[50] Before serving at
Harvard as Preacher to the University, he pastored Madison
Avenue Presbyterian Church of New York City, a large congregation whose members included Henry Luce, founder of *Time* magazine. During the 1950s, working as a writer and mainly as an editor,
Buttrick orchestrated his most enduring achievement: a luminous
twelve-volume set of Biblical criticism known as the *Interpreter's
Bible*. Because this large work is both substantive and highly
readable, it quickly became a standard desk reference for thousands
of moderate and liberal Protestant clergy.[51]

Like his analysis of Dives and Lazarus and the rich fool, "On
Being a Good Neighbor," King's initial treatment of the good
Samaritan, came from Buttrick. Both Buttrick and King begin by
explaining that Jesus told the parable during an exchange with a
Jewish lawyer. After they had talked briefly, the lawyer inquired,
"Who is my neighbor?" Running parallel are Buttrick's and King's
accounts of this exchange and of the lawyer's likely motivation.
Buttrick and King offer the same view of the lawyer's question—
that he was "taking up the cudgels of debate."[52] Both interpreters
then analyze Jesus's response as grasping the question and setting it
on a "dangerous" highway near Jerusalem.[53] Paraphrasing Luke,
both relate the tale of the beaten man, the priest, the Levite, and the
Samaritan. Buttrick's description of the latter—"He was a half-
breed, of a race . . . with which [the Jews] had "no dealings"—
becomes King's "a certain Samaritan, a half-breed from a people
with whom the Jews had no dealings."[54]

King replays Buttrick when he describes the road the victim was travelling:

BUTTRICK: Jerusalem was some two thousand feet above sea level and Jericho over one thousand feet below it. The twenty miles between the cities wound through mountainous country, whose limestone caves offered ambush for brigand bands, and whose sudden turns exposed the traveller to unforseen attack. The road became known as the "Bloody Pass."[55]

KING: When Mrs. King and I visited the Holy Land, we rented a car and drove from Jerusalem to Jericho. . . . Jerusalem is some two thousand feet above and Jericho one thousand feet below sea level. The descent is made in less than twenty miles. Many sudden curves provide likely places for ambushing and expose the traveler to unforseen attacks. Long ago the road was known as the Bloody Pass.[56]

Furthermore, Buttrick and King distill Jesus's story to the claim that "neighbor" belongs to no particular nationality or group but is anyone "in need."[57] Both writers seize the parable as an opportunity to criticize the limited, culture-bound scope of neighborly sentiment that characterizes much human behavior. To support this point, both supply examples of provincial loyalties interfering with universal compassion and brotherhood. They note that Jews were forbidden to kill fellow Jews but were allowed to kill certain non-Jews; they add that ancient Greeks did not treat their slaves as neighbors.[58] Greatly expanding Buttrick's point about race, King adds to Buttrick's exegesis a detailed protest against segregation.

Portions of another King sermon, "Good Samaritan," repeat material in "On Being a Good Neighbor" that King had borrowed earlier from Buttrick. However, King organizes the remainder of "Good Samaritan" differently, dividing it into three sections, each corresponding to a different outlook. The robber exemplifies the first perspective, the priest and the Levite the second, and the Samaritan the third. By mugging someone and stealing his money, the robber says, in effect, "What's yours is mine . . . I'll take it from you." By walking hurriedly past the victim, the priest and the Levite seem to say, "What is mine is mine and what is yours is yours." By aiding the beaten man, the Samaritan obeys the precept of "What is mine is yours, and I'll give it to you."

In a famous lecture from 1926, Charles Reynolds Brown originated King's three-part arrangement based on the attitudes of the robber, the priest and Levite, and the Samaritan.[59] King also reiterated Brown's argument. However, just as King altered other sources, he changed this one as well. Although Brown's lecture expressed a potent social gospel, Brown never mentioned race. King however, included a detailed analysis of degrading, racist housing in Chicago.

In both sermons about the good Samaritan, King rescored and reorchestrated an utterly familiar, utterly mainstream homiletic topic for the purpose of attacking racial injustice. Once again, he wrapped his protest in the impeccable garb of orthodoxy.

He followed a similar procedure in "Prodigal Son," another sermon about a standard topic. By dissecting every human being as a perplexing paradox of good and evil, he reiterated the main contention of *Horns and Halos*, Hamilton's book-length examination of the prodigal.[60] After asking, "And how many men are in every man?" Hamilton answers his own question:

HAMILTON: There is a bit of the coward in the bravest man and a bit of the hero in the meanest. A bad man looks like a good man sometimes— when his baby is sick, for instance; and a good man looks like a bad man when someone takes his parking space. There is always something in our enemy that we admire, and something in our closest friends that we don't admire.

Shakespeare put it down in two great speeches. In "Hamlet" he sees the halos: "What a piece of work is man, how noble in reason, in action how like an angel, in apprehension how like a god." Then something happened to Shakespeare, between "Hamlet" and "King Lear." In "King Lear," he rubs against the horns: "Man is false of spirit, bloody of hand; a fox in stealth, a wolf in greediness, a lion in prey."[61]

In "Prodigal Son" King meditates on the divided self, observing, ". . . each of us is two selves." Echoing Hamilton, he explains this split:

KING: Do you know that there is a bit of the coward in the bravest of us? And a bit of the hero in the meanest of us. A bad man looks like a good man sometimes, for instance, when his baby is sick. And a good man looks like a bad man sometimes, for instance when somebody takes his parking space. There's always something in our enemy that we admire. And there's always something in our closest friends that we don't admire. . . . Shakespeare one day thought of the fact that there are halos within man and within human nature. He wrote in *Hamlet,* "What a piece of work is man! How noble in faculty! How infinite in reason! . . . In action how like an angel, in apprehension how like a God." . . . Later on Shakespeare wrote *King Lear.* And he knew that man did not only have halos in his being, but he also had horns. And so in *King Lear* he wrote, "Man is false of spirit, bloody of hand, a wolf in greediness, a lion in prey."[62]

In addition, Hamilton and King harness an anonymous poem:

> There's so much good in the worst of us,
>   And so much bad in the best of us,
> That it doesn't behoove any of us
>   To find fault with the rest of us.[63]

Other leading preachers also spotlighted the prodigal as the Biblical paradigm of the divided self, the perfect example of the war within a single person. During the late 1920s Buttrick reflected on the prodigal: "Self-will is not our true self."[64] A sermon from 1940 featured the same anonymous poem that Hamilton and King used later.[65] During the mid-1940s—ten years prior to *Horns and Halos*— Fosdick remarked, "He was not one self but—a prodigal and a son. He was both. . . ."[66] During the year that *Horns and Halos* appeared, C.L. Franklin explained, "So the record is that when [the prodigal son] found himself in the pigpen, he came to himself, which means that he was not at himself when he left home."[67] In short, this parable is an extremely well-known story, the prodigal often represents the divided self, and that division (or mixture) of good and evil is classic Christian theology.

But unlike Buttrick, Fosdick, Hamilton, and even Franklin, King compares America to the prodigal and links the story to American racism. Insisting that a prodigal America strayed to a far country of discrimination, King analyzed at length the devastating effects of segregation and poverty.

The topic of the prodigal served King in two ways. First, interpreting every person as good and evil meant placing all people on the same plane and reinforcing his basic argument against racial superiority. No race can be altogether superior or inferior if every individual is sometimes good and sometimes evil. Second, preaching on the divided self meant, once again, packing his polemic against racism into a box of homiletic orthodoxy.

King purposefully chose material that was widely used and highly intertextual. By at least the middle of his career (and probably near its beginning), he discovered abundant parallels and correspondences among sermons by Fosdick, Buttrick, Hamilton, and others. Consider his "Antidotes for Fear," based on John 4:18 ("There is no fear in love; but perfect love casteth out fear . . .).[68] More complexly intertextual than any of King's other works, "Antidotes" draws on a voluminous, highly interwoven literature. For this sermon, he directly used five sources—one sermon by Fosdick; one by Buttrick; one by McCracken; *Peace of Mind*, by popular radio preacher Rabbi Joshua Liebman; and *The Courage to Be* by Tillich.[69] With the exception of Tillich's book, these remarkably similar texts—and King's—overlap at many points. And they strongly resemble a host of other sermons about fear.

In the long introduction to "Antidotes," King borrowed directly from Liebman, Fosdick, and Buttrick.[70] Then, using a conventional, four-part arrangement, he separated his sermon into four sections, each of which features a solution to fear. For his initial remedy, he declares that one must first confront fear. In the second section he advocates matering fear through courage, in the third through love, and in the fourth through faith.

The first cure—confronting fear—parallels one that McCracken endorsed.[71] For his discussion of the second cure, courage, King borrowed several sentences from *The Courage To Be*—one of the extremely few instances that King the public figure ever borrowed from Tillich.[72] (King, however, clearly subordinates Tillich's single solution to fear to the multiple solutions offered by popular preachers.)[73] King's analysis of love as a remedy to fear reflects his scriptural cornerstone—"Perfect love casteth out fear." In their sermons about fear, Fosdick and Buttrick cite the same Biblical verse and, of course, propose love as a solution to fear.[74] Finally Fosdick, Buttrick, McCracken, and Liebman all presage King's contention that faith conquers fear.[75]

Undoubtedly many preachers faced a widespread demand for help in overcoming fear. McCracken once observed: "I notice that when I preach on 'What To Do with Our Fears' the request for copies of the sermon is greater than when the theme is 'The Christian View of History.' "[76] Writing in *Pulpit*, another minister also remarked the popularity of this topic: "It is no accident that modern sermons come back so often to the problem of our fears and anxieties, for every one of us will agree that it is one of the persistent problems. Ours is called 'the age of fear.' "[77] The age of fear may have begun in 1873, when Henry Ward Beecher sermonized on "Perfect love casteth out fear."[78] Beginning with E.F. Tittle's homily in 1932, a veritable river of sermons (and other works) about fear flooded bookstores as literally dozens of preachers addressed the topic.[79] Like the texts about fear that King consulted, most of this outpouring (including a sermon by Hamilton) features remarkably similar remedies for fear.

Together, Fosdick, Buttrick, Liebman, McCracken, Tillich, and King added only a small tributary to this river. However, by borrowing directly from Fosdick, Buttrick, Liebman, and McCracken, King took pains to ensure that his sermon reflected a broad homiletic consensus.

In addition, he undoubtedly knew that many of his literary quotations were just as standard as his antidotes for fear. Consider four examples. He quotes two complete quatrains and half of another by Omar Khayyam. One or more of these popular poems surfaces in a book by Thurman and in sermons by Fosdick (twice), Buttrick (twice), Hamilton, Niebuhr, and at least three other clergy.[80]

King also cites four extremely popular lines from John Bowring:

In the cross of Christ I glory,
Towering o'er the wrecks of time;
All the light of sacred story
Gathers round its head sublime.

This verse adds luster to volume after volume of sermons. Gladden broadcast it in 1904. Fosdick incorporates it in no fewer than six books. Bowring's rhyme also brightens works by Buttrick, Hamilton, Sockman, and at least six other preachers, not to mention a compilation of illustrations.[81]

In addition, King recalls a cynical line from Shakespeare equating life with "a tale told by an idiot. . . ." Fosdick includes this metaphor in five volumes of sermons; Buttrick features it twice; and Weatherhead, Thurman, Luccock, Sockman, Tittle, Chalmers, and Johns all refute the metaphor from *Macbeth*.[82]

Finally, King's use of Swinburne's proclamation—"Glory to Man in the highest! for man is the master of things"—had many precedents among ministers, who invariably enjoyed ridiculing it. The exclamation circulates in a total of thirteen books by Fosdick, Weatherhead, Kennedy, Bosley, Buttrick, Luccock, and Bonnell. It also surfaces in Niebuhr's most important treatise.[83]

The very familiarity of these quotations endeared them to many preachers, including King. Just as he borrowed sermons from the most popular ministers, he also wielded the most popular quotations available. Neither of these practices is accidental. Rather, his repeated use of highly intertextual material testifies to his awareness of homiletic intertextuality, an awareness that helped him transport black demands into a white universe.

King's mainstream sermons proved highly persuasive not because they reflected his study of canonical texts of Western philosophy and theology, but because he planted them firmly in Protestant homiletic traditions. He succeeded because he demonstrated his absolute mastery of standard subjects, themes, quotations, and other important elements of liberal preaching. Members of Ebenezer Church and other black audiences rejoiced at his ability to weave traditional black protest into the fabric of formal, orthodox statements about well-known Biblical texts.

King's stock themes, reliable quotations, and four-square orthodoxy offered assurance to those who either wondered about or were upset by his disruptive politics. His advocacy of body-and-soul dualism—dust and divinity—established his voice as one of moderation. So did his call for balanced, three-dimensional Christian life and his advice about combining the wisdom of a serpent and the harmlessness of a dove.

Explicating the parable of the good Samaritan enabled him to erect his pleas for brotherhood on a beloved Biblical foundation that could never be challenged. Calling for Samaritan-like altruism and compassion validated his politics as an expression of concern for the needy and stigmatized his opponents as avatars of selfishness and privilege. Moreover, advocating the gospel of brotherhood helped him stake out high moral ground and indict America for flouting what it claimed to hold dear.

Articulating the devilish paradox of good and evil also served the cause of civil rights. By embracing the paradox, King avoided ideologically equating his movement with pure goodness and his opponents with evil incarnate—an equation that Malcolm X and other radical leaders did not hesitate to make. King's decision had important consequences. Some reformers stand with Amos and call for justice to roll down like waters but are unwilling to build any irrigation ditches. By contrast King not only called for justice to roll down like waters, he actually sat down with business leaders and government officials to channel and direct the waters of justice. His argument about good and evil within each person granted him the flexibility to negotiate with allies and bargain with adversaries. Without becoming a hypocrite, he could counsel Presidents Kennedy and Johnson about the shape of civil rights legislation and negotiate with a mayor who singlehandedly ruled Chicago. And, during a crisis of confrontation, he could hammer out an agreement to desegregate the downtown stores of Birmingham.

Such mediation was absolutely crucial, for it proved that protests actually brought tangible results. Thus, King's orthodox themes undergirded his customary strategy of orate, demonstrate, negotiate. Because Malcolm X, Stokely Carmichael, and other radicals identified powerless blacks as pure good and powerful whites as pure evil, they could not engage in such mediation.

For King, prescribing cures for fear also had practical benefits. He demonstrated to whites that he and his movement could master fear during a tumultuous period. And he fortified activists to face police dogs, fire hoses, beatings, jail, and even death. Texts from Fosdick, Buttrick, Liebman, and McCracken provided entirely conventional steps for eliminating fear that had already been sifted and tested by a large religious community. For this reason—not because they resulted from the solitary thought of a gifted philosopher—the solutions were as close as any Protestant could come to unimpeachably authoritative, foolproof answers that could sustain protestors even unto death.

Yet, despite his unswerving orthodoxy and willingness to negotiate and compromise, King was far from a simple moderate. Borrowing mainline themes meant presenting his radical tactic of civil disobedience as something far less threatening than it would otherwise have appeared. Standard literary quotations and other homiletic boilerplate made his goals of an immediate end to poverty, segregation, and war seem far less radical than they actually were. His use of theologically soothing material did much to establish his simultaneous identities as both a mainstream thinker and a radical leader, as a "conservative militant."[84]

As he adapted sermonic boilerplate and refined and retested his best original material, King skillfully inserted his arguments against segregation into a web of ideas and phrases that moderate and liberal white Protestants had already approved. Undoubtedly, many of King's Northern white supporters who annually poured money into his organization had listened for years to Fosdick's nationally broadcast radio sermons. Many of them had heard their own pastors emulate the liberal pulpit manner of Fosdick, Buttrick, and Hamilton—an approach their clergy had assimilated at seminary. King validated himself by borrowing passages carefully attuned to his core white audience and by reciting them again and again as he hopscotched the nation. Using words his listeners had already heard, he reinforced what they already believed.

Literary quotations comprised an important part of King's rhetorical arsenal. Had he studiously examined volumes of Shakespeare, Carlyle, Khayyam, Swinburne, and other canonical authors, he might have ransacked new selections as apt as those he took from other preachers. However, such fresh citations would never have resonated as well as those he actually used because his audiences would never have heard them before. The intertextual quality of King's language enhanced and invigorated his appeal.

By incorporating into virtually all of his mainline sermons the old-fashioned, yet radical black demand for equality, King accomplished a feat that no one else had ever achieved. He reached white audiences and thereby turned the traditional black demand into something it had never been before—a mainstream American idea.

FIVE

DARKNESS CANNOT DRIVE OUT DARKNESS

A loud explosion rocked the front of the house. Glass from the windows blanketed the floor. Underneath swirling smoke that smelled of dynamite, part of the front porch was blown asunder, and a hole had opened in the concrete underneath it. Inside their home a woman and her baby were fine, though they could have been killed. When a crowd of several hundred blacks gathered in front of the porch, many were ready to tear apart the city of Montgomery. Some adults were armed. Young boys carried broken bottles.

The presence of the mayor and the police commissioner did nothing to assuage the anger. A boycott of city buses had found city fathers unyielding in their refusal to meet the most modest black demands. The minority community had not asked city officials to end bus segregation, merely to make it slightly less degrading. But white leaders had brushed them aside. And now this.

When police instructed the crowd to disperse, no one moved. One man threatened a shoot-out. Upon arriving, a young minister waded through the crowd and entered his home, where others were already meeting. After conferring with his wife, he listened to the mayor's regrets. The principal of the city's largest black high school told the mayor that apologies meant little when the mayor's own anti-Negro, "get-tough" policy had encouraged this act of violence. Unable to answer, the mayor and police commissioner stood mute. Around the porch the crowd grew more menacing. The police were visibly frightened, and white reporters, who wanted to file their stories, hesitated to move.

At that moment the youthful minister mounted what remained of his front porch. When he began speaking, everyone hushed. Though it lasted only three or four minutes, the Sermon on the Porch was the most important address this man ever made. If he failed to control his emotions, if he failed to talk nonviolence, if he failed to preach love, and—most importantly—if he failed to disarm the mob, nonviolence would fail, the boycott would fail, love would fail, and he would fail. If the Sermon on the Porch fizzled, M.L. King, Jr., would have remained M.L. King, Jr.—the name his parents and Rosa Parks knew him by, the name he himself preferred.[1] He would never have become Martin Luther King at all.

King told his infuriated listeners to set aside their weapons. Violent retaliation, he insisted, would not succeed. He quoted Jesus: "He who lives by the sword will perish by the sword." And again, "Love your enemies, bless them that curse you." He finished by proclaiming that, whatever happened to him, God would ensure the victory of the boycott.

Some wept. Several yelled, "Amen!" Others announced their support. But when the police commissioner rose to speak, people reacted angrily. Only when King asked for quiet did their yelling subside. After the commissioner and mayor vowed to arrest the culprit, the crowd gradually dispersed. And all through that day and night—indeed throughout the entire boycott—the African-American community steadfastly refused to retaliate despite this and many other bombings directed against it.[2]

Here and on literally thousands of other occasions, King measured violence, which sprang from hatred, against nonviolence, which sprang from love. The incident at the porch provided a unique opportunity to preach nonviolence in a dramatic political context. The contrast between violence and nonviolence that he sketched in the Sermon on the Porch was vividly manifest in the contrast between the explosion and the boycott. Anyone hearing about the porch incident (or reading about it in his book, *Stride Toward Freedom*) could see that, quite unlike a bus boycott, racist violence threatened to kill an innocent woman and her baby. By contrast his followers had put down their swords.

The pattern of nonviolent protest met by violent retaliation occurred throughout the bus boycott and throughout the early 1960s. Hundreds of innocent activists suffered bombed homes and churches, gunshot wounds, and cracked skulls. Others were martyred. King himself was stabbed in the chest and almost lost his life. He also faced blows by fists and rocks, a bombed hotel room, and endless death threats. Publicized by the news media, incidents of peaceful protest and violent reaction supplied extremely powerful and vivid examples of the contrast King tirelessly drew between nonviolence and violence.

This stark contrast propelled a Second American Revolution at the Bunker Hill of Montgomery, the Valley Forge of Birmingham, and the Yorktown of Selma. But what prompted King's devotion to nonviolence? Countless books, essays, and articles claim that King learned nonviolence from Mahatma Gandhi. But King did not develop his pacifism from a single-handed wrestling match with Gandhi. In fact, Gandhi exerted very little direct influence on King. Instead, King learned nonviolence almost entirely from American sources.

Nor did King's nonviolence reflect the powerful influence of Reinhold Niebuhr, as many have maintained.[3] Except for reinforcing King's father's teachings about sin, Niebuhr never exerted a significant impact on King. Instead, his nonviolence developed as he listened to, conferred with, and read works by black and white pacifists, especially a group of mentors affiliated with Howard University. Moreover, his devotion to nonviolence and his political/religious orientation grew directly from the African-American folk religion of his father and grandfather.

In "Pilgrimage" King reports that he first became interested in Gandhi when he heard Mordecai Johnson preach about Gandhi's achievements.[4] This presentation was "so profound and electrifying," King notes, that he immediately "bought a half-dozen books on Gandhi's life and works."[5] However, King fails to mention a speech and an essay about Gandhi that supply most of the analysis of nonviolence that appears in "Pilgrimage." Portions of his explication of nonviolence, including several quotations from Gandhi, stem from Harris Wofford's speech "Nonviolence and the Law: The Law Needs Help," which Wofford published in 1957. Note:

WOFFORD: "Rivers of blood may have to flow before we gain our freedom but it must be our blood," [Gandhi] said to his countrymen. . . . What was Gandhi's justification for this ordeal to which he invited his countrymen, for this mass political application of the ancient doctrine of turning the other cheek? . . . there should be little that a lawyer need say to convince you of the educational potentialities of suffering. "Things of fundamental importance to people are not secured by reason alone but have to be purchased with their suffering," said Gandhi. "Suffering is infinitely more powerful than the law of the jungle for converting the opponent and opening his ears, which are otherwise shut, to the voice of reason."

If the jails must be filled, let them be entered, as Gandhi urged his countrymen, "as a bridegroom enters the bride's chamber."[6]

KING: "Rivers of blood may have to flow before we gain our freedom, but it must be our blood," Gandhi said to his countrymen. . . . If going to jail is necessary, [the nonviolent resister] enters it "as a bridegroom enters the bride's chamber."

One may well ask: "What is the nonviolent resister's justification for this ordeal to which he invites men, for this mass political application of the ancient doctrine of turning the other cheek?" . . . Suffering, the nonviolent resister realizes, has tremendous educational and transforming possibilities. "Things of fundamental importance to people are not secured by reason alone, but have to be purchased with their suffering," said Gandhi. He continues: "Suffering is infinitely more powerful than the law of the jungle for converting the opponent and opening his ears which are otherwise shut to the voice of reason."[7]

Other segments of King's explanation come from William Stuart Nelson's essay "Satyagraha: Gandhian Principles of Non-Violent Non-Cooperation," which also appeared in 1957.[8] Moreover, King's summary of Gandhi's theories incorporates a sentence from Richard Gregg's *Power of Nonviolence*, which was apparently one of the half-dozen volumes that King examined after hearing Johnson's speech.[9]

Explaining nonviolence in "Loving Your Enemies" and "Antidotes for Fear," King relies not on Gandhi or Niebuhr but on an anti-war tradition of Fosdick and other preachers. In "Loving Your Enemies" he borrows a discussion of nonviolence from E. Stanley Jones's 1948 volume, *Mahatma Gandhi: An Interpretation:*

JONES: The weapons Gandhi chose were simple: We will match our capacity to suffer against your capacity to inflict the suffering, our soul force against your physical force. We will not hate you, but we will not obey you. Do what you like, and we will wear you down by our capacity to suffer. And in the winning the freedom we will so appeal to your heart and conscience that we will win you. So ours will be a double victory; we will win our freedom and our captors in the process.[10]

KING: To our most bitter opponents we say: "We shall match your capacity to inflict suffering by our capacity to endure suffering. We shall meet your physical force with soul force. Do to us what you will, and we shall continue to love you. . . . But be ye assured that we will wear you down by our capacity to suffer. One day we shall win freedom, but not only for ourselves. We shall so appeal to your heart and conscience that we will win *you* in the process, and our victory will be a double victory."[11]

King reiterated Jones's paragraph on many occasions. "Loving Your Enemies" also offers an analysis of violence and nonviolence that King located in Hamilton's *Horns and Halos:*

HAMILTON: The Christian technique of forgiveness is to get rid of enemies by getting rid of enmity.[12]

At the height of the Civil War, when feeling was bitterest, at a White House reception [Lincoln] dropped a kindly remark about the South, and a woman there flared up, shocked that he could speak kindly of his enemies when he should want to destroy them. Lincoln looked at her and said slowly, "Madam, do I not destroy my enemies when I make them my friends?"

But now we have come to the place where it is a case of "forgive—or else!" These multiplying hatreds can destroy us. This chain reaction of evil—hate begetting hate, wars making more wars, violence begetting more violence . . . —must be broken.[13]

Darkness cannot drive out darkness; only light can do that. . . . More evil cannot drive out evil; only goodness can do that.[14]

KING: Darkness cannot drive out darkness; only light can do that. Hate cannot drive out hate; only love can do that. Have we not come to such an impasse in the modern world that we must love our enemies—or else? The chain reaction of evil—hate begetting hate, wars producing more wars—must be broken.

. . . we get rid of an enemy by getting rid of enmity. It was this same attitude that made it possible for Lincoln to speak a kind word about the South during the Civil War when feeling was most bitter. Asked by a shocked bystander how he could do this, Lincoln said, "Madam, do I not destroy my enemies when I make them my friends?"[15]

For "Antidotes for Fear" King updates an analysis of fear and violence that Fosdick published in *Hope of the World*:

FOSDICK: Now, the old remedy for fear was great armaments. Armed to the teeth, a nation said, we shall not fear. But how futile that old remedy is in the new world! Great armaments are not a remedy for fear. They are the major cause of fear. . . . Not battleships and poison gas but only organized goodwill can ever give the nations real security and cast out fear.[16]

KING: We have armed ourselves to the nth degree. . . . The nations have believed that greater armaments will cast out fear. But alas! they have produced greater fear. . . . Not arms, but love, understanding, and organized goodwill can cast out fear.[17]

In *Stride* King also explains nonviolence by replaying long segments of Wofford's "Nonviolence and the Law: The Law Needs Help."[18] Both Wofford and King reject the Old Testament maxim of "an eye for an eye," because such a practice "leaves everybody blind." Both define nonviolence as a middle alternative between aggression and passivity, and both sketch protestors' calm and directness, their willful disobedience after their words had failed, and their readiness to die for their testimony. Both recount Nehru's summary of India's campaign against the British. Both then turn to Montgomery and Little Rock, contending that a generation of black children would profit from the bravery demonstrated by children in Little Rock. Both offer an identical quotation from Gandhi and claim that nonviolence will help bury the apathy generated by racism.[19] In the middle of his discussion, King inserts a paragraph from E. Stanley

Jones's *Mahatma Gandhi: An Interpretation*—the same passage he
uses in "Loving Your Enemies" and on many other occasions.[20]

Like the thoughts of Jones, Hamilton, and Fosdick, King's
principles of nonviolence express his Christian faith. King always
subordinated Gandhian notions to Christianity, constantly interpreting nonviolence as the collective expression of Christian love.
As the best-known minister in the nation, he tirelessly preached
Christianity. In "Address to Holt Street Baptist Church," his first
civil rights speech, he failed to mention Thoreau or Gandhi. In "I
Have a Dream" he likewise ignored Gandhi. Although "Letter from
Birmingham Jail" represents his most sophisticated explication of
civil disobedience, "Letter" also omits any reference to Gandhi. Yet
the Holt Street address, "I Have a Dream," "Letter," and virtually
all other examples of King's discourse are Bible-soaked and explicitly Christian. Although he often espoused and interpreted love
without mentioning Gandhi, he never espoused Gandhi apart from
Christianity.

While King frequently explained the relationship between
Christianity and nonviolence, he did so best in a remarkable,
unpublished letter to the editor of the *Christian Century*. In his
column, editor Harold Fey had worried that Gandhi was overtaking
Christ as a figure of devotion in the civil rights movement.[21] As
evidence, Fey cited the establishment of the Gandhi Society, which
King and his associates had initiated as a mechanism for raising
funds. Fearing the rise of Gandhi as a cult figure, the editor attacked
the Gandhi Society and called for increased dedication to Jesus
Christ. Even though Fey raised his argument in a short column—
not a full-length essay—King understood the respect that the
Christian Century commanded among Northern religious liberals.
For that reason, despite the incalculable demands on his time, he
responded with an extremely thoughtful, four-page, single-spaced
letter to Fey.

King's letter angrily, yet very lucidly rebuts Fey's charge,
reaffirming the Messiahship of Christ while observing that
". . . God worked through Gandhi, and the spirit of Jesus Christ
saturated his life." He continued, "It is ironic, yet inescapably true
that the greatest Christian of the modern world was a man [Gandhi]
who never embraced Christianity."[22] In King's eyes, Gandhi was
the greatest modern Christian because Gandhi's protests amounted
to a collective expression of Christ-like love. According to King, Fey

wrongly believed that Gandhian thought and practice formed an alternative to Christ's teachings. Instead, King argued, Gandhian nonviolence was the *embodiment* of Christianity.

No one should be surprised by King's response to Fey, for King's father and grandfather had long seen nonviolent protest as an expression of the Christian gospel. The tenets of Christian love and nonviolence that King first learned at Ebenezer Church were reinforced and elaborated through several influences during his adult life.

Among them was the anti-war preaching of Fosdick, Hamilton, and other liberals, who nurtured King's understanding of nonviolence and whose words registered a huge impact on King's audiences. King found preachers' analyses of war so agreeable that he frequently reiterated them as his own. By borrowing their language, he unavoidably borrowed their thought, for thought and language are inextricably intertwined.

King gravitated toward Fosdick and other pacifist preachers because their anti-war tradition was homegrown, not imported from overseas. While they occasionally discussed Gandhi, their opposition to war was specifically American, specifically Christian, and not especially indebted to Gandhi. Commanding hundreds of pulpits and many radio microphones, pacifists both famous and ordinary extolled love and denounced war to literally millions of moderate and liberal Protestants.[23] Between the two world wars, their audiences comprised a large percentage of the entire American population. The peace-minded pulpit became a fixture in American life, and many thousands of Americans became pacifists or near-pacifists.

When King celebrated nonviolence as an expression of Christian love, he reinvigorated a dormant, but longstanding advocacy of pacifism in the liberal pulpit. This tradition was extremely important for King's audiences, who frequently reassimilated its language as King spread his gospel of nonviolence. When audiences applauded him, they applauded words many of them had literally heard or read before. His appeals for nonviolence succeeded in part because he reached a crucial group of Northern, white progressives through anti-war language they already knew and relished.

A predominantly black group affiliated with Howard University played an even more important role in shaping King's devotion to nonviolence. In 1935, while teaching at Howard University,

Howard Thurman traveled to India to confer with Gandhi. In a conversation with Thurman, Gandhi prophesied that American blacks would perfect his methods in their crusade for racial equality.[24] Inspired by Thurman's expedition, other luminaries at his institution repeated his journey to India to learn the ways of peaceful protest. They included the well-known, larger-than-life president of the institution, Mordecai Johnson, and two succeeding deans of the School of Religion, Benjamin Mays and William Stuart Nelson. Like Thurman, his friend and former student, Mays sought lessons in nonviolence from Gandhi himself.[25] Harris Wofford also ventured to India to study nonviolence before enrolling at the law school of Howard University.[26]

After returning from their odysseys to India, the Howard University sojourners—especially Wofford, Nelson, and Johnson—spread the word about Gandhi. In 1950 Wofford and his wife wrote a book about nonviolence in India. Nelson advocated collective protest in 1944; five years later he argued, "Negroes would find a potent instrument in the type of sacrificial spirit of non-cooperation which has proved so successful in India."[27] Johnson preached on Gandhi to a number of audiences, including one at Crozer Seminary that included King.

Listening to Johnson, however, was only one of King's many chains of contact with black academics and others who actively propagandized Gandhian theory and strategy. By 1957, when he wrote "Pilgrimage," he "loved and respected Thurman" and was personally acquainted with and/or had heard lectures by Mays, Johnson, Wofford, and possibly Nelson—each of whom had trekked to India to study nonviolence and two of whom had conversed directly with Gandhi.[28] At the time of the Montgomery bus boycott or shortly thereafter, Wofford sent King a copy of his speech "Non-Violence and the Law: The Law Needs Help." In 1956 he accepted King's invitation to discuss peaceful protest at the Institute on Nonviolence sponsored by King's organization in Montgomery.[29] Probably in 1957 or early 1958 Nelson mailed King a copy of his essay "Satyagraha: Gandhian Principles of Non-Violent Non-Cooperation."[30] By 1957 King also knew James Lawson, a black Christian pacifist roughly his own age. Lawson spent thirteen months in prison as a conscientious objector to the Korean War and lived in India between 1952 and 1955, studying Gandhian methods.[31] King later met Richard Gregg, a white pacifist who had lived in India and known Gandhi personally. In 1959, a decade after Gandhi's death, King retraced the footsteps of Thurman, Johnson, Nelson, and Mays by travelling to India to visit with Gandhi's followers and learn about nonviolence.

For King, the influences of anti-war preachers and American Gandhians converged in the persons of Mays, Thurman, and Johnson—who shared platforms with Fosdick and other pacifists—and in the person of E. Stanley Jones.[32] A long-time missionary to India, Jones knew Gandhi fairly well, published prolifically in the United States and England, and preached at the Chicago Sunday Evening Club and other stops on the pulpit circuit.

As early as 1925—four years before King was born and seven years before Niebuhr's *Moral Man* appeared—Jones wrote "Jesus Comes Through Irregular Channels—Mahatma Gandhi's Part," a chapter in his *The Christ of the Indian Road*. Here Jones calls Gandhi "the most successful man who has lived in East or West in the last ten years."[33] Three years later Jones penned *Christ at the Round Table*, a set of reflections on Christianity in India and on Gandhi's meeting with the British at the Round Table Conference. By the time Jones had written *Mahatma Gandhi: An Interpretation* in 1948, he had already spent more than two decades ruminating about Gandhi's leadership and deciding what he liked about Gandhi—namely, the theory and techniques of nonviolent dissent. For King, borrowing Jones's 1948 treatment of nonviolence meant borrowing ideas that the thoughtful Jones had developed carefully over a period of twenty-three years. Although King probably did not read Jones's "Jesus Comes Through Irregular Channels—Mahatma Gandhi's Part," King's response to Harold Fey's attack on the Gandhi Society is quite consistent with thoughts about the Mahatma that Jones expressed several decades earlier. Reading Jones's *Mahatma Gandhi: An Interpretation* reinforced an understanding of Gandhi that King developed under the tutelage of the American Gandhians from Howard University.

During the Montgomery bus boycott, King also benefited from the direct counsel of pacifist advisors. He received advanced lessons in nonviolence from Wofford; from Glenn Smiley, a white pacifist employed by the Fellowship of Reconciliation (FOR); and from Bayard Rustin, a black pacifist who had previously worked for the FOR.

Smiley's and Rustin's views about nonviolence were remarkably consistent with those of Jones, Gregg, Lawson, and the Gandhians of Howard University. Fosdick and other anti-war preachers only occasionally invoked Gandhi's name. Unlike Gandhi, they offered no practical method for organizing grassroots protest. Nonetheless their calls to eradicate war were quite compatible with Gandhian thought.

Obviously King did not begin the process of applying Gandhi to America, as many people believe. Serving as King's mentors, members of the black religious intelligentsia and other Gandhians molded and filtered King's conception of nonviolence. Filled with a desire to introduce Gandhian strategy to the black struggle, these teachers sought to persuade college students, seminarians, and ministers to adopt Gandhi's ideas. In the case of King, Farmer, and others who heard their presentations and read their writings, they succeeded magnificently. In turn, King, Farmer, and Lawson coaxed and instructed a new generation, igniting campaigns of massive civil disobedience that none of their mentors had been able to spark.

In Montgomery and elsewhere King grafted Gandhian principles onto the worldview of African-American Protestants. The African-American social gospel had propelled his interest in Gandhi in the first place—just as it had propelled his black models to visit India to inquire firsthand about the vision and tactics of nonviolence. For these pioneers and for King and his followers, Gandhi's methods were simply a means of implementing Christian love and achieving the long-sought goal of black Americans: this-worldly deliverance from oppression.

The anti-war stance of these white and black pacifists dramatically contrasts with Niebuhr's position. As King explains, in *Moral Man* Niebuhr contends that nonviolence and violence share the same ethical ambiguities and therefore are morally almost indistinguishable.[34] Without exception, all of King's pacifist coaches strongly disagreed with Niebuhr, as did Fosdick and other anti-war preachers. Unlike Niebuhr, they wholeheartedly endorsed nonviolence as a morally praiseworthy alternative to violence. They uniformly hailed Gandhi's methods and achievements and expressed no significant reservations. Unlike Niebuhr, they consistently maintained that neither nonviolence nor violence is ethically ambiguous. Instead, they insisted: nonviolence is good, and violence is evil, pure and simple.

In the Sermon on the Porch and throughout his entire career, King sketched precisely the same contrast. In contrast to Niebuhr, who minimized the distinction between nonviolence and violence, King exalted that distinction. The contrast is especially evident in the sentences King borrowed from Jones, which starkly oppose the "soul force" of nonviolence to the "physical force" of violence.

King's difference with Niebuhr is also apparent in his use of two of Niebuhr's well-known, paired phrases. In his 1944 work *Children of Light and Children of Darkness* (which King apparently read), Niebuhr defined "children of light" as "those who seek to bring self-interest . . . in harmony with a more universal good."[35] For Niebuhr the category "children of light" includes Christians and "secularized idealists."[36] Qualifying as utopian idealists are such diverse figures as Adam Smith, Hegel, Marx, Marxists, and many liberal Protestants.[37] In contrast to these figures, Niebuhr denotes "children of darkness" as "moral cynics" who act simply from self-interest.[38] Essentially Niebuhr minted his phrases to articulate what was arguably his favorite theme—the dangers of utopian thought and utopian social movements.

In *Stride* King retools the phrase "children of light" to refer to racial moderates in the South who were aware of injustice but afraid to speak about it. He contrasts these people to the South's "children of darkness," presumably ardent racists and segregationists.[39] Whereas Niebuhr wields his paired phrases to analyze global philosophical and political movements, King employs them to refer strictly to two species of white Southerners with diverging attitudes about race. Thus King substantially alters the meaning of Niebuhr's phrases, which originally had nothing to do with race. He does so in a book that, like all his other discourse, demands a high-minded idealism able to vanquish racism.

Significantly, in *Stride* King does not substantially alter the texts of Wofford and Jones, or those of the six other writers who supply sources for "Pilgrimage"—most of whom would fit Niebuhr's definition of irresponsible idealists, as would King himself. He borrows without alteration a sentence from Richard Gregg, whose idealism Niebuhr specifically attacked.[40] He also failed to change the idealistic anti-war expressions of Hamilton and Fosdick that he incorporates into "Loving Your Enemies" and "Antidotes for Fear." By explaining nonviolence through the unchanged sentences of Jones, Fosdick, Hamilton, and the American Gandhians, King unmistakably signals his enormous debt to the pacifists of Howard University and the white pacifist pulpit—not to Niebuhr's blatant anti-pacifism, which King clearly rejected.

Far from being mere conduits through which King encountered Gandhi, the American Gandhians dramatically shaped and edited King's version of Gandhi. King ignored many of Gandhi's most fundamental religious values and practices. Unlike Gandhi, he never became a vegetarian, never obeyed any strict dietary regimen, never advocated sexual abstinence, and never adopted a weekly day of silence to facilitate spiritual awareness. Unlike Gandhi, he never shed material possessions and never embraced voluntary poverty.[41] Nor did he imitate Gandhi's decisions to found a commune and establish small-scale handcrafts (e.g., homespun cloth) as alternatives to products sold by the oppressor. Furthermore, he never seriously examined Gandhi's Hinduism or any other Eastern religion. And, unlike Cesar Chavez, he never ventured Gandhi's most dramatic form of protest—a hunger strike. Indeed, he almost never grappled with many of Gandhi's pivotal convictions.[42] Rarely, if ever, did he seriously consider myriad features of Gandhi's religion and politics that Gandhi himself viewed as vitally important.

King failed to do so because his black religious models, Gandhian advisors, and E. Stanley Jones had already screened off these Gandhian notions as largely or entirely irrelevant to American life. They paid little or no attention to the communal Gandhi, the cloth-spinning Gandhi, the vegetarian Gandhi, the ascetic Gandhi, the celibate Gandhi, the Hindu Gandhi, and the fast-unto-death Gandhi. Instead they concentrated on the nonviolent Gandhi who orchestrated massive campaigns of civil disobedience. And, following the thinking of his American mentors, so did King.

King's oratorical genius and his choreography of massive, nonviolent protests explained Gandhi to the entire nation, so successfully that King's Gandhi became America's Gandhi. But King's interpretation of the spiritual mentor of India was hardly the result of King alone. Indeed he never considered anything remotely resembling an unedited Gandhi. Rather, King's Gandhi is a Gandhi that leaders of Howard University and others had carefully screened and molded.

Their own black Christianity led Thurman, Johnson, Mays, and Nelson to define Gandhi as they did. They undertook their odysseys to India because, as open-minded Christians, they realized that the non-Christian Gandhi was busily perfecting a Christian means of overcoming oppression. They viewed Gandhian nonviolence as a loving, Christian method of demanding, hastening, and implementing this-worldly deliverance from segregation. For that reason they filtered the religion of Gandhi into a readily digestible message of nonviolence and civil disobedience. This message is precisely what King and Farmer learned from their teachers and precisely what they popularized during the 1950s and 1960s.

But when King first met the American Gandhians, he heard nothing terribly surprising. Instead, advanced lessons in Gandhi served mainly to confirm and elaborate what he was always taught as a child and adolescent. One older member of Ebenezer Church observes that he originally "learned nonviolence from his mother."[43] He also absorbed nonviolence from his father, J.H. Edwards, and other leaders in and around Ebenezer Church. Gandhian theory largely amounts to a relatively formalized, systematic explanation of the assumptions underlying the newspaper boycott of King's grandfather and the voting rights march of King's father. Though neither of these protests seem influenced by Gandhi, except for their smaller scale and lack of national publicity, they strikingly resemble the boycotts and marches that Gandhi and King, Jr., led.

While King's early training was incalculably successful, the themes of that training were hardly unique. For many generations, the black church had preached oppression and deliverance and had schooled its members in Christian love. Had the church failed to do so, masses of black churchgoers would never have responded enthusiastically to King. Had his ideas seemed alien, supporters would never have followed him into jail cells, accepted beatings, or risked their jobs and their lives for his cause. Successful political organizers never organize outside the experience and the values of their own people.

Applying Gandhian tactics, King arranged confrontations in the form of medieval morality plays that television relayed to the nation. Starring in these dramas were nonviolent activists, who faced police dogs, fire hoses, cattle prods, and clubs—all wielded by the forces of "law and order." By repeatedly committing acts of violence against peaceful agitators, segregationist police and vigilantes volunteered for the role of "bad guys." In Montgomery,

Birmingham, and Selma, they played their part perfectly in King's villains-and-heroes melodramas.[44] Time after time the nonviolence of demonstrators and the violence of racists refuted Niebuhr and repeatedly illustrated and underscored King's point: nonviolence means love, violence spells death.

Not only did peaceful demonstrations and violent retaliation actualize this contrast, such acts also made King a prophet. Whenever marchers sang "We Shall Overcome," they exemplified the beloved community that he had already described, promoted, and predicted. When authorities or the Klan responded with violence, they brought the destruction and death that he had already explained as the product of their evil system. Beginning in Montgomery, the contrast he drew between nonviolence and violence interpreted actions of activists and their enemies *before they ever took place.*

This prophecy formed only one side of King's leadership. For other elements of his general orientation, he also looked to black and white preachers, not to Gandhi or to prestigious Euro-Americans.

For example, when King measured the gospel of love and nonviolence against the challenge of Communism, he turned not to Niebuhr but to Robert McCracken, who inherited Fosdick's pulpit at Riverside Church. Unlike other themes important to King, his view of Communism apparently grew mainly (and possibly initially) from his studies at Crozer and Boston, not from his earlier experiences at Ebenezer Church.

King's section on Communism in "Pilgrimage" derives from a sermon in McCracken's 1951 collection *Questions People Ask.* In "Pilgrimage," King explains his attitude as a response to reading Communist works. Compare:

MCCRACKEN: [Communism] is avowedly secularistic and materialistic. . . . Again, Communism is a heresy because it acknowledges no transcendental standards or values. . . . Since for the Communist there is no Divine government, no absolute moral order, there are no fixed, immutable principles. . . . Any means—force, violence, imprisonment, torture, terrorism, lying, murder—justify that millennial end.[45]

KING: For the first time I carefully scrutinized *Das Kapital* and *The Communist Manifesto.* I also read some interpretive works on the thinking of Marx and Lenin. In reading such Communist writings I drew certain conclusions that have remained with me as convictions to this day. First, I rejected their materialistic interpretation of history. Communism, avowedly secularistic and materialistic, has no place for God. . . . Second, I strongly disagreed with Communism's ethical relativism. Since for the Communist there is no divine government, no absolute moral order, there are no fixed, immutable principles; consequently almost anything—force, violence, murder, lying—is a justifiable means to the "millennial" end.[46]

King also repeats McCracken's view of the positive qualities of Marxism:

MCCRACKEN: [William Temple, the late Archbishop of Canterbury,] once described Communism as a "Christian heresy." . . . He meant that Communism had laid hold on certain truths which are an essential part of the Christian scheme of things and which every Christian should acknowledge and profess, but that it had bound up with them concepts and practices which no Christian can ever acknowledge or profess. . . . First, Communism is the story of men aflame with a passionate concern for social justice. . . . Consider a second conception basic in Communism but also an integral element in the Christian outlook, the conception of a classless society. . . .[47]

KING: The late Archbishop of Canterbury, William Temple, referred to Communism as a Christian heresy. By this he meant that Communism had laid hold of certain truths which are essential parts of the Christian view of things, but that it had bound up with them concepts and practices which no Christian could ever accept or profess. Communism . . . should challenge every Christian . . . to a growing concern about social justice. . . . Communism in theory emphasized a classless society, and a concern for social justice. . . .[48]

Furthermore, both McCracken and King criticize the loss of freedom under Communist dictatorship and both invoke Jesus's first sermon as an expression of Christian concern for the poor.[49]

King's sermon "How Should a Christian View Communism?" also overlaps McCracken's text. As in "Pilgrimage," King follows McCracken by balancing the vices of Communism against its virtues.[50] Like McCracken, he begins by interpreting Communism as the most serious rival of Christianity. Both preachers compare and contrast the successes and shortcomings of Marxism to those of

Christianity. On the minus side of the ledger, King incorporates McCracken's quotation from Lenin ("We must be ready to employ trickery, deceit, lawbreaking . . ."). He then repeats McCracken's view of the unprincipled, totalitarian nature of Communism and reiterates McCracken's antipathy toward atheism. He represents an atheist perspective through an anonymous four-line poem cited in Hamilton's *Horns and Halos*.[51]

Echoing McCracken, King balances this harsh criticism with a positive response to Communists' passion for social justice and racial equality. Replaying McCracken's quotations, he illustrates these points with a line from the Magnificat ("He hath put down the mighty from their seats . . .") and with the text of Jesus's initial sermon.[52] He also harnesses Fosdick's proclamation of the social gospel—a slightly altered version of the same statement he employs in "Pilgrimage" and "What Is Man?"[53]

King's rejection of war as the solution to Communism further reflects McCracken's anti-war impulse, as does his suggestion for impassioned Christian evangelism as the proper, positive response to Communism.[54] Like McCracken, King criticizes the church for harboring racial bigotry.[55] He contrasts the ethics of early Christians to those found in the modern church, whose eleven A.M. hour of worship is "the most segregated hour of the week"—an observation made by several preachers.[56]

McCracken's and King's two-sided interpretation of Communism was articulated in many other pulpits as well. For example, in 1937 E. Stanley Jones prefigured McCracken by weighing the virtues of Communism against its vices. Jones objected to Marxism for its "dogmatic atheism, its denial of liberty, its economic determinism, its materialism, its class war and compulsions." Against these gross errors and failures, Jones spotlighted positive features of Communism, which, he explained, "stands for principles that are interracial and international." Jones contended that, when Communism "bases its economic life on 'to each according to his need,' it draws close to the original Christian society, based upon the same principle." The famous missionary also preceded McCracken and King by approving of a professor's notion that both Christians and Marxists aim for a classless society.[57] In 1949 Jones used the same quotation by Lenin that later appealed to McCracken and King.[58]

In 1948 Leslie Weatherhead also antedated McCracken's and King's objections to Communism for its unscrupulous methods, its totalitarianism, and its rejection of God. Like Jones, Weatherhead anticipated McCracken and King by measuring this criticism against a favorable notice for certain features of Communism. After declaring that Marxism expressed its founders' sympathy for the poor, Weatherhead wielded the same quotation from the Magnificat that McCracken and King employed later. Weatherhead also applauded Communists for treating all races as one.[59]

Other religious liberals made similar points. In his *Christianity and Communism* of 1948 John C. Bennett, a visible Protestant leader, predated McCracken in citing Archbishop Temple's observation that Communism constituted "a Christian heresy."[60] Branding Communism as tyrannical and atheistic, Bennett balanced these objections with the observation that Communism "has acted as a reminder of the responsibility of Christians . . . to seek the realization of more equal justice in society."[61]

Lecturing at Yale University in 1952, Mays disdained the atheism and dictatorship of Communism. But he also hailed Russia for its refusal to sanction racial segregation.[62] During that same year Mordecai Johnson joined others in rating the vices of Soviet Communism—dictatorship, violence, and deception—against its praiseworthy attempt to eliminate poverty and racism.[63]

As part of his balanced appraisal in "Pilgrimage," King complained about capitalism, arguing that it "may lead to a practical materialism that is as pernicious as the theoretical materialism taught by Communism." His editor toned down this view from his original statement that capitalism promoted a materialism "far more pernicious" than that of Communism.[64]

Although McCracken did not criticize capitalism, other homilists did. In 1937 Jones protested "ruthless [economic] competition," designating it as poisonous and calling for its replacement by "co-operation" and the use of "brotherhood economics."[65] Fosdick also objected to unbridled capitalism, matching his criticism of Marxism with objections to capitalist greed.[66] Weatherhead's 1948 text also criticized both Communism and capitalism. *Horns and Halos* explicitly rejects both Communism and economic individualism.[67] Calling one of his 1955 meditations "Between Individualism and Communism—The Kingdom," Jones locates Christianity as a midpoint between the two fiercely antagonistic ideologies.[68] In 1960, another preacher described the "stance of the Christian between Communism and capitalism."[69]

Like McCracken and King, almost all these other clergy claimed that true Christianity would eliminate the Communist threat.[70] If Christians actually practiced their religion, they maintained, Communism would disappear. For that reason, war was not needed to destroy Communism.[71] Christian zeal would naturally triumph, and it was far preferable to anti-Communism, which was *against* something and not *for* anything.

During the late 1940s and early 1950s these preachers' attitude toward Communism was truly extraordinary. In the heyday of Joseph McCarthy, when many Americans viewed Communism as the Anti-Christ, McCracken and his cohorts failed to promulgate the rigid anti-Communist line popular among millions of Americans. Although liberal preachers did not embrace the Russian Revolution in the manner of Paul Robeson, neither did they brand the Russian system as totally evil.

Their balanced response to Marxism sharply contrasts with Niebuhr's judgment, especially with Niebuhr's consistently strident anti-Communism during the late 1940s and early 1950s. This stridency is particularly evident in *Irony of American History*, the final book Niebuhr completed before his debilitating stroke. His biographer rationalizes the unequivocally harsh anti-Communism of *Irony* by declaring that such a view "was to be expected in 1951," when Niebuhr delivered the second series of lectures forming the body of the book.[72]

However, while the McCarthyite atmosphere of that time heightened Niebuhr's anti-Communism, it did not influence McCracken's sermon about Communism, which appeared in 1951.[73] Instead, McCracken ignored anti-Communist hysteria and courageously reiterated the evenhanded interpretation of Communism that had firmly established itself in the liberal pulpit. In the hands of McCracken, Johnson, Mays, and Hamilton, the independent progressive pulpit withstood the winds from the right that Niebuhr failed to resist.[74]

During the early years of his public career—the middle 1950s—King joined McCracken, Mays, and others in refusing to embrace blanket anti-Communism. In "Pilgrimage" and his sermon about Communism, he combines his critique of Marxist vices with an assessment of capitalist shortcomings. His response to Communism was never Niebuhrian, and what Wofford terms his "gradual, Mississippi River-like development" as a person paralleled the general evolution of his thinking from liberalism to radicalism.[75] This evolution moved in the opposite direction of Niebuhr's change between the 1920s and the 1950s, when Niebuhr shifted from radicalism to conservatism.[76] However, King did not change as much as Niebuhr, for King's evaluation of Communism and capitalism never deviated notably from that of earlier preachers.

By condemning Communist totalitarianism and atheism, the civil rights leader distinguished his cause from Marxism, which he was constantly accused of supporting. However, because Communists agitated for racial equality and in theory embraced the ethical ideals of Judeo-Christianity, King felt no desire to denounce Communism in the unequivocal manner of Richard Nixon or John Kennedy. Instead, he looked to McCracken for balanced thinking.

King's refusal to repudiate Marxism wholesale helped retain the confidence of leftists who upheld civil rights, including members of his New York Kitchen Cabinet, two of whom once belonged to the Communist Party.[77] More importantly, in the face of McCarthyite hysteria about all things Marxist, McCracken's mixed assessment of Communism passed muster with listeners and readers.[78] McCracken's success in differentiating the strengths and weaknesses of Communism gave King reason to believe that liberal Protestants would accept his balanced appraisal and might even like it. McCracken's ability to say something good about Communism without being stoned or silenced encouraged King to do the same.

The independence of the liberal pulpit did not end with the issues of nonviolence and Communism. Not only did McCracken and other, like-minded preachers adopt a rare attitude toward Communism, they also advocated nonconformity in general. So did King, who maintained that upholding love, brotherhood, and nonviolence meant practicing nonconformity. Like their homiletic models, three sermons in *Strength*—"Paul's Letter to American Christians," "Knock at Midnight," and "Transformed Nonconformist"—proclaim the virtues of nonconformity.

Early in "Paul's Letter to American Christians" King quotes Romans 12:2 ("Be not conformed to this world. . . ."). He interprets

Jesus's metaphors "salt of the earth," "light of the world," and Paul's "leaven in the lump of the nation" as encouragement for nonconformity. He borrowed this analysis from Fosdick's *Hope of the World.*[79]

King based "Knock at Midnight," on Luke 11:5–6 ("Which of you who has a friend will go to him at midnight . . ."). His source was D.T. Niles's "Summons at Midnight."[80] Exploring the same passage of scripture, Niles and King chose the same commanding metaphor for their sermons: living at midnight means living under grim conditions, when every color turns gray. Niles and King noted the traveler's interruption of the stillness of midnight and defined the church as the "one familiar landmark" that travelers seek at midnight.[81] Both concentrated on the role of the contemporary church. Departing from Niles, King criticized the church for its conformity to the social order. Incorporating a passage from Fosdick, he explained that the Russian Orthodox Church died because it refused to question the czars.[82]

Basing "Transformed Nonconformist" on Romans 12:2, King again used the scripture to challenge the conformity of the church to an unrighteous society. He invoked a passage from Paul's letter to the Philippians ("We are a colony of heaven"), echoing Fosdick's analysis:

FOSDICK: Do you remember what Paul called [Christians] in his letter to the Philippians? "We are a colony of heaven," he said. The Philippian Christians would understand that figure, for their city of Philippi was a Roman colony. When Rome wanted to Romanize a province, it took Roman people and planted them as a colony in the midst of it. There, as a powerful minority, they stood for Roman law, Roman justice, Roman faith and Roman custom. . . .[83]

KING: To the Philippian Christians, Paul wrote, "We are a colony of heaven." They understood what he meant, for their city of Philippi was a Roman colony. When Rome wished to Romanize a province, she established a small colony of people who lived by Roman law and Roman customs. . . .[84]

King joined Fosdick in hailing "maladjustment":

FOSDICK: Professor Seelye Bixler . . . has lately made some shrewd comments on our new psychological talk about the well-adjusted life. At its finest, the well-adjusted life is so beautiful. . . . But in much of our popular rendition the well-adjusted life settles down into contentment with the status quo. . . . The sacredest obligation of the Christian is to be maladjusted—to the war system, to the inequities of an acquisitive economic order, to the wrongs of race prejudice, to the vulgarities of popular morals, to the crude sectarianisms of the churches. . . . The deepest obligation of a Christian, I should suppose, is to be maladjusted to the status quo.[85]

KING: Some years ago Professor Bixler reminded us of the danger of overstressing the well-adjusted life. We must, of course, be well-adjusted to avoid neurotic and schizophrenic personalities, but there are some things in our world to which men of goodwill must be maladjusted. I confess that I never intend to become adjusted to the evils of segregation and the crippling effects of discrimination, to the moral degeneracy of religious bigotry and the corroding effects of narrow sectarianism, to economic conditions that deprive men of work and food, and to the insanities of militarism and the self-defeating effects of physical violence. Human salvation lies in the hands of the creatively maladjusted.[86]

Other portions of "Transformed Nonconformist" also overlap Fosdick's text.[87]

Another important source for King's text is "The Peril of Conformity" by a relatively obscure, outspoken preacher named Eugene Austin. Austin delivered this homily at King's Crozer commencement ceremony in 1951.[88]

Like McCracken and unlike Niebuhr, Austin stoutly resisted McCarthyism. Indeed, he bravely confronted right-wing paranoia when almost no one else would. King's text incorporated Austin's trenchant critique of conformity:

AUSTIN: Millions of Americans fear nothing more terrible than to be identified with a position that stands out, sharp and clear, as different, setting them apart from other men. . . . Increasingly the typical ambition . . . is to belong to something that is . . . ambiguous enough to include anything, and popular enough so that everybody will want to belong.[89]

We can continue traveling down this road toward thought-control, business-control, freedom-control, until we land in totalitarianism.[90]

KING: Many people fear nothing more terribly than to take a position
which stands out sharply and clearly from the prevailing opinion.
The tendency of most is to adopt a view that is so ambiguous that it
will include everything and so popular that it will include everybody.[91]

If Americans permit thought-control, business-control, and freedom-
control to continue, we shall surely move within the shadows of
fascism.[92]

This little-known preacher warned that Joseph McCarthy "would
whip himself" into "a frenzy" if Thomas Jefferson were to reap-
pear. Jefferson, Austin continued, would face "investigation by a
dozen congressional committees" because "the tide of independent
thought and courageous individualism is running out."[93] Adapting
Austin, King asked, "Have we permitted the lamp of independent
thought and individualism to become so dim that were Jefferson to
write and live . . . today we would . . . investigate him?"[94]

By borrowing Austin's powerful anti-McCarthy rhetoric, King
again rejected Niebuhr's thought in favor of that of liberal preachers. In 1952, when Niebuhr bashed Communism in *Irony* and
ignored McCarthy's witchhunt, Austin berated McCarthy. King
adopted Austin's message in an attempt to warn against the
ultra-patriotism advanced by McCarthy and disregarded by Niebuhr.

Here King also draws on other sources. He contends that
Christians should be thermostats transforming society, not thermometers recording the temperature of popular opinion. This
double metaphor apparently stems from "Thermometers Versus
Thermostats," a sermon that H.H. Crane preached at the Chicago
Sunday Evening Club. King's quotation from Emerson was pre-
viewed in McCracken's "Peril of Conformity" (which appeared in
the same year as Austin's sermon of the same title).[95] Like Fosdick
and Austin, McCracken remarked the limitations of individualism
and encouraged Christians to question the status quo.[96]

These preachers were not alone in valorizing nonconformity.
Their colleagues also hailed individualism and attacked the numb-
ing effects of social convention. Basing a sermon on Romans 12:2,
Tillich saw the Biblical text as a statement of God's approval of bold
originality.[97] Vernon Johns and another preacher also include this
scripture in sermons.[98]

Applying Paul's discussion of the "colony of heaven," Luccock calls for the church to serve as a vanguard for political and corporate reform. Published in 1928, Luccock's interpretation of the "colony of heaven" anticipated the substance of Fosdick's comment in *Hope of the World*.[99] In 1960 Paul's figure of speech inspired another liberal to write *God's Colony in Man's World*—yet another work defining the church as an institution properly devoted to social transformation. In that writer's words, "A faithful church is always in a colonial situation."[100] The "colony of heaven" metaphor also appealed to workaday preachers whose sermons never appeared in print.[101]

Even without the verses from Romans and Philippians, well-known progressives found ways to chastise stagnant Christians for failing to challenge entrenched injustice. During the mid-1920s Sockman scorned an everyone-does-it morality.[102] In the mid-1940s, Weatherhead warned, "Official religion . . . has always been the greatest enemy of the kingdom of heaven."[103] In 1951 Kennedy endorsed Christian nonconformity by quoting with approval most of John Bunyan's statement that later appealed to Austin and King.[104] A year earlier, Kennedy became a brave nonconformist when he blasted the "buffoon tactics of a certain congressional committee" and "embryo demagogues" who would "smear decent men with the term 'un-American' just because they happen to disagree with them."[105] This criticism of McCarthyism anticipates the complaints Austin made a year later. And in one of his final books, Fosdick titled a chapter, "What To Do about the Curse of Conformity?"[106]

One of the most withering of all attacks on a conforming, hypocritical church comes from Vernon Johns, the most prophetic nonconformist in all of twentieth-century Protestantism:

> "We preach Christ crucified," shouts Paul. But moderns are wont to preach him a political and social and financial success, far removed from the "down and outs." He has the finest army on the planet. He is fast draining the resources from every heathen community in the world and piling them up beside a glittering cross. His women wear the finest furs and the haughtiest airs to be found in this sad, half naked world. Under the transforming magic and artistry of our emphasis we make Christianity anything but what its Founder made it! Bruce Barton is a typically modern Christian when he stands forth

The Man Nobody Knows as a prototype of the high-powered
business executive. One wonders why Jesus did not build the little
shop at Nazareth into a Sears Roebuck concern.[107]

Clearly preachers' calls for nonconformity reinterpreted and
reapplied the old-time religion of the social gospel. Building Paul's
"colony of heaven" meant rejecting corrupt social practices and
"official religion" in favor of a *"higher allegiance"* to Christ-like
principles—a loyalty that could remedy the pervasive shallowness
of American life.[108]

When King proselytized for nonconformity, he repeated the
message of Fosdick and many others. By the early 1950s, when
Austin delivered his sermon at Crozer, nonconformity had become
a standard motif in the liberal pulpit. Austin's bold homily simply
applies this traditional theme to McCarthy's witchhunt. When King
published "Transformed Nonconformist" in 1963, individualism
was a homiletic mainstay, one of the more common themes of the
Protestant pulpit. Nonconformity had become a convention.

Of course, nonconformity was not unusual in the black church,
which originated through acts of defiance. Many slaveowners
prohibited their slaves from worshipping God—sometimes at the
cost of their lives.[109] Other slaves were forced to listen to white
preachers who lectured them on the need to obey their masters.
Hostility toward authentic slave religion often prompted slaves to
hold religious celebrations in secret. Frequently they shouted, sang,
preached, and praised God late at night while meeting deep in the
woods.

Northern whites also suppressed black Christians. During the
eighteenth and nineteenth centuries, blacks were literally forced
out of white churches when they attempted to worship. Resisting
these efforts to stymie their faith, Richard Allen and other African-
American leaders organized churches and denominations among
those expelled from white congregations.

Whites always remained somewhat uneasy about African-
American religion, for the church served as virtually the only
institution that blacks operated entirely on their own. Active white
opposition to Southern black religion returned during the early
1960s, when Ku Klux Klansmen and other white supremacists
burned and bombed scores of churches in Mississippi, Alabama,
and elsewhere. Of course these churches supported the civil rights

movement, and their pastors endorsed the nonconformist, antisegregationist position of A.D. Williams, Vernon Johns, King, Sr., and King, Jr. The erudite, determined Johns tirelessly excoriated his listeners, including churchgoers at Dexter Avenue Baptist Church of Montgomery. By the mid-1950s, when the younger King succeeded Johns at Dexter Church, he addressed members whom Johns had repeatedly lashed for their conformity to the ways of segregation. By the time of Rosa Parks's arrest in Montgomery, members of Dexter Church and other congregations responded jubilantly to King's call for a defiant, nonconformist boycott of segregated buses.

Championing nonconformity also helped King with white audiences. The theme provided Biblical validation for marches, demonstrations, and boycotts. By seizing Fosdick's point that the early church had stopped infanticide and gladitorial displays, King justified his use of black and white churches as a political base. He could do so persuasively only by hailing a nonconformist church that could interrogate social practices instead of sanctioning them uncritically. Fosdick's 1933 sermon served as a resource for King's effort, as did Austin's denunciation of McCarthyism and warnings against gray-flannel-suit Americanism.

Just as the theme of nonconformity proved durable, it also proved flexible, for King adapted it to particular circumstances. For example, he adjusted his material on nonconformity when Julian Bond was denied his seat in the Georgia legislature. Although Bond had been duly elected to his position, legislators refused to accept him because he opposed the Vietnam War. Defending Bond in the sermon "Nonconformist—Julian Bond," King illuminated Bond's situation by applying Paul's familiar statements about nonconformity, Fosdick's quotation from Emerson, Crane's double metaphor, Fosdick's condemnation of "jumboism," and McCracken's argument that war will not stop Communism.

The theme of nonconformity proved most useful in helping King justify the radical tactic of civil disobedience and the massive disruption caused by the freedom struggle. Biblical and homiletic support for nonconformity made the upheaval more acceptable as white and black activists became the transformed nonconformists their preachers had long implored them to be.

SIX

HE WANTED TO BE AN OUTSTANDING PREACHER

Nothing mattered more to King than being an outstanding preacher.[1] To this end he embraced sermonic argument, rejected ambivalent white attitudes toward borrowing, and mastered forms of voice merging from the black folk pulpit. These strategies account for much of King's oratorical magic, not only in his sermons but also in "I Have a Dream," "I've Been to the Mountaintop," and other landmark speeches.

The strategies are quite distinct from—and often opposed to—those of law, philosophy, and theology. For example, in the courtroom and the legislature, speakers convince listeners on the basis of informal logic and evidence, establishing truth as the conclusion of a well-supported chain of reasoning.[2] Unable to appeal to any authority to determine whether or not a defendant committed a crime, a lawyer can only hope to marshall evidence and shape it into a pattern that an opposing lawyer cannot dismantle. Attorneys do not even attempt to produce absolute proof, and judges and juries do not expect it. Lawyers seek only to approximate truth within some degree of probability. In this rhetorical universe, no person is found absolutely guilty, but only guilty beyond a reasonable doubt.

Because sermonic argument proceeds from the Word of God, it contrasts sharply to legal language and other forms of secular discourse. In Christian sermons, the authority of the Bible serves as its own warrant and proof, and the truth of the Bible defines and judges human truths. Other sources of knowledge do not provide external proofs to validate the truth of scripture, for scripture requires no external proofs. Scripture validates itself. Although preachers can misapply scripture by misconstruing a contemporary situation, the fault never lies in the Bible; for the Bible, properly understood, invariably sheds light on any and all human experience.

The structure of sermons reflects this assumption. Sermons traditionally begin with the reading of scripture (unless the scripture has been read earlier in the service), followed by the preacher's exegesis of the Biblical verse. This analysis clarifies the historical context of the scripture and its meaning within that context. Much more than a convention, this practice stems from the assumption that knowledge proceeds from Biblical authority. A preacher discerns truth in a particular scripture and develops that truth or theme deductively. Beginning deductively allows a preacher to subordinate all other means of ascertaining truth to the truth already proclaimed by the Bible.[3]

Then, for the larger, second portion of the sermon, a pastor, "draws upon signs, examples, and commonplaces from the beliefs of his audience to demonstrate inductively the same principle originally derived deductively."[4] At this point preachers extract evidence from other sources of knowledge. These sources—which include everything from scientific investigations to government statistics to literary insights—simply illustrate and recapitulate the revealed truth of the Bible. Preachers summon wise contemporaries—psychologists, best-selling novelists, or anyone else—who, either knowingly or unknowingly, unmask Biblical truth disguised in modern garb. The insights of great masters of world literature also help explicate God's everlasting Word. Because the inductive part of the sermon simply reinforces and elaborates what has already been gleaned deductively, the sermon manifests "a pattern of thematic reduplication." Following this pattern, the deductive and inductive segments of the sermon are "logically redundant."[5]

Fosdick and other modern preachers often vary the traditional arrangement by beginning a sermon with a discussion of current problems. This variation, however, does not substantially alter the deductive-then-inductive form of homiletic argument. In such modern sermons, scripture still functions as the self-validating, authoritative source of God's revealed truth. And scripture applies deductively. Other sources of truth simply reinforce and elaborate the truth already proclaimed in the Bible.

Not only do ministers assume that the Bible serves as a self-validating source of truth, they also rely on other, related assumptions about knowledge.

They assume, for example, that God's fundamental truth is repeated and repeatable, unmodified in its essentials as one generation of Christians passes it to another. While preachers adapt to shifting circumstances, they also reiterate a message shared by all other Christians living and dead. Therefore, like much other religious language, sermons are in part ritualistic, both in form and content.

Preachers further assume that truth is shared by a large religious society that includes both the uneducated and the well-schooled. Christians hold that their entire community filters the truth, endorsing some messages from the pulpit while rejecting others. No one becomes a great preacher merely by pleasing an elite; rather, an outstanding homilist must command the ears and the respect of many, many ordinary people.

Similarly, preachers presuppose that, for the most part, truth is communicated orally. Jesus wrote nothing. Paul regarded his letters as a poor substitute for speaking in person.[6] The four gospels were not written until several decades after Jesus's death and resurrection. Like Jesus, Paul, and other early Christians, preachers continue to privilege oral communication. Printed sermons are mere transcriptions of oral performances. In the prefaces of their books of sermons, many preachers—including Fosdick—explain their reluctance to print messages best expressed from the pulpit, not the page.[7] African-American preachers also prize oral communication. Only a tiny fraction of black American preachers have ever seen a single one of their sermons in print.

Preachers further presume that, to a large degree, truth reveals itself through narrative. The Bible consists mainly of stories. Jesus taught chiefly through stories, each of which the gospel writers frame within the larger, master narrative of his life, death, and resurrection. To a large degree the purpose of sermons is to explicate and apply the meaning of all these narratives. Not only are preachers Biblical interpreters, they are also inveterate story-tellers, relating countless illustrations, anecdotes, and tales from world literature.

Each of the rhetorical assumptions underlying homiletics— truth as derived from the Bible and deductively applied, truth as repeatable, truth as shared, truth as best communicated orally, and truth as expressed in story—diverges from the system of knowledge known as Western philosophy. In fact, philosophy rests on a set of assumptions that starkly oppose those undergirding sermons.

In contrast to homiletics, philosophy refuses to acknowledge the Bible as its own warrant and proof. Whereas preaching emanates from the ultimate authority of God Almighty as expressed in scripture, philosophy pursues truth by challenging authority. It interrogates every species of received wisdom, including the views not only of religious authorities but of the most outstanding philosophers as well.[8]

In the universe of philosophy, a well-constructed argument always defeats any traditional view. Although philosophers sometimes synthesize the conclusions of previous thinkers, one can almost say that one becomes a great philosopher by attacking and replacing the work of another great philosopher. Or by overturning some other, established system of beliefs. Thus, Plato sweeps aside the sophists, Aristotle builds around Plato, Hume bulldozes Aquinas, Kant responds to Hume by reviving metaphysics, Kierkegaard assaults Hegel, Nietzsche scorns Christianity, empiricists dismiss metaphysics, and so forth ad infinitum. In philosophy, truth advances dialectically as the sturdiest body of thought reigns until the next substantial challenge either modifies it or overpowers it.

Here nothing is final—not tradition, not the achievements of the most laudable philosophers, not the rules of logic, and not even the basic tenets of common sense. All these matters are subject to revision, redefinition, or repudiation. Philosophy acknowledges only one ultimate—the dialogue itself, a game in which every champion waits to be dethroned by a mighty contender from the future.

As it advances dialectically, philosophy does anything but reiterate what has already been validated by a large community.

Unlike preachers, philosophers share no agreed-upon set of conclusions. Because philosophy invariably develops via new combinations of ideas, the content of philosophy never repeats itself and thus is rarely, if ever, ritualistic.

Moreover, in contrast to homiletics, philosophy presumes that truth is grasped by an intellectual elite. Philosophers write mainly for each other and certainly for a scholarly readership that cares about abstractions. Western philosophers have little to say to anyone lacking powerful intellectual interests, and ordinary people have no say in deciding which philosophers are read from one generation to the next.

The esoteric nature of philosophy dictates that it exist mainly on the page. Although professors regularly lecture on philosophy, books and essays serve as the primary means of transmitting its dialectical message. Even the best philosophical lectures can only supply a general sense of Plato's dialogues and Kant's intellectual project. In order to grapple with the intricacies of philosophy, one has no choice but to scrutinize texts carefully.

Finally, unlike homiletics, philosophy assumes that abstract ideas—not narration—serve as the best means of discovering and communicating truth. Largely avoiding story-telling, philosophers relegate illustrations to a minor role in argumentation. And, until recently, they have seldom reflected on narratives.

In contrast to both homiletic and philosophical persuasion, theology systematically explains God, the universe, and humanity. Christian theologians accept fundamental church doctrines and refine, extend, or modify those doctrines in hope of achieving a more satisfactory worldview. Theological argument is not as easily defined as homiletic and philosophical argument, for theology embraces certain traditional religious principles while also incorporating secular modes of argument. Thus, in an effort to rehabilitate traditional Christian language, Tillich wed Heideggerian thought to Christianity, characterizing God as the Ground of Being. Thus, Niebuhr examined the interface between orthodox Protestant doctrines and American political life, combining traditional Christian dogma with sociopolitical analysis. For Tillich and Niebuhr, mixing sacred and secular epistemologies meant refusing to subsume either mode of thought under the other.

While theologians usually affirm core doctrines of the faith, they also introduce novelty through various reinterpretations of

God's revelation through Christ. Though King's dissertation criticizes Tillich and Henry Nelson Wieman for defining God impersonally, King wrote about Tillich and Wieman because they defined God in relatively new, unorthodox terms. Had they failed to do so, they never would have become major theologians, and King would never have written about them. Because theology cannot succeed without novelty, it is much less ritualistic than homiletics.

Like philosophers and unlike preachers, theologians appeal to an elite. Masses of people have never read major theological works, and they never will. Only a small religious intelligentsia determines who qualifies as an important theologian.

Like philosophers and unlike preachers, theologians develop extensive systems of thought best communicated in print. Tillich preached to those who had difficulty reading his theology, which he considered his primary work.[9] Unlike theologians, preachers attempt to change people's lives by winning them to Christ and inspiring their thoughts. For preachers, truth is exemplified every day in the lives of good Christians; for theologians, truth is an intellectually satisfying religious system.[10] Theologians typically reflect on the content of the Bible, not its narrative elements.

Failing to resemble works of philosophy and theology, King's sermons follow distinctly homiletic forms of argument. Like other preachers, King assumes that the Bible serves as its own warrant and proof. He invariably reflects upon a verse of scripture and proceeds deductively, using the Bible to elucidate contemporary experience. Illustrations, quotations, and other material serve to highlight, amplify, and apply the truth of scripture—never to argue for its likelihood or demonstrate its validity. Following the deductive-then-inductive pattern of development, his inductive material repeats and reinforces themes that he has already expounded deductively. His arguments proceed directly from the revealed Word of God and conform to the uniquely homiletic scheme of thematic reduplication.

King's preaching also sprang from the assumption that God's Word is repeated and repeatable. He clearly aimed to uphold the traditional Christian message. Borrowing texts meant using language that had already been welcomed by liberal Protestants— both listeners and readers. Borrowing thus granted his sermons a ritualistic quality that resonated with those who had heard or read similar or identical themes.

Preaching before hundreds of thousands of people, King clearly assumed that truth is shared by a large, diverse religious community and is judged by that community. He leapfrogged the nation on literally hundreds of occasions to speak to the broadest possible range of people—from Harvard PhDs to impoverished slum dwellers—who often heard the same material.

King also concentrated on oral communication, devoting far more time to his thousands of addresses than to his writing.[11] Although he often employed ghostwriters for his essays and books and occasionally for speeches, he seems never to have done so for sermons.[12] Like Fosdick, Buttrick, and many other preachers, he used the preface of his sermonic collection to explain his reluctance to publish a message best explained aloud, not on the page. Plainly he preferred to speak to people rather than to write for them. Like Jesus, Paul, Fosdick, and Buttrick—and unlike Tillich and most other theologians—he valued sermonizing and speech-making over writing.

Like all other good preachers, King delighted in narrative. He frequently examined stories in the Bible, especially parables from the New Testament, and filled his sermons with anecdotes gleaned from others' sermons and compilations of illustrations. He also shaped his own experiences into illustrations, and many of these stories spilled over into his speeches, essays, and books.

While King organized all his sermons according to the deductive-then-inductive pattern, the deductive structures of "Love in Action," "Shattered Dreams," and "Death of Evil" are particularly noteworthy.

"Love in Action" employs a deductive chain to organize the motifs of blindness and forgiveness. Borrowing from Fosdick, he begins with Christ's exclamation from the cross: "Father, forgive them; for they know not what they do."[13] Fosdick and King interpret the crucifixion of Christ by blind, stupid people as the supreme expression of a tragic deed recurring throughout history. Both preachers relate the archetypal nature of the "spiritual blindness" responsible for the crucifixion.[14] In King's words, "History reverberates with testimonies of this shameful tragedy."[15] Noting other heroic figures hounded by a benighted society, the preachers begin their lists with the trial of Socrates.[16] Fosdick's examples include the persecution of Joan of Arc and Galileo.[17] King cites

Saul's suppression of the early Christians, the horrors of the Inquisition, and opposition to Copernicus and Darwin.[18]

Again echoing Fosdick, King explains that the series of tragic stupidities continues into the present. He comments that the arms race reflects "this [same] tragic blindness" of stupid people "who know not what they do."[19] But, unlike Fosdick's catalogue, King's examples of blindness include slavery and segregation. Refuting claims that black people are inferior, he cites Ruth Benedict and other leading anthropologists—all of whom insist that no race is superior or inferior to another.

What is striking about King's discussion of anthropologists is the location of that reference within a long, deductive chain. At the end of a series of horrific events whose archetype is the crucifixion and whose cause is stupidity, King cites slavery and segregation as the latest examples of the sequence. In this argument, he does not allow the testimony of anthropologists to stand on its own feet. Instead, he plainly subordinates that testimony to his extended deductive argument: Benedict and her colleagues merely illuminate another example of archetypal "tragic blindness." They testify that blacks are, in effect, crucified by stupidity, just as Christ, Socrates, and others were crucified. Far from constituting self-validating expertise, anthropologists' views simply clarify and repeat a conclusion already deduced from scripture. As part of the inductive portion of King's sermon, these views form logically redundant support for the Biblical truth that King had proclaimed through a long, deductive chain beginning with Christ's prayer from the cross.

A similar process can be seen in King's "Shattered Dreams." Serving as the scriptural foundation for this sermon is Paul's statement in Romans 15:24 ("When I take my journey to Spain, I will come to you."). Although Paul wanted to reach Spain, his imprisonment and death prevented him from spreading the gospel to the western Mediterranean. Paul's unfulfilled ambition provided an opportunity for Hamilton, King, and others to reflect on frustration.[20]

Portions of King's highly intertextual sermon link together through two chain-like series of actions. King first elucidates how Roman jailers dashed Paul's glorious dream of evangelizing on Spanish soil. He then initiates the first chain by recounting a concatenation of noble dreams stymied by insuperable obstacles:

the division of India and Pakistan destroyed Gandhi's dream of a unified nation; the Senate denied Woodrow Wilson an effective League of Nations; and the South refused to free those slaves who died before Lincoln proclaimed emancipation.[21] Each of these frustrations amounts to a repetition-with-variation of Paul's blocked ambition to visit Spain. Paul's failure serves as a Biblical type that both portends and illuminates a sequence of future disappointments.

Borrowing from Leslie Weatherhead and Howard Thurman, King describes several flawed responses to frustration.[22] Then he relates a second chain of events repeating Paul's triumph despite his hardship. In King's deductive-then-inductive argument, Paul's achievement despite his "shattered dream" serves as a harbinger for other, parallel victories. In King's series each hero also "exchanged their thorns for crowns": Darwin defeated sickness, Robert Louis Stevenson withstood tuberculosis, Helen Keller overcame severe handicaps, Handel triumphed over paralysis, and early Christians expressed joy when facing lions.[23] None of these figures deserves detailed examination, however, for their lives simply repeat the Pauline pattern of attaining heights despite enormous difficulties.

The lives of slaves also exemplify Paul's archetypal failure to reach Spain. Unlike other modern frustrations, slaves' hardships merit a detailed treatment borrowed from Thurman:

THURMAN: . . . slavery was a dirty, sordid, inhuman business. When the slaves were taken from their homeland, the primary social unit was destroyed, and all immediate tribal and family ties were ruthlessly broken. This meant the severing of the link that gave the individual African a sense of persona. There is no more hapless victim than one who is cut off from family, from language, from one's roots.

For the slave, freedom was not on the horizon; there stretched ahead the long road down which there marched in interminable lines only the rows of cotton, the sizzling heat, the riding overseer with his rawhide whip. . . .

In instance after instance, husbands were sold from wives, children were separated from parents. . . .

. . . the slave women were constantly at the mercy of the lust and rapacity of the master himself, while the slave husband or father was powerless to intervene. . . .

There is a bottomless resourcefulness in man that ultimately enables him to transform "the spear of frustration into a shaft of light."[24]

KING: Slavery was a low, dirty, and inhuman business. When slaves were taken from Africa, they were cut off from their family ties and chained to ships like beasts. Nothing is more tragic than to be divorced from family, language, and roots. In many instances, husbands were separated from wives and children from parents. When women were forced to satisfy the biological urges of white masters, slave husbands were powerless to intervene. Yet, in spite of inexpressible cruelties, our foreparents survived. When a new morning offered only the same long row of cotton, sweltering heat, and the rawhide whip of the overseer, these . . . men and women dreamed of a brighter day. . . . Their bottomless vitality transformed the darkness of frustration into the light of hope.[25]

Significantly, unlike Thurman, King does not allow this analysis of slaves' lives to stand on its own, but instead places it as a link in the archetypal chain of failures and successes beginning with Paul's experience in prison. King locates contemporary blacks on the chain as well. Finding themselves "in the prison of segregation," African Americans can, like Paul, triumph despite the jail cell in Rome/America that prevents their arrival in Spain.[26] Arguing deductively from scripture, King suggests that Paul's frustration is an archetypal experience that continues to define and shape human lives, especially those of black people.

In "Death of Evil" King views the liberation of the Hebrews from their Egyptian manacles as an archetypal event that God cycles and recycles throughout history, particularly during the twentieth century. As he explains, Gandhi and other Moses figures have liberated Third World peoples "from the Egypt of colonialism." When Lincoln announced the Emancipation Proclamation, he led the blacks "nearer to the Red Sea," but "the pharaohs" thwarted their escape by creating an "Egypt of segregation." Then the Supreme Court divided the waters in the case of *Brown v. Topeka;* now, through their persistence, blacks can "reach the promised land."[27] Throughout King's text, each variation of the Exodus follows archetypally and deductively from the Biblical text, and each variation serves as a link in a deductive chain holding together substantial portions of the sermon.

While the deductive nature of King's argument is especially

clear in "Love in Action," "Shattered Dreams," and "Death of Evil," his other sermons also rest on the assumption that the Bible serves as its own warrant and proof and they invariably proceed deductively from the Bible. His penchant for deductive appeals to authority carries over into many speeches as well, including the most famous ones. In "I Have a Dream," for example, he argues from the authority of Lincoln, Jefferson, Amos, Isaiah, Jesus, and others. In "Mountaintop" he argues from the authority of Amos, Moses, and Jesus, among others.

Not only does King's sermonic argumentation fail to reflect the influence of Marx, Hegel, Spinoza, and other philosophers, his deductive-then-inductive persuasion constitutes the polar opposite of the epistemology and organization of Western philosophical argument. His typical form of argument also owes virtually nothing to the systems of knowledge and arrangement that characterize theological discourse. Instead his argument is decidedly homiletic.

King's sermons gained additional authority from his ability to blend elements of folk sermons and liberal, white homilies.

Most African-American folk sermons are loosely organized in associational clusters. Related images, phrases, and ideas form together in clusters that are sometimes—but not always—framed by a larger homiletic conception mentioned in the introduction. Floating freely from one sermon to another, certain set pieces, subthemes, and formulaic expressions also bind folk sermons together.

Favoring a loose homiletic form, folk preachers can easily engage in call-and-response with their congregations, adjusting their messages to listeners' reactions. When churchgoers react audibly, a preacher may extemporize on the point that evoked the reaction. Because no extended portion of the sermon is tightly structured, spontaneous comments do not sidetrack listeners from a formally planned development. This relaxed sense of homiletic structure can also help a folk preacher in trouble. If a sermon is failing altogether, a homilist can abandon a topic in midstream, choosing another that seems more promising. The minister might link the two subjects in some way or simply ignore the initial topic altogether during the second half of the performance.[28]

Unlike folk homilists, seminary-trained white preachers prefer to plan their sermons entirely in advance. During the 1940s and 1950s, white seminaries taught their students numerous more-or-less formal schemes for organizing sermons. Halford Luccock explicates many (but not all) of these patterns in his popular book from 1944, *In the Minister's Workshop*. One form, the Ladder Sermon, begins with a commonly held proposition; moves up to a less ordinary, but reasonable second step based on the first; progresses to a third step based on the second; and so forth, culminating in an unusual conclusion the preacher has skillfully prepared listeners to accept. The Jewel Sermon involves the examination of many facets of a single notion, which a preacher displays like a gem. The Roman Candle Sermon consists of a set of loosely related points analogous to a sequence of fireworks set off by a Roman candle. The Key Sermon allows a homilist to define a problem, try one possible solution (or key), other possible solutions (or keys), then conclude with a key that unlocks the problem.[29] A minister could also choose the Thesis-Antithesis-Synthesis Sermon, which begins with a thesis, continues with an antithesis, and concludes with a synthesis.[30] Homileticians also offered the Classification Sermon, Skyrocket Sermon, Twin Sermon, Springboard Sermon, Surprise or Mouse-trap Sermon, and other homiletic forms.[31]

While studying with professor Robert Keighton, King and other Crozer students learned the Ladder Sermon, the Jewel Sermon, the Roman Candle Sermon, the Classification Sermon, and other methods of arrangement.[32] Some of Crozer's black students laughed at these labels and invented a few of their own, including the Rabbit in the Bushes Sermon. They reasoned that, just as someone with a rifle might fire into a moving bush in hope of killing a rabbit, a preacher might repeat an idea upon hearing a congregation respond to it.[33] This thinking reflected their background in folk religion, for the system of call-and-response popular in the folk pulpit encouraged preachers to interact spontaneously with their congregations.

While King frequently engaged in call-and-response, he often preferred formal patterns instead of the associational clusters of folk preaching. He sometimes used deductive chains to organize his presentations—a pattern he may have learned from Fosdick and that comports nicely with slaves' typological view of history. Because he often classifies major and/or minor points, a number of his homilies qualify as Classification Sermons.[34]

Moreover, like other preachers, King frequently blends methods of organization, often joining classification with some other pattern. For example, basing his "Answer to a Perplexing Question" on one sermon by Phillips Brooks and another by Hamilton, King follows Brooks in combining the Key Sermon with the Thesis-Antithesis-Synthesis sermon. After raising the question of eliminating evil, King first tries the key of humanism and discovers that it does not unlock the problem. Then he tries the key of passive reliance on God, but it also fails to resolve the dilemma. Then he synthesizes these solutions by calling for cooperation between people and the Almighty. This key unlocks the problem of evil.[35]

At times an awareness of standard arrangements enabled King to improve sermons that served as his sources. For example, whereas McCracken lists the virtues of Communism before he considers its weaknesses, King uses his knowledge of the Ladder Sermon to rearrange McCracken's argument. King's text begins by analyzing the failures of Communism—an analysis his audiences would readily accept—then explains its strengths, which his audiences would now more easily grant.

Like his published sermons, many of King's unpublished homilies reflect the patterns of his sources and his own use of structures familiar to white audiences. However, on hundreds of occasions he organized speeches and sermons by rearranging parts of old addresses in new combinations. This system of composing enabled him to reuse the same material in scores of presentations while preventing his fans from hearing the same speech twice. This mix-and-match form of composition came from his exposure to the folk pulpit. For, unlike their liberal, white counterparts, folk preachers freely transferred phrases, set pieces, and themes from one sermon to another and from other preachers' works into their own.

Instead of dissolving his homiletic patterns when he mixed and matched, King usually opened the forms and stirred part of one address into another. However, during his last two years—the most stressful period of his life—he sometimes jettisoned formal sequences in favor of old-fashioned, freely arranged folk sermons. In a number of his loose-jointed later sermons—especially those protesting the Vietnam War—he completely abandoned white structure in favor of pure associational clusters. In one such sermon—a late edition of "Sleeping Through a Revolution"—he provided a long introduction then explained his loose organization:

". . . and I think you can take a subject like [sleeping through a revolution], and just put almost anything in. . . ."[36] Then he did just that.

King consistently rejected white Protestants' deep and unresolved ambivalence about homiletic borrowing. During his lifetime and before, many professors of homiletics and eminent preachers decried the use of secondhand language. Issuing commandments to preachers, Gerald Kennedy advised, "Thou shalt not steal another man's material. . . ."[37] Another leading minister branded encyclopedias of illustrations "a snare."[38] Labeling books of homiletic plans "First Aids to the Lazy," Charles Reynolds Brown also counseled preachers to discard such works.[39] Expressing a sweeping opinion, Luccock admonished, ". . . Do not use anything found in the sermons of other men."[40] The advice of Kennedy, Brown, and Luccock was not unusual. After carefully surveying attitudes about borrowing in the pulpit, one scholar observed: "Upon no subject was there greater unanimity [among homileticians] than that of the ruinous effect of the constant use of collections of illustrations. . . . Generally, a touch of satire pervaded the mode of attack on these compilations."[41]

Seminaries, however, gave their students another message as well. While virtually every seminary library included books objecting to the use of collections of illustrations and outlines, the same library shelf also held the very collections that prompted these objections. The Gerald Kennedy who warned against borrowing was the same Gerald Kennedy who published two popular collections of homiletic illustrations. The very purpose of these collections was to help preachers borrow each other's material. Attempting to resolve the profound ambivalence toward borrowing, some homileticians accepted the occasional practice of recycling illustrations while prohibiting other borrowing.[42] But many preachers had difficulty reiterating illustrations without also borrowing the points that were illustrated. After all, an illustration by definition is not a free-floating anecdote and instead illustrates a particular point.

Although homiletic borrowing was often ridiculed, it was extraordinarily common. One homiletician protested against "plagiarism" but candidly admitted, "Everybody borrows."[43] In fact, the frequent complaints about borrowing testify to its popularity.[44]

For their sources, pastors commonly looked to the greatest homilists of the era, especially Fosdick. Once he was introduced to a group of ministers as someone "whose sermons you have heard and preached."[45] At another gathering, a colleague jokingly sympathized with Fosdick because he was the only minister unable to borrow from Fosdick.[46] Once Fosdick responded to a minister who wanted to publish a Fosdick sermon under the minister's own name; Fosdick endorsed the idea, wishing "to have [his] message spread in any way whatsoever."[47]

Hamilton's musings also enjoyed wide circulation. His widow attests that ministers often relied on her husband's work:

> Sometimes Wallace would hear men preach his sermons. They used his material faster than he could produce it. He said he would change lines of poetry perhaps according to his own sense of rhythm. He said, "I know preachers got illustrations from me because they would make identical changes in a story or poem that I had made." Speaking of his books of sermons, preachers would say, "Please send more. My congregation loves [hearing me deliver] them."[48]

Many ministers borrowed because they enjoyed little time to compose sermons. During the first six decades of this century, both black and white Protestant clergy generally assumed most or all of the following responsibilities: delivering sermons every Sunday morning and Sunday evening; courting prospective members; counselling the troubled; consoling the bereaved; visiting the sick; marrying the engaged; burying the dead; writing and producing a weekly church newsletter; directing programs in religious education; overseeing the church board and all its committees (none of whose members could ever be given an order or fired); organizing and attending religious conventions, retreats, and summer camps; reading religious books and journals; raising extra funds to build a new building or buy a new organ, pews, or a church bus; and fulfilling sundry other obligations, such as the unofficial—but very real—duty of finding an appropriate spouse and raising model children. All these duties left ministers little time to write sermons.

But time constraints alone do not account for borrowed sermons. Another major reason was the assumption that Christian truth is repeated and repeatable. Communicating a common gospel, ministers never produce novel language in the manner of a spider spinning a web from its body. After all, how many truly original sermons are possible on Luke's account of Christ's birth, the parable of the good Samaritan, or the last week of Christ's life? Yet tens of thousands of preachers are obliged to sermonize on these topics. Paul emphasized the importance of preaching a shared message when he declared, "Woe is me if I preach not the Gospel!"

Moreover, the alternative to borrowing is not always wondrous. Homespun sermons are not always good sermons, and some ministers are entirely capable of preaching homilies that are highly original, yet perfectly dreadful.

Also, preachers realized that borrowing was a time-honored practice. Chaucer and other medieval writers relied extensively on sources. So did Renaissance authors—including Shakespeare, who created few original plots. And, as Leslie Weatherhead explained in 1944, "The very parables Jesus used are not original."[49] Indeed Jesus and Paul often quoted the Old Testament and other Jewish sources, and they never supplied footnotes.[50] In addition, by midcentury, liberal ministers realized that the writers of the Gospels of Matthew and Luke had incorporated most of the Gospel of Mark into their texts and had drawn upon other texts as well. The gospel writers offered no acknowledgment whatsoever.

Despite the procedures of New Testament authors, one might ask: why not acknowledge sources? Mainly because acknowledging sources means impeding the flow of thought. Writing shortly after he taught King at Crozer, Robert Keighton ventured, ". . . the sermon is a means, not an end." He further explained that the function of a sermon is inspirational—not scholarly—and that a sermon "is not an essay, a lecture, a paper, or a thesis."[51] For Keighton and other homileticians, a sermon is not an elegant, literary construction but a way of changing lives. If a sermon inspires a deeper faith and better living, it succeeds; if not, it fails. Nothing else matters.

Concurring with Keighton, thousands of workaday clergy have acted on the assumption that preaching is a means, not an end. They have also agreed that a sermon is not self-expression and that it cannot be judged by formal standards. Agreeing with Paul as well, these ministers in effect held that a sermon was successful if it communicated the message of Jesus Christ. If it did not, then, though it might ring as sounding brass or a tinkling cymbal, it carried no meaning at all.

Unlike their white counterparts, African-American folk preachers have never felt ambivalent about borrowing sermons. Their attitude continued well into the civil rights era. Juanita Abernathy, widow of Ralph Abernathy, recalls, "A lot of preachers preached Ralph's sermons." She remembers that, on one occasion, a man delivered an Abernathy homily even though he recognized Abernathy in the audience. Black pastors, she reports, did not believe that recirculating sermons amounted to plagiarism.[52]

Folk preachers created themselves not only by reiterating sermons, but also by embedding familiar passages of scripture, formulaic phrases, and beloved lyrics. They often elaborated that material and welded it to their own. Concluding their sermons, they often interwove their own sermons into the lyrics and then led congregational singing. Consider, for example, the conclusion of a 1946 sermon by E.O.S. Cleveland, a master of embedding:

> And with Jesus Our Leader, we shall Mount Up on Wings and Try the Air, and FLY–FLY–FLY–FLY–AWAY to our Heavenly HOME. . . .
>
> Thank God I know How To Fly. Yes—I KNOW HOW TO FLY. . . .
>
> Some glad morning when this life is over, I'll fly away
> To a home on God's celestial shore, I'll fly away. . . .[53]

The final two lines and several succeeding lines serve as the lyrics of the famous hymn "I'll Fly Away." Cleveland's earlier declaration, "I KNOW HOW TO FLY," anticipates the lyrics of the hymn. Who is this "I"? The "I" is the person in the pulpit, but the "I" is also the narrative voice of the hymn, as Cleveland merges his identity with the narrator of "I'll Fly Away." After such voice merging, folk sermons typically do not end but instead turn into hymns, which churchgoers join the preacher in singing. Each member of the congregation then becomes the "I" of the lyrics. In addition, the "I" is everyone alive or dead who has ever vocalized the hymn. The identities of all these people converge through the remarkable voice merging undertaken in the pulpit and the pews.

Famous folk preacher C.L. Franklin often embedded lyrics and scripture. Consider how he identified his voice with the narrator of a hymn as he led his church in singing, interjecting sermonic comments along the way. He began with four lines of "I'm Going Through" then added his own material:

> I'm going through . . .
> I'll pay the price whatever others do.
> I'll take the way of the Lord's despised few.
> I started with Jesus and I'm going through.
> Some people don't want to pay the price. . . .
> They feel like sacrifice is too much. . . .
> You that turn away from God
> You are paying a greater price than I'm paying
> By travelling with Jesus. For you see,
> The man who turns his back on God
> Is not only paying with your body . . .
> But paying with your soul. . . .
> And what does it profit a man to gain the whole world
> And then lose his soul? . . .
> I wondered about what my reward would be.
> I'd heard about crowns.
> I'd heard about slippers.
> I'd heard about golden streets and golden gates. . . .
> I'm going through. Yes, I'm going through. . . .
> I started with Jesus and I'm going through.[54]

When Franklin declares,

> You that turn away from God
> You are paying a greater price than I'm paying
> By travelling with Jesus

who is the "I" of this statement? The "I" is Franklin, but the "I" is also the voice of the hymn—a voice that Franklin repeats and elaborates throughout the passage. Threading the lyrics into his sermon and rethreading his sermon into the lyrics, Franklin weaves a seamless quilt of discourse. Into this quilt he also sews a question from Jesus ("And what does it profit a man to gain the whole world and then to lose his soul?") and familiar folk imagery of heavenly crowns and heavenly slippers, golden streets and golden gates. Franklin locates his homiletic self within lyrics and scripture and embroiders lyrics and scripture through his preaching. In this sacred world of folk pulpit, Franklin, Jesus, and "I'm Going Through," all speak in the same voice.[55]

On another occasion Franklin preaches:

> I've been through the storms.
> I've been through the beating rains.
> I've been up in the high mountains.
> I've gone down through the valleys.

Then he immediately sings:

> I will trust in the Lord.
> I will trust in the Lord.
> I will trust in the Lord til I die.[56]

Here Franklin, the "I" who has experienced storms and rains and who has journeyed through mountains and valleys, is the same "I" as the narrative voice of the hymn "I Will Trust in the Lord."

Franklin also practices embedding in a sermon based on a statement by Paul that Franklin partly quotes and partly paraphrases as "Nothing will separate me from the love of God":

> Nothing will separate me from the love of God. Nothing.
> I've made up in my mind that
> Nothing will separate me from the love of God.
> Let the clouds roll.
> Let the thunder clap. I said nothing.
> Let the winds blow. Nothing. . . .
> I said nothing shall separate me from the love of God.
> He's been too good to me. . . .
> He's opened doors that have been closed in my face. . . .
> Nothing will separate me from the love of God.
> I'm committed now.
> I'm disciplined now.
> So that nothing will separate me from the love of God.[57]

Who is the "me" here? Because Paul originally announced (in effect), "Nothing shall separate me from the love of God," the "me" plainly indicates Paul. But because Franklin extends the sentence with his own declarations, the "me" also designates Franklin, who skillfully merges Paul's identity with his own. Here, as before,

Franklin constructs an expansive persona with and within the rhetoric sanctioned by his community. Unlike the preacher from the 1930s who seemed to have eaten breakfast with Moses and Daniel, Franklin and Paul do not eat breakfast together. Instead, they speak through the same mouth. Franklin does not claim to be Paul's equal; instead, he renders Paul's message vivid and immediate nineteen hundred years after his death. Paul's revelation becomes Franklin's revelation and that of every other Christian—not through the worthiness of Paul or Franklin but through God's grace.

Biblical typology, borrowed sermons, and embedded quotations enable preachers to create themselves and to introduce sacred time. Summoning important events from the past (such as Paul's revelation about God's love), ministers dissolve chronological time and reenact important moments. By invoking sacred time, they grant meaning to history, preventing it from becoming a junkheap of isolated voices, unrelated experiences, and forgettable characters.

Like folk homilists before him, King created himself and introduced sacred time by using typology, borrowing sermons, and embedding quotations.

King's typology scandalizes the system of Biblical interpretation he learned in seminary. There he studied the Bible with two distinguished scholars, James Pritchard and Morton Scott Enslin. Following the practice of Rudolph Bultmann, Pritchard and Enslin claimed that one could understand the Bible properly only by carefully reconstructing the historical contexts of Biblical authors and events. After all, they reasoned, scripture was written with a specific meaning at a specific time by a specific writer for a specific audience. Only by paying close attention to a historical situation could anyone hope to discover what a scripture means.

This "demythologizing" approach stripped away the colorful legends and folklore of the Bible and located its literal, historical characters and authors once the layers of myth were peeled away. Pritchard practiced "demythologizing" when he contended that Moses may never have lived. And Enslin dismissed portions of the four gospels as myth.[58]

Underlying this interpretation is the assumption that history is a linear arrangement of discrete events and discrete human beings. In this "commonsense" view, historical dynamics and Biblical principles may be long-lasting or even eternal, but specific Biblical situations and characters are unique and nonrepeating.[59] Along with King's professors, Euro-American philosophers, theologians, and preachers all assumed that Biblical characters were locked in a timebound sequence.[60]

Clearly his professors' practice of "demythologizing" and their "commonsense" view of history did not reinforce notions King absorbed from the folk pulpit. While at Crozer and Boston, though, he was apparently swayed by his professors' modernist ideas about the Bible.[61]

However, by 1956, when he delivered "Death of Evil," he had entirely abandoned his professors' practice of reconstructing Biblical occurrences as discrete, unrepeatable events. Instead of scrutinizing the historical context of the Bible, he constantly lifted Biblical events and writers out of their situations and installed them in the present. Extracting the Bible from the straitjacket of the past, he explained that archetypal Biblical acts continually spiral through history. These recurring events structure not only the era of Moses and Jesus, but all subsequent experience as well.

King's interpretation of the Bible recapitulates and reenacts the archetypal, typological view of slave religion and the folk pulpit. From late 1956 until his death, he electrified his followers by reawakening the slaves' sense of sacred time and archetypal view of the Bible. Evoking repeatable Biblical events, he directly contradicted the "demythologizing" approach of his professors.

Like Cleveland, Franklin, and other folk preachers, King created himself by repeating, merging, expanding, and intertwining various historical identities. Reviving sacred time, he erased time and geography, shoved Biblical occurrences—particularly the Exodus—into the present, conjugated two thousand-year-old Biblical sentences into the present tense, and developed a self within well-known and richly resonant patterns of human personality.

King's entire sermon "Paul's Letter to American Christians" projects the Biblical past into the present. Plucking Paul out of ancient Rome, King reads a letter from Paul to twentieth-century Americans. Paul urges his/King's readers to eradicate segregation.

King also awakens sacred time in the "Remaining Awake through a Great Revolution." Nearing his climax, he mentions the deplorable conditions observed by Jeremiah, who asked "Is there a balm in Gilead?" King then adds Thurman's sketch of the horrors of American slavery and reports the slaves' response to Jeremiah. As

King explains, despite their hardships, slaves "took Jeremiah's question mark and straightened it out to an exclamation point and said, 'There *is* a balm in Gilead to make the wounded whole!'"[62] Slaves treated Jeremiah's centuries-old interrogative as something directed squarely at themselves, a question they were supremely qualified to answer. If slaves could triumph over their adversity, then, King insists, we should accept the slaves' reply to Jeremiah. There is a balm in Gilead because the defeat of slavery portends the defeat of segregation, a disguised version of slavery. Through King's invocation of sacred time, Jeremiah, the slaves, King, and his listeners become contemporaries holding a conversation and answering each other's questions.

King also violates his professors' assumption when he adapts a line from the Book of Job that serves as the poetic conclusion of literally dozens of his speeches and sermons. The scripture reads, "The morning stars sang together and the sons of God shouted for joy"; King alters the statement, declaring, "The morning stars will sing together and the sons of God will shout for joy." By switching verb tenses, he changes the event from one that has already happened to one that will someday occur. Thus he gives this Biblical declaration an eschatological meaning it did not originally possess. Only a universe of sacred time enables a speaker to treat past, present, and future events as acts occurring simultaneously. And only a typological theology empowers a speaker to regard Biblical events as acts replaying archetypally throughout the past, present, and future.

Yoking Biblical quotations together is another way that King violates the method of reconstructing texts proposed by his professors. Instead of patiently reviewing the historical contexts of Biblical authors and situations, he time after time compresses scriptural voices—especially Old Testament oracles—into a single prophecy. Consider a diversity of Biblical texts:

> But they shall sit every man under his fig tree, and none shall make them afraid.
> —*Micah 4:04*

> . . . what does the Lord require of you but to do justice, to love mercy, and to walk humbly with your God?
> —*Micah 6:08*

> Let justice roll down like waters and righteousness like a mighty stream.
>
> *—Amos 5:24*

> The lion shall lie down with the lamb.
>
> *—Isaiah 11:06 (First Isaiah)*

Toward the end of a long series of parallel sentences condemning slums and segregated housing, King orchestrates this memorable declaration:

> Let us be dissatisfied until every state capital houses a governor who will do justice, who will love mercy, and who will walk humbly with his God.
> Let us be dissatisfied until from every city hall justice will roll down like waters and righteousness like a mighty stream.
> Let us be dissatisfied until that day when the lion and the lamb shall lie down together, and every man will sit under his own vine and fig tree and none shall be afraid.[63]

Who are the "us" here? The "us" are King and his listeners, but the "us" also include Micah, Amos, and First Isaiah, who initiated the phrases King uses. Here Micah, Amos, First Isaiah, and King all speak the same words with the same meaning. Together, this choir performs a beautiful chorale.

Note King's single sentence that weds the eschatological visions of First Isaiah and Micah. Although these Biblical writers lived in different generations and under different circumstances, King expertly fuses their separate expressions into a single image. As the lion and lamb lie down together, every man sits nearby under his own vine and fig tree and is not afraid—either of other humans or of nearby lions, who are now tame. King's imaginative voice merging enables First Isaiah and Micah to envision a single, harmonious scene instead of the two entirely separate images that occur in scripture.[64]

King mastered voice merging because he grew up in a culture where homiletic borrowing was commonplace. Ordained as a minister before leaving home for seminary, he almost certainly learned borrowing and voice merging before arriving at Crozer. There and at Boston University he received mixed signals. Failing to treat sermons as wealth created by everyone and owned by no one, American print culture defined all texts as commodities to be copyrighted, packaged, and sold to earn money for authors.

While King heard this message, he also heard something else. Taking a course on the four gospels, he recorded in his notes the well-established scholarly view that the authors of the Gospels of Matthew and Luke incorporated most of the Gospel of Mark.[65] They did so without acknowledgment. In effect, King was taught that two of the gospel writers regarded the story of Christ as a communal treasure, not private property. He also learned that oral sermons sometimes overlapped and that—like the four gospels themselves —published sermons were often highly intertextual. And he found one extremely reputable preacher, Gerald Kennedy, who encouraged borrowing by assembling an anthology of usable illustrations.

Though he encountered powerful contradictions in religious attitudes toward borrowing, King the graduate student received relatively little reinforcement for his initial training in language. Despite some preachers' eagerness to deliver or publish partly unoriginal sermons, American print culture officially defined the Word as copyrightable private property to be sold on the marketplace. No homiletician and none of King's professors openly examined, questioned, or challenged this definition. They failed to examine it even though it directly contradicted the practice of many preachers and two gospel writers.

Despite his years of immersion in academia, however, King never conformed to print culture. Quite unlike white preachers and homileticians, he displayed no ambivalence whatever about borrowing sermons. Like folk preachers before him, he borrowed freely, treating sermons as shared blessings, not personal belongings. His socialization in folk culture led him to ignore the bedrock assumption of print culture, namely, that publication dictates ownership.

While typically failing to acknowledge his sources, King never seemed self-conscious about his borrowing and made no great effort to hide it. When an interviewer asked him about Phillips Brooks's influence on one of his sermons, he could have ducked the question. Or he could have acknowledged that Brooks influenced the single sermon that the interviewer spotted. Instead, he forthrightly volunteered that Brooks had affected much of his preaching.[66] Moreover, had he wanted to conceal his borrowing, he would have recirculated obscure texts, not sermons by the best-known ministers in the land. Had he felt ashamed of his borrowing, he would certainly have avoided using the titles that Fosdick, Hamilton, and Luccock employed. Instead, like the folk homilists who delivered "Dry Bones in the Valley" and "The Eagle Stirs Her Nest," he did not hesitate to recycle the titles—as well as the content and form—of previous sermons.[67]

King also replayed sermons throughout his entire public career, from beginning to end. According to Larry Williams, he borrowed his very first sermon at Ebenezer Church.[68] He also borrowed much of "Three Dimensions," the first homily his bride-to-be Coretta Scott ever heard him deliver and one that doubled as his trial sermon in Montgomery.[69] Two months before his assassination he mined Hamilton's text for "Drum Major Instinct"; he also turned to Luccock and others for parts of a sermon he delivered five days before his death. Like folk preachers before him, he obviously felt comfortable using other ministers' material.

When King borrowed these texts, he merged voices and enhanced his status by selecting themes that were not only useful but also authoritative. He usually chose sermons from famous preachers, texts that had previously demonstrated broad popularity. Before he seized his themes, they had already passed several litmus tests for doctrinal soundness and congregational appeal.

This process of composing is analogous to a method used by Jesus and Paul, who often repeated and adapted material from the Old Testament and apparently from oral rabbinic sources as well. Some of this material—such as the Deuteronomic phrase "eye for an eye" and portions of the Ten Commandments—was highly familiar to Jesus's Jewish listeners. Other material was not well-known, especially to the non-Jewish listeners whom Paul proselytized on the Northern rim of the Mediterranean Sea. Scholars describe Jesus's and Paul's use of Old Testament and rabbinic sources as a kind of argument from authority, a strategy of citing a sacred text to bolster a point.

Although King may never have considered Jesus's and Paul's persuasion by citation, he often made similar arguments, frequently mentioning and quoting John Donne, Shakespeare, Carlyle, Emerson, Lincoln, Jefferson, and other Western icons. For King and others, borrowing sermons also served as a way of arguing from authority. By lauding certain preachers, the Protestant community had in effect placed upon their sermons its Good Housekeeping Seal of Approval. When King reiterated their texts, he evoked the authority of those certified by all of liberal Protestantism. Like folk preachers before him, he gained an authoritative self in part through ideas and language that were known and honored by those who had already heard them. For that reason, his borrowing has an epistemological significance. He gained authority by evoking a sanctified tradition and demonstrating his ability to embody that tradition.

Furthermore, King frequently embedded scripture and lyrics. For example, he often ended his sermons with the lyrics of hymns, spirituals, and gospel songs. Carrying this practice from the folk pulpit to the political stage, he capped many speeches with the same lyrics.[70] Indeed he concluded almost every major speech by merging his identity with the narrative voice of a religious song.

King used embedding brilliantly when he explained his most important religious experience—a revelation that took place during the Montgomery bus boycott. This epiphany is one that he often discussed, for the memory of it refreshed him throughout long years of tribulations.[71] The experience occurred when, harrassed by death threats, he rose in the middle of the night and went to the kitchen to make a cup of coffee. He explains that during this moment, "Religion had to become real to me and I had to know God for myself." He continues:

> It seemed . . . that moment that I could hear an inner voice saying to me: "Martin Luther, stand up for righteousness! Stand up for justice! Stand up for truth! And lo I will be with you even to the end of the world.[72]

King's description of his sacred experience is a variation of a conversion report, a popular species of Christian testimony in general and black Protestantism in particular.[73] Henry Mitchell once told his homiletics students that, if they could think of nothing else to preach about, they should expound upon their own conversion experiences. After all, a preacher should be able to relate this story well, for it requires no research.[74] Conversion testimony presents a problem only if one was born and raised a Christian. In such a case, one modifies one's testimony by explaining that Christianity did not seem "real" until a crisis occurred and God provided revelation and renewal.

The son of a preacher, King had no single, blinding experience that led him to his faith.[75] For that reason, instead of relating his conversion, King's account of his epiphany in the kitchen describes the moment when God seemed overwhelmingly immediate and palpable. To this standard variation of a conversion story, King skillfully adds a social gospel twist. Unlike the narrators of traditional conversions, he faltered not from personal weakness or temptation, but from the strain of leading a social crusade. His description testifies to a social gospel, for God offered him strength —not to resist personal temptation—but to continue leading the bus boycott. By translating the social gospel into a conversion narrative, he expertly blends this-worldly and otherworldly redemption, just as the ministers Gardner Taylor heard as a child blurred the two forms of liberation. He carefully fuses personal gospel and social gospel, just as his father and grandfather had fused them before.

Note King's statement that God told him, "Lo, I will be with you even to the end of the world." This sentence echoes the conclusion of the Great Commission, Jesus's final assurance to His disciples. One can ask: who is the "you" of King's statement? The "you" signifies the disciples, who heard Jesus's promise and circulated it orally until it was preserved in writing. The "you" also refers to King himself, for God spoke to the disciples and to King with the same archetypal declaration: "Lo, I will be with you even to the end of the world." By referring to himself through Biblical language, King merges his identity with that of the disciples. He does not seem egotistical because he displays himself as weak and faltering and God as powerful and enabling.

Continuing to describe the same revelation, he offers metaphors from nature:

> I've seen the lightning flash, I've heard the thunder
>   roll.
> I've felt sin's breakers dashing, trying to conquer my
>   soul.

But I heard the voice of Jesus saying still to fight on.
He promised never to leave me, never to leave me alone.
No, never alone. . . .[76]

These five lines form the first verse and chorus of the hymn "Never Alone."[77] Who is the "I" of "I've seen the lightning flash"? The "I" is King and the "I" is also the narrative voice of the hymn. As he often does, King here unites his persona with the narrative voice of treasured lyrics.

Finally he merges his voice with the lyrics of "There Is a Balm in Gilead." Consider the spiritual:

Sometimes I feel discouraged,
I feel my work's in vain.
But then the Holy Spirit
Revives my soul again.
There is a balm in Gilead.

Compare King's testimony:

Sometimes I feel discouraged.
And I don't mind telling you this morning that
Sometimes I feel discouraged.
I felt discouraged in Chicago.
As I move through Mississippi and Georgia and Alabama,
I feel discouraged.
Living every day under the threat of death,
I feel discouraged sometimes. . . .
And feel my work's in vain.
But then the Holy Spirit
Revives my soul again.
There is a balm in Gilead![78]

Who is speaking here? In King's address the voice is obviously the narrator of the spiritual. Yet the voice certainly belongs to King as well: he met frustration in Chicago, Mississippi, Georgia, and Alabama; survived assassination attempts; and received death threats frequently. The persona of the nineteenth-century slave song and King speak in the same voice as King the folk preacher fuses his identity with the narrator of the spiritual.

In a single description of his epiphany in the kitchen, King creates a self by interweaving New Testament language and the social gospel into the fabric of his black conversion narrative. He also blends his identity with that of the disciples and with the narrative voices of a gospel song and a spiritual. Here African Americans relating their conversion epiphanies; the narrative voices of "Never Alone" and "There Is a Balm in Gilead"; and King, the once faltering but now rejuvenated disciple of Christ and leader of the boycott, all speak the same words with the same meaning. They do so through King's reanimation of the sacred time and typology of folk religion.

By recirculating outstanding sermons, mastering the time-honored procedures of voice merging, and astutely blending this-worldly and otherworldly liberation, King simultaneously created majestic discourse and an authoritative self. He expanded folk preaching in significant ways, taking the major step of adapting procedures of the folk pulpit to the universe of print. Reading supplied him with a pool of discourse much larger than anything a folk preacher could hold in memory. Writing afforded him the chance to reach an audience far beyond the walls of a church or an auditorium. By enlarging the pool of discourse and the size of audiences, print altered King's rhetorical universe without disturbing its premise that words are shared assets, not personal possessions.

He also enlarged folk preaching when he used it to lead a much stronger movement than any political effort black America had previously mounted. He communicated the central message of the folk pulpit—the necessity of liberation—with greater force and to a far larger audience than anyone else had ever dared to imagine.

Had King stepped down from Boston University and sounded like Spinoza or Tillich, no one would have listened. Had he sounded like a professor talking about Spinoza or Tillich, no one would have listened. He succeeded largely because he steadfastly refused to imitate either prestigious philosophers or professors who talked about them. He rejected their forms of argument, their ice-cold language, and many of their ideas and assumptions. Philosophical and theological discourse failed to impinge on his sermonic language and has almost nothing to do with his persuasiveness.

In their form, content, system of knowledge, structure, and delivery, King's sermons are thoroughly and strictly homiletic— not philosophical or theological. Most of his speeches—especially the best ones—are homiletic as well. His essays and books also contain large amounts of homiletic material and sometimes reflect sermonic forms and sermonic argument.[79]

By appropriating the language of well-established white preachers, King created and maintained a self who grappled with urgent public issues and was also a scholar, a philosopher, and a theologian. His magisterial image as a philosopher and his consummate political skill disproved whites' patronizing and stereotypical views of black preachers as uneducated souls ranting in the pulpit to wildly emotional followers. But, while King's philosophical image was an utterly necessary fiction, it was a fiction. Today it is no longer necessary or useful. We should no longer allow this image to conceal his relationship to the folk pulpit, which served as the wellspring of almost all his ideas and values. He triumphed because, by adapting the traditions of the folk pulpit to a massive white audience, he became the greatest folk preacher of all.

SEVEN

VOICE MERGING IN WASHINGTON AND MONTGOMERY

On August 28, 1963, one hundred fifty thousand or more demonstrators sweltered in Washington, D.C., listening to fine music from Marian Anderson, Joan Baez, and other singers. On the steps of the Lincoln Memorial an endless procession of speakers droned and droned. Despite the interruption of John Lewis's impassioned eloquence, the perspiring crowd began to wilt. Then, late in the afternoon, Mahalia Jackson revived everyone. With her hat pinned firmly to her hair, the unaccompanied Queen of Gospel swayed to a rhythm entirely her own, arousing weary listeners with the slave spiritual "I Been 'Buked and I Been Scorned":

> *I been 'buked and I been scorned.*
> *I'm gonna tell my Lord when I get home*
> *Just how* long *you've been treating me wrong.*[1]

Here Jackson merged her voice with the narrator of the lyrics, identifying her experiences with those of slaves. Through this song, the slaves' indignity became her indignity and that of thousands of blacks hearing her, all of whom had been 'buked and scorned. The slaves' cry became her cry, the slaves' protest her protest.

Following this spirited performance, King stepped to the microphone to launch the profoundly paradoxical "I Have a Dream."[2] Wearing his normal funereal suit, white shirt, and black tie, he, like Jackson, evoked the woebegone past to demand a sparkling future. He cited Jefferson, alluded to Lincoln, and embraced Old Testament prophets and Christianity, presenting an entire inventory of patriotic themes and images typical of Fourth of July oratory.[3] But, despite these nostalgic references, the first half of "I Have a Dream" did not celebrate a dream. It catalogued a nightmare. King damned an intolerable status quo that demeaned the Negro, who existed "on a lonely island of poverty" and was an "exile in his own land."[4]

Then King merged his voice with others. He enlisted Amos as a spokesman for his cause:

> There are those who are asking the devotees of civil rights, "When will you be satisfied?"
>
> We can never be satisfied as long as the Negro is the victim of the unspeakable horrors of police brutality.
>
> We cannot be satisfied as long as our bodies . . . cannot find lodging in the motels of the highways or the hotels of the cities. . . .
>
> No . . . we will not be satisfied until justice rolls down like waters and righteousness like a mighty stream.[5]

Who are the "we" of this passage? The devotees of civil rights—the disenfranchised blacks whom King represented. But the "we" of the last sentence includes more than blacks. This line harnesses a famous exclamation from an Old Testament prophet—Amos's cry "Let justice roll down like waters and righteousness like a mighty stream!" So Amos is also speaking here as King merges Amos's persona with his own. This union reflects back to the immediately preceding sentences: the "we" who cannot be satisfied until justice rolls down are the same "we" who seek lodging in the motels of the highways and the hotels of the cities. The voice of King/Amos calls for justice to run like a river and for Congress to open the dam by mandating integration. The words of Amos gave an unimpeachably authoritative tone to King's demands.

In the most famous passage of all his oratory, King again engaged in voice merging:

I have a dream that one day this nation will rise up. . . .

I have a dream that my four little children will one day . . . not be
judged by the color of their skin but by the content of their
character.
I have a dream today! . . .
I have a dream that one day every valley shall be exalted and every
hill and mountain shall be made low, the rough places will be
made plain, and the crooked places will be made straight, and
the glory of the Lord shall be revealed, and all flesh shall see it
together.[6]

Who is the "I" here? The "I" is surely King, the father of four young children. But who is the "I" of the last sentence? The dream is not simply King's dream. Isaiah initially sketched the scene of valleys exalted, mountains laid low, and rough places made plain—impossible geography symbolizing the coming of the kingdom of God. Jesus reaffirmed this powerful conception by quoting Isaiah's visionary language. Then Handel enshrined it in the lyrics of the *Messiah*, the most famous long piece of Christian music. Uniting his persona with those of Amos, Isaiah, Jesus, and Handel's narrator, King built his identity by evoking a sanctified past. Underlying this process of self-making is the typology of slave religion and the folk pulpit. King assumes that personality reasserts itself in readily understandable forms governing all human history. Scripture, music, and sermons describe and illuminate these patterns.

Although these forms are reliable, they can be flexible as well. Following the "I have a dream" litany, King again evoked Biblical eschatology by reworking imagery from the prophet Daniel: "With this faith we will be able to hew out of the mountain of despair a stone of hope."[7] Interpreting a famous dream of King Nebuchadnezzar, Daniel describes a stone that smashes a figure made of precious metals, iron, and clay. Hewn from a mountain by God, the stone symbolizes God's ideal kingdom that destroys all petty, earthly kingdoms and itself endures forever. In King's speech, however, human beings extract the stone from the mountain without waiting passively for God to create the new kingdom entirely by himself. Represented by the stone from the mountain, the arrival of Daniel's ideal kingdom coincides with the arrival of Isaiah's realm of valleys uplifted and mountains levelled. King expertly merged the mountain symbols from Daniel and Isaiah into a single image of a perfected community. He also merged his dream with Nebuchadnezzar's dream.

Joining King's choir of voices was the most distinguished of all possible members: God Almighty. King orchestrated the divine voice in several ways. One was through his status as a Baptist minister. (Six years earlier he literally donned his pulpit robe to address a crowd of twenty-five thousand gathered at the same spot.) He also expressed God's Word by reiterating the vision of the prophets and Jesus, who spoke directly for God. And he used the cadences of the black pulpit to heighten his demands.

He began by invoking patriotic authority—the Declaration of Independence, the Gettysburg Address, and the Emancipation Proclamation. Religion did not enter the speech overtly until Amos spoke at the halfway point. Like other folk preachers, King here (and elsewhere) began to accentuate rhythm and vocal contrasts in the middle of his presentation. When the words of Amos emerged, so did the vocal dynamics of the folk pulpit. At exactly the same point he offered a cornucopia of rhetorical figures, packing together seven series of repeating phrases (e.g., "We are not satisfied . . ." and "I have a dream . . ."). His chockablock use of these parallelisms added another religious element, for such sequences were standard practice in the folk pulpit.

By enlisting the divine voice, King did more than create a homiletic self. Just as C.L. Franklin assumed the mantle of a Biblical prophet, so did King in "I Have a Dream." His expert application of Biblical prophecy through folk preachers' techniques signified that God spoke through him.

As he catalogued an American nightmare, King essentially argued that the finest secular presences, including Jefferson and Lincoln, had failed miserably. The "architects of our republic" offered a "promissory note" that pledged liberty. But for blacks the note proved "a bad check," a check "marked insufficient funds."[8] By introducing divine authority after secular authority, which had proven inadequate, this new Biblical prophet suggested that an impatient God would now overrule secular forces and install justice without delay. When God ordains for justice to roll down like waters, the flood must eventually cross the Mason-Dixon line. When valleys are exalted, racism will end. When the stone of hope emerges from the mountain, it will smash the flawed kingdom of segregation. Why? Because, in the holistic vision of slaves, God redeems his children in both the next world and this world, for in the end the sacred and secular worlds are inseparable.

As usual King practiced voice merging in his conclusion. The prophet adjusted and refined a passage from his acquaintance and fellow black pastor, Archibald Carey.[9] Consider the final portion of Carey's 1952 address to the Republican National Convention:

> We, Negro Americans, sing with all loyal Americans:
> *My country 'tis of thee,*
> *Sweet land of liberty,*
> *Of thee I sing.*
> *Land where my fathers died,*
> *Land of the Pilgrims' pride*
> *From every mountainside*
> *Let freedom ring!*
>
> That's exactly what we mean—from every mountain side, let freedom ring. Not only from the Green Mountains and White Mountains of Vermont and New Hampshire; not only from the Catskills of New York; but from the Ozarks in Arkansas, from the Stone Mountain in Georgia, from the Blue Ridge Mountains of Virginia—let it ring not only for the minorities of the United States, but for . . . the disinherited of all the earth—may the Republican Party, under God, from every mountainside, LET FREEDOM RING![10]

Here the "My" of "My country" is both the narrator of Samuel Smith's "America" and Carey and "all Negro Americans." Through voice merging, Carey enlists the first verse of "America" as an agent not for self-satisfaction but for radical political change. He unites his identity with the ultra-patriotic voice of our unofficial national anthem.

In his peroration King refined Carey's words:

> This will be the day when all of God's children will be able to sing with new meaning:

> *My country 'tis of thee,*
> *Sweet land of liberty,*
> *Of thee I sing.*
> *Land where my fathers died,*
> *Land of the Pilgrim's pride,*
> *From every mountainside*
> *Let freedom ring!*

So let freedom ring from the prodigious hilltops of New Hampshire.
Let freedom ring from the mighty mountains of New York.
Let freedom ring from the heightening Alleghenies of Pennsylvania. . . .
Let freedom ring from Stone Mountain of Georgia.
Let freedom ring from Lookout Mountain of Tennessee.
Let freedom ring from every hill and molehill in Mississippi.
From every mountainside, let freedom ring.[11]

This entire litany extends the lyrics of "America." King used "Let freedom ring"—the last three words from the song—to establish his concluding series. By initiating each thought, these three words organize the entire sequence. This extension is metaphorical as well as stylistic, for the narrator of "America," Carey, and King compare freedom to a mighty bell whose peal will echo across every mountain. In effect King composed another verse for the anthem as he merged his voice with "America." Surely the "My" of "My country" indicates King and "all of God's children" as well as the narrative voice of the song. He also used this sequence to apply Isaiah's dream of valleys turned upside down. In the new landscape of Isaiah/King, even the hills and molehills of Mississippi, a low-lying state, will be exalted into mountains prodigious enough to echo the peal of freedom.[12]

Hailing Isaiah's and Carey's utopian future, King envisions a day when everyone will dismantle social barriers and merge voices by singing "America." Here he simultaneously engages in voice merging and reflects on a future of massive voice merging that will collapse all racial distinctions. He thereby takes the harmonious, heavenly vision of folk religion and sets it down squarely on earth.

In his final sentence King reinforced this entire rhetorical process by quoting yet another source:

... when we allow freedom to ring ... from every village and every hamlet, from every state and every city, we will be able to speed up that day when all of God's children—black men and white men, Jews and Gentiles, Protestants and Catholic, will be able to join hands and sing in the words of the old Negro spiritual: "Free at last! Free at last! Thank God Almighty, we're free at last!"[13]

The "We" of "we're free at last" is not only King and his ensemble of authoritative voices. "We" are all people—blacks and whites, Jews and Christians—who experience the long-awaited coming of the kingdom of God. Reinvigorating the sacred time of folk religion, King announced that Isaiah's prophecy will finally come true: the glory of the Lord will be revealed and all flesh will see it together. All flesh, all human beings will hold hands, merge voices in song, and celebrate the fulfilled vision of slaves, Jefferson, Lincoln, Amos, Isaiah, Daniel, Jesus, Handel's narrator, Carey, and King. Through sacred time, all their hopes and longings will fuse into the same hope and the same longing, which will finally be satisfied.

Here King again simultaneously engaged in voice merging and explained his hope for massive voice merging in an eschatological future of racial justice. Through the language of his inclusive, harmonious choir, he projected the end of history, when brotherhood will triumph, identities will converge, and sacred time will reign. Justice will pour down like waters, valleys will become mountains, and the stone hewn from the mountain will smash all racist, earthly kingdoms. On this day Americans will finally create themselves and their nation.

While "I Have a Dream" is a great folk sermon, some of King's speeches are not folk sermons at all. In sharp contrast to this speech is a largely ghostwritten anti-war address delivered in April 1967 at Riverside Church, the institution of Fosdick and McCracken.[14] An important presentation, "A Time to Break Silence" was King's first fully publicized attack on the war in Vietnam.

Before reviving McCracken's view that only true Christianity could defeat Communism, King provided an extended political analysis of the history of Vietnam and a detailed argument about Ho Chi Minh and his followers. He then reminded listeners of the deadly effects of American firepower and argued that the majority of the enemy, the National Liberation Front, were nationalists, not Communists.

While King began by alluding to his career, he dispensed with his usual argument from authority. Apart from a brief mention of the good Samaritan, he made no significant references to the Bible. Nor did he invoke great American presidents. Refusing to argue deductively, he did not claim that all war violates Christian principles. Instead, his argument succeeded or failed on the merits of his inductive assessment of the history of Vietnam, the intentions of the Viet Cong, and the appropriateness of American intervention. Thus "A Time to Break Silence" clearly embodied an inductive argument replete with inductive logic. In this respect it resembles several of his other ghostwritten speeches.

By contrast "I Have a Dream" and virtually all of King's other memorable speeches operate by way of a deductive structure similar to that of his sermons. In "I Have a Dream" King argues from the authority of Jefferson, Lincoln, "America," and the Bible—all of which he applies deductively to the situation of black America. According to the logic of "I Have a Dream," segregation is wrong, but not for reasons unveiled in a detailed analysis, which never surfaces in the speech. Rather segregation is wrong because it eviscerates the Emancipation Proclamation, scandalizes Jefferson's vision, violates Amos's demand, stymies Isaiah's longings, and contaminates the freedom celebrated in "America." Essentially "I Have a Dream" contends that segregation is wrong because it prevents the highest deductive truths of the nation and the Bible from governing human relations. Enacting these deductive truths means eradicating segregation.

The deductive nature of "I Have a Dream" is obvious not only in contrast to "A Time to Break Silence" but also in the context of the other speechifying at the March on Washington. Virtually all other addresses at the March concentrated on inductive appeals. In his censored but still militant speech, John Lewis talked of a pregnant activist in Albany, Georgia, whose brutal beating took the life of her fetus. Lewis and other speakers related other recent events and complained about the congressional bottleneck preventing passage of civil rights legislation. Identifying culprits of injustice, Lewis named names and wondered aloud about creating a new political party.

By contrast, "I Have a Dream" alluded to no recent incidents. Unlike Lewis and the other orators, King mentioned not a single, living person by name and referred only to his four children and to one other specific, living human being—the governor of Alabama. Unlike the array of other speakers, who discussed the importance of a civil rights bill, King made no direct reference to Congress or to the pending legislation, which became the most important civil rights law in American history. Only by considering the context of "I Have a Dream"—not by listening to any of its lines—can anyone even tell that the speech has anything to do with John Kennedy's civil rights proposal.

Instead of talking historical particulars in the manner of "A Time to Break Silence" and other ghostwritten speeches, "I Have a Dream" and King's other sermonic speeches repeatedly enunciate overarching, deductive principles and insist that these principles demand the repeal of segregation. The argument of King's most eloquent speeches owes nothing to formal Western philosophy. The argument of his sermonic speeches—including all his spectacular oratory—is never philosophical or inductive. Rather, the argument is invariably deductive, and stands as a variation of sermonic argument.

To make such arguments King often borrowed from himself, moving material freely from speeches to sermons and sermons to speeches. The strikingly similar appeals of his memorable speeches and his sermons enabled him to interchange material through his mix-and-match method of composing. Because he generally used deductive argument in both sacred and secular orations, most of his material fit equally well into speeches and sermons, which is why his speeches seem like sermons and his sermons seem like speeches.

In "I Have a Dream" King summarized a deductive contention that he wove into many speeches and sermons: ". . . unearned suffering is redemptive." Occurring near the halfway point of "I Have a Dream," this statement explains the relationship between the nightmare of the first half and the dream of the second half. Given the "bad check" that the Founding Fathers had given blacks and given blacks' status as "exiles in their own land," there would seem little reason for hope. But King maintains that African Americans' undeserved suffering will help implement the brightest visions of Biblical prophecy.

King never tired of elaborating and justifying his belief in redemptive suffering. In fact none of his arguments is more important than the claim that unmerited suffering saves those who suffer—a notion that proved absolutely crucial to the movement. He repeated this point frequently because his followers endured suffering that demanded explanation. Faced with brutality and murder that often went unpunished, organizers wondered about the nightmare engulfing them. Nearly overwhelmed by pain, activist Anne Moody related the terror that prompted her to question God:

> . . . I had witnessed killing, stealing, and adultery committed against Negroes by whites throughout the South. God didn't seem to be punishing anyone for these acts. On the other hand, most of the Negroes in the South were humble, peace-loving, religious people. Yet they were the ones doing all the suffering, as if they themselves were responsible for the killing and other acts committed against them. It seemed to me now that there must be two gods, many gods or no god at all.[15]

Like Moody, King often recounted racists' crimes and the more quotidian hardships imposed on millions of African Americans. He needed a definite answer to Moody's question: how could a loving God permit such evil? He also answered another question: how could the sacrifices of innocent people improve the state of black America? In "I Have a Dream" and elsewhere he claimed that improvement occurs not in spite of unearned suffering, but because of it.

King provided historical examples of redemption brought on by suffering. For example, in "Shattered Dreams," "Death of Evil," and "Remaining Awake," he elucidated the condition of slaves, who answered Jeremiah by affirming "There *is* a balm in Gilead" and who achieved freedom after years of hardship. The Apostle Paul and many other heroes enumerated in "Shattered Dreams," "Making the Best of a Bad Mess," and elsewhere eventually triumphed in spite of or, more likely, because of their deprivations.[16]

The freedom struggle supplied further examples of redemptive suffering. In "Antidotes for Fear," "Letter from Birmingham Jail," and many other addresses and essays, King related a favorite story of an old woman who supported the Montgomery bus boycott by walking every day across the city. When offered a ride, Mrs. Pollard refused, saying, "My feets is tired but my soul is rested." Her physical exhaustion uplifted her spirit. Her tiredness, a mild form of suffering, relieved her soul. Persuaded that her testimony stood as an emblem for the entire crusade for civil rights, an editor chose *My Soul Is Rested* as the title of his outstanding oral history.[17] This title reiterates Mrs. Pollard's and King's point about the value of suffering.

More extreme suffering also served a lofty purpose. In Montgomery, homes and churches were often bombed. After an earlier bomb had inspired the Sermon on the Porch, a second, undetonated explosive was found smoking on the same porch. When a crowd gathered, King counselled, ". . . unearned suffering is redemptive."[18] In effect he claimed that the bombings directed at African Americans would help end bus segregation in Montgomery.

When dynamite killed four black girls attending Sunday School in Birmingham, King eulogized the victims by remarking their dignified deaths as "martyred heroines of a holy crusade."[19] The loss of these innocent children, he argued, would introduce a measure of goodness into people's lives. In his words, "History has proven over and over again that unmerited suffering is redemptive." He suggested that the girls' deaths might redeem Birmingham, the South, and even America itself.[20] In his eulogy for Jimmie Lee Jackson, a martyr of the Selma campaign, he again observed that such a death "must prove that unmerited suffering does not go unredeemed."[21]

Affirming redemption through suffering, King often went voluntarily to jail. He maintained that he and his supporters did not deserve arrest because the laws they violated were unjust and unconstitutional. And he hoped that the experience of going to jail, an act of unmerited suffering, would spotlight injustice and thus help overcome it.

The saving power of undeserved suffering is not a motif King borrowed from texts. Instead it stands as a variation of the central message of Christianity. At its core Christianity asserts that Jesus Christ experienced a tortuous death and rose from the dead. By sacrificing his life, Christ liberated humanity from sin, offering salvation to all who recognize his sacrifice and accept him as Lord. Because Jesus was entirely without sin, his pain on the cross was totally unwarranted. Yet his suffering transformed history by rescuing sinners.

While Christians certainly view the Christ event as unique, they often regard it as the epitome of a recurring experience.

According to most believers, early Christians devoured by lions did not die in vain but instead popularized their divinely inspired religion. Moreover, instead of impeding Christianity, the cruel, unmerited deaths of Stephen and Paul spread the Gospel. Far from suffering for no purpose, Joan of Arc and other saints communicated the Christian gospel despite, or because of, the persecutions they endured. Indeed the entire conception of Christian martyrdom signifies that the suffering and death of the innocent serves to advance the faith.

In his eulogy for the four murdered girls, King subtly underscored the connection between their deaths and Christ's sacrifice when he mentioned the redemptive power of the girls' "innocent blood" and "spilt blood."[22] Christians often use these phrases while celebrating the sacrament of the Last Supper, which includes the ritualistic drinking of wine representing Christ's blood.

Accompanying the theme of redemptive suffering is that of God's conquest of evil, a feat the Almighty usually accomplishes through unwarranted suffering. In "Death of Evil," "Our God Is Able," and "Answer to a Perplexing Question," King locates that theme in the Bible and argues for it deductively. In "Death of Evil" King presents the Exodus as a harbinger of liberating events that will eventually include freedom from segregation. In "Our God Is Able" he keeps repeating his title phrase, maintaining that God consistently defeats evil. The sermon proceeds deductively from that scriptural premise. Based on texts by Brooks and Hamilton, "Answer" cites Jesus's ability to exorcise a demon as proof that God and humanity together can vanquish evil. Like Brooks and Hamilton, King examines how God and human beings can work cooperatively to eliminate evil.[23]

For the inductive portions of his sermons and speeches, King often assembled one or more thematically related aphorisms to reassure audiences that an unfailing God ruled a universe where goodness invariably vanquishes evil. These lines and their original sources are as follows:

Those who live by the sword will die by the sword.
—*Jesus*

You're going to reap what you sow.
—*Apostle Paul*

Weeping may spend the night, but joy comes in the morning.
                                              —*Psalmist*

There is a balm in Gilead to make the wounded whole.
                                              —*slave spiritual*

Only when it's dark can you see the stars.
                              —*anonymous, cited by Charles Beard*

There's a divinity that shapes our ends,
Rough-hew them how we will.
                                              —*Shakespeare*

No lie can live forever.
                                        —*Thomas Carlyle*

Truth crushed to earth will rise again.
                                —*William Cullen Bryant*

The arc of the moral universe is long, but it bends toward justice.
                                —*attributed to Theodore Parker*

Truth forever on the scaffold, Wrong forever on the throne,—
Yet that scaffold sways the future, and, behind the dim unknown,
Standeth God within the shadow, keeping watch above his own.
                                        —*James Russell Lowell*

The non-Biblical sayings are valid because they provide inductive support for the Biblical sayings, which are valid because they are Biblical. The adages from Beard, Carlyle, Bryant, and Lowell amounted to homiletic boilerplate broadcast by Fosdick and many other preachers. So did the maxim from Shakespeare.[24]

During the Sermon on the Porch, King replayed the "live by the sword" proverb; he also employed it as the final sentence in *Stride*.[25] Shakespeare's lines brighten "Death of Evil," while Beard's undergird "Death of Evil" and "Mountaintop."[26]

Often yoking these truisms together, King especially favored those of Carlyle, Bryant, and Lowell, which he frequently combined to form an oratorical set piece sometimes augmented with other commonplaces. Adjusting this material, he formed ringing conclusions for scores of addresses. For example, the 1956 rendition of "Death of Evil" featured the good-over-evil aphorisms of Carlyle, Bryant, and Lowell. He also included them in many, many other addresses.[27] For a version of "Knock at Midnight," he orchestrated the familiar maxims from Lowell, Bryant, Carlyle, and the Psalmist to cap a powerful conclusion.[28] In the recorded version of "Remaining Awake," he launched a peroration that listeners in Cincinnati greeted with rapture:

> We shall overcome . . .
> Because Carlyle is right: no lie can live forever. . . .
> Because William Cullen Bryant is right:
> Truth crushed to earth will rise again. . . .
> Because James Russell Lowell is right:
> Truth forever on the scaffold, wrong forever on the throne
> Yet that scaffold sways the future, and behind the dim unknown
> Standeth God within the shadow keeping watch above His
>   own. . . .
> There *is* a balm in Gilead to make the wounded whole.

In 1965 King marshalled several of the truisms when he spoke at the end of the famous march from Selma to Montgomery. They helped rouse an estimated crowd of fifty thousand people, who had gathered at state capitol of Alabama to demand the right to vote.

He began "How Long?" by recounting the suffering of his audience, several hundred of whom had just finished the fifty-mile trek. He reminded them of the sunburn on their faces and the rain that soaked their bodies. Relating his story about Mrs. Pollard, he reflected on their aching feet and applied Mrs. Pollard's words to them: ". . . our feet are tired, but our souls are rested." Like Mrs. Pollard's tiredness, the hikers' physical exhaustion refreshed their spirits. Their suffering elevated their souls.[29]

King then enumerated vicious resistance—church burnings, house bombings, and murders whose perpetrators escaped justice.[30] He candidly admitted that brutalities had not ceased: "We are still in for a season of suffering. . . ." Yet this grimly realistic expectation should not preclude hope. Three sentences later he declared: "We will be able to change all of these [deplorable] conditions."[31]

He concluded "How Long?" by answering his own question about when justice would come:

> I come to say to you this afternoon . . . it will not be long, because truth pressed to earth will rise again.
> How long? Not long, because no lie can live forever.
> How long? Not long, because you still reap what you sow.
> How long? Not long, because the arc of the moral universe is long but it bends toward justice.
> How long? Not long, because mine eyes have seen the glory of the coming of the Lord . . .
> He has loosed the fateful lightning of his terrible swift sword.
> His truth is marching on.[32]

King probably repeated "How long?" because he had heard folk preachers sounding the same refrain. In 1951 a folk homilist spurred his listeners by asking, "How long?" An observer noted, *"For rousing the audience, 'How long?' is now placing a match to gasoline."* He added, "The words 'how long' suggest to the Negro his apparently endless chain of trials. How often he has wondered *how long* the lord would permit his chosen servant to be mistreated. . . ."[33] This preacher and King used the phrase "How long?" for the same purpose—to recall the unending frustrations of African Americans.

Framed by the words "How long?", King's thematically related maxims explained the basis for hope. Radical change can occur because—as the Bible guarantees and the homiletic aphorisms attest—God overpowers evil. By communicating this metaphysical truth, the commonplaces and the other good-over-evil material performed the extremely important function of interpreting protest, death, and disruption as events occurring within a reliable universe. This universe was as upright and old-fashioned as a Victorian sofa, but far more comfortable. For that reason King's message reassured both his followers and undecided white listeners who heard portions of the speech on television.

King's dependable, beneficent cosmos guaranteed that unmerited suffering would pay long-term dividends. The unearned suffering of the Hebrews inevitably led them out of Egypt and into the Promised Land. Christ's unmerited crucifixion inexorably implied his resurrection. The undeserved cruelties experienced by slaves impelled the signing of the Emancipation Proclamation. When crushed, truth ineluctably rebounds. Liars' words will never endure. People will surely harvest what they plant. The moral universe will always curve in the right direction. And, by refusing to suffer, those who live by the sword ensure that they will never die in their sleep. If these interpretations are valid, King insists, then protests, civil disobedience, and demands for racial equality will *necessarily* occasion the rebirth of Southern society.

The related themes of suffering and deliverance were extremely advantageous for King. The conception of suffering as liberatory reassured blacks tempted to question the Almighty. All Christians face the tough challenge of reconciling the claim that Christ was God's ultimate revelation against two thousand years of ambiguity and tragedy following the arrival of Christ. King addressed the problem by arguing that redemption purchased by Christ's undeserved suffering served as the ultimate model for a process recurring continually in human history. Even though goodness triumphs, evil always returns to create additional unearned suffering. In turn, this new suffering necessitates the triumph of goodness. Or, as King explains in "Death of Evil," ". . . the death of one tyranny is followed by the emergence of another tyranny."[34] The Christ event is ultimate because it both enacts and illuminates the underlying, recurrent meaning of all history. Essentially, King told followers that their undeserved hardships and pain did not refute Christianity but instead reenacted it and thus reaffirmed it. Moreover, his cyclical view of good and evil repeated the archetypal and cyclical view of history evident in his typology, his borrowing of sermons, and his practice of embedding.

In addition, the themes of suffering and deliverance were extremely elastic. If redemptive suffering could explain hundreds of years of slavery, then it could easily account for anything that bigots could dish out in Alabama or Mississippi. Similarly a modest success, such as concessions made by business leaders in Birmingham, could be seen as the dawn of a new day achieved by unearned suffering.[35] When segregationists reacted to these concessions by murdering four black girls, then blacks were involved in more unearned suffering. This theme made King a prophet, for it enabled him to explain *in advance* almost anything that could happen in or to the civil rights movement. Almost every new event involved either a new round of unearned suffering or a victory resulting from previous unearned suffering.

The themes also revived the aphorisms by testing them under exceedingly rugged conditions. Wielding familiar religious and patriotic maxims, King essentially argued that maintaining segregation meant refuting cherished beliefs and truisms. If segregation were to continue, then the Hebrew people would never escape Pharaoh's Egypt, a lie would thrive forever, truth crushed to earth would never rebound, truth on the scaffold would die unnoticed, evildoers would never harvest a bad crop, those who live by the sword would die quietly, and no balm from Gilead would heal the wounded.

King's insistent precepts and the Exodus typology invited listeners to interpret events within the context of a stable universe. They also challenged hearers to support his crusade and thereby prevent the triumph of chaos. Borrowing adages helped King make it difficult for audiences to reject his leadership without also rejecting a beneficent universe. Coupling this fundamentally conservative argument with his deliberate strategy of provoking Southern police, King turned the tables on advocates for the status quo. Commonplaces, Exodus typology, and his political tactics revealed King as the advocate of conservative order and his adversaries as promoters of chaos. In this universe, racists had temporarily upset cosmic justice with the disorder of racial injustice. Here order did not forbid revolution—order *demanded* revolution, a revolution will never end until Biblical prophecy is realized and the kingdom of God is at hand.

EIGHT

LETTER FROM JAIL

In the spring of 1963 Cleo Kennedy, a soloist at St. Luke's Church in Birmingham, began her a cappella rendition of "Swing Low, Sweet Chariot."[1] The slow, lullaby-like tempo of the most famous of all spirituals fit perfectly with the quiet joy of its lyrics. The resplendent expression of a calm expectation to reach heaven, "Swing Low" is a perfect song of religious contemplation. No one would ever tinker with it. But someone did. Without warning, organist Carlton Reese and his choir dove into Kennedy's solo and began belting "Rock Me, Lord," a pounding, extremely upbeat variation of "Swing Low." The pews began to quiver as Reese's whitehot solo proved beyond doubt that every jazz pianist should have played the organ instead. Sopranos leapt boldly into the few spaces the skittering organist left open. And the low, steady bass notes riveted the building to its foundation, which it threatened to desert.

The crowd shouted, clapped, and stomped, celebrating not only the heavenly music, but also their own earthly crusade to eliminate segregation from their city, a bastion of American apartheid.

King stepped up to the pulpit, into the excitement generated by sublime music and by a grassroots protest that had galvanized the attention of the world. He addressed the church in placid, measured tones, transforming his followers' zeal into calm as he prepared them to face the wrath of the city. He and they realized that Sheriff Bull Connor would continue to confront peaceful marchers with powerful fire hoses and angry police dogs. But he insisted that, though greeted with dogs and hatred, protestors should remain nonviolent and patiently accept jail sentences for themselves and their children.[2]

Nonviolence was finally winning the Battle of Birmingham. King and SCLC had already dispatched twenty-five hundred people to jail, for the first time meeting their objective of literally filling the jails.

The Birmingham movement gained the sympathy of millions of Americans, who were horrified by police violence, especially when applied to innocent black children. But police brutality in Birmingham and elsewhere did not automatically signify that segregation was evil. The public needed to understand police barbarism as symptomatic and symbolic of an entire racist system. King and the movement had to convince America that Connor was no aberration, that everyday segregation was just as horrific as Connor's police. By sacrificing themselves to the hoses and dogs, King's activists essentially claimed that Connor's violence represented the hidden, daily violence of racism.

Just as police brutality served as an apt symbol for the less dramatic, quotidian evil of segregation, so did jail. As they presented themselves for jail, African Americans in effect argued that jail symbolized racism.[3] They could stand jail because segregation already locked them in jail. If segregation was already a prison, then why not go behind bars?

Providing this equation explicitly in "Shattered Dreams," King equates Paul's suffering in prison with the experience of enslaved and segregated blacks. He argues that African Americans in "the prison of segregation" recapitulate Paul's experiences in prison.[4] King's "Letter from Birmingham Jail" implicitly offers the same comparison: life in jail matches life under segregation.

King could provide this equation because his conception of religious leadership came from the Old Testament prophets, the

Apostle Paul, and the black church. Early in this letter he compares himself to the eighth-century Old Testament prophets and to Paul.[5] His readers realized that Paul was often incarcerated and wrote letters from jail. Like the prophets, Paul was simultaneously a preacher, a theologian, and a disturber of the peace. And Paul made no distinction between his sermons, his theology, and his letter-writing. Refusing to cultivate an elite, he preferred to evangelize anyone who would listen.

Long before King was born, black churches often insisted on vesting in a single person the duties of theologian, preacher, and activist. In many black communities, mastering all these roles has been almost a requirement for becoming an authoritative religious leader. Until the advent of black theology about the time of King's death, blacks rarely recognized theology as something distinct from sermons. Believing that the brightest and best-educated people should instruct whole congregations, African-American leaders have historically gained authority by combining the roles of expert and public speaker. The finest black theologians—Richard Allen, Henry Highland Garnet, Vernon Johns, C.L. Franklin, and others— delivered theology through their sermons, not by way of erudite theological prose. They also engaged in protest; indeed, their church "was born as a protest movement."[6] And, while its impulse to protest has sometimes remained dormant, the impulse has never died.

By contrast, in the first half of this century liberal white Protestants treated sermons, theology, and social protest as discrete concerns. No one regarded Fosdick, Buttrick, and Hamilton as theologians. Nor were they activists of any note. Though Tillich often preached, his reputation rests on his theological volumes, which he clearly valued more than his sermons. Though Niebuhr ventured across the tidy demarcations of religious roles, he, like Tillich, regarded his theology—not his sermons—as the most important expression of his thought. In fact, the extremely prolific Niebuhr never published a collection of sermons and never used theology to organize a movement.[7] Like other white Protestants, King's professors regarded theology, homiletics, and social ethics as separate subjects to be taught in separate classes.

While many would rank King as the greatest American preach-er of the century, one could easily wonder how he could become a stellar homilist and essayist while also directing a social revolution. He managed to become both the most accomplished preacher and the most successful reformer of the century partly because he did not begin the process of fusing the roles of preacher, theologian, and activist. Unlike white religious leaders, he preached by protesting, protested by preaching, and wrote theology by stepping into a jail cell. His successful theology consists of his sermons, speeches, civil rights essays, and political career—not his formal theological work. Had he accepted the white division of theology, homiletics, and politics, he never would have gone to jail to gain the authority to speak. By rejecting white models, he achieved the apotheosis of his own community's understanding of religious leadership, an understanding the nation came to cherish.

Nowhere is this black conception of theology more evident than in "Letter from Birmingham Jail." Along with the Sermon on the Porch, the essay is more completely inseparable from the civil rights movement than any other example of King's discourse. Indeed a better match between words and deeds is difficult to imagine. King perfectly tailored his letter to the particulars of Birmingham in 1963, including its recent mayoral election and an unsolved rash of bombings. The principles outlined in "Letter" mandated his trip to jail, and a stay in jail mandated the explanation supplied by "Letter." Getting arrested set the stage for "Letter," "Letter" set the stage for future arrests.

Yet, as King masterfully performed the simultaneous roles of preacher, theologian, and activist, he wrote an essay that, unlike his other discourse, actually reflects his study of Euro-American philosophy and theology. "Letter" also manifests the powerful and more familiar influences of the black folk pulpit, *Christian Century*, Fosdick, Wofford, and two other religious writers. All these influences converge in this extraordinary essay.

Although King's epistolary essay was inspired by Paul, his more immediate stimulant was *Christian Century*.[8] In 1959, six months after joining the editorial staff of the journal, he informed its editor that he wanted to write "occasional articles and letters" that could reach "the Protestant leadership of our country."[9] The editor agreed that his readership would appreciate "an occasional personal letter which you could write."[10] Six months later the editor gave more explicit instructions, telling King and his other editors-at-large to write Christmas letters "in such a form that they can actually be sent to the people to whom they are addressed as well as appearing in the columns of the magazine."[11] The recipients responded with a set of public letters printed in the Christmas issue of the journal. Like "Letter," these letters ostensibly focused on their real-life addressees but actually on readers of *Christian Century*. Like "Letter," some of them combined a cordial and respectful tone with forceful criticism of their addressees. Although King did not write a public letter on this occasion, he did so a few years later in Birmingham.

Ostensibly serving as King's response to eight moderate clergy, "Letter" first surfaced in *Christian Century*, *Liberation*, and *Christianity and Crisis*—three left-of-center journals—and in pamphlets disseminated by the Fellowship of Reconciliation (FOR) and another leftist, pacifist organization, the American Friends Service Committee.[12] Soon afterwards other readers encountered King's epistle in *The Progressive*, *Ebony*, and other liberal periodicals. Publication in the *New York Post* and the *San Francisco Chronicle* further expanded King's readership. (He claimed that "nearly a million copies . . . have been widely circulated in churches of most of the major denominations."[13]) He also installed the instantly popular essay as the centerpiece for *Why We Can't Wait*, his longer account of the Birmingham movement.

Given that King wrote "Letter" for *Christian Century* and other left-of-center outlets, one can say that its original and primary audience was not the ostensible audience of eight moderate clergy. Nor was it other moderate readers. Instead, King carefully crafted a letter that could actually be mailed to its addressees while engaging the readers of *Christian Century* and other liberal Protestants. The progressive ministers and laity who raved about King's sermons at Cathedral of St. John, Riverside Church, the Chicago Sunday Evening Club, and elsewhere were the same people who subscribed to *Christian Century*. Because this journal had promulgated racial equality not merely for years, but for several decades prior to "Letter," the vast majority of its subscribers wholeheartedly agreed with King's attack on segregation long before he wrote his essay. Had the editors of the journal failed to sympathize with King, they would not have published "Pilgrimage" several years prior to "Letter." Nor would they have welcomed him as an editor-at-large every year from 1958 until a year after the publication of "Letter." Equally sympathetic were those who read "Letter" in other liberal forums. Although the essay eventually reached large numbers of moderates, King's main purpose was to convert the converted and reinforce their earlier support. He carefully preached to the choir, targeting an audience of liberals by asking them to invoke the role of moderates. The essay was so well written that it reached a large, spillover audience of moderates as well.

All readers perused an essay composed under trying conditions. By every account, King entered Birmingham jail with nothing to read and with no notes or examples of his own writing. However, he remembered earlier speeches and sermons and insinuated several familiar passages into his essay, including material he had originally obtained from sources. Because he relied on his memory —not directly on texts—the borrowed passages in "Letter" do not resemble his models as closely as usual. Still, several of his sources can be clearly identified.

For his arguments about nonconformity, he recalled his own sermon "Transformed Nonconformist," including passages that came from Fosdick's *Hope of the World* and from a sermon by H.H. Crane:

FOSDICK: We Christians were intended to be that [creative] minority. We were to be the salt of the earth, said Jesus. We were to be the light of the world. We were to be the leaven in the lump of the race. . . . That is joining the real church. . . . *ecclesia* . . . a minority selected from the majority. . . . There was a time . . . when Christianity was very powerful. Little groups of men and women were scattered through the Roman Empire. . . . They were far less than two per cent and the heel of persecution was often on them, but they flamed with a conviction. . . .

Do you remember what Paul called them . . . "We are a colony of heaven," he said . . . [Christianity] stopped ancient curses like infanticide. It put an end to the . . . gladitorial shows.[14]

CRANE: Consider first the thermometer. Essentially, it . . . records or registers its environments. . . . Instead of being *conformed* to this world, [man] can *transform* it. . . . For when he is what his Maker obviously intended him to be, he is not a thermometer; he is a thermostat. . . . there is a thermostatic type of religion . . . and its highest expression is called vita Christianity.[15]

KING: There was a time when the church was very powerful. . . . In those days the church was not merely a thermometer that recorded the ideas and principles of popular opinion; it was a thermostat that transformed the mores of society. Whenever the early Christians entered a town, the people in power . . . immediately sought to convict the Christians for being "disturbers of the peace". . . . But the Christians pressed on in the conviction that they were a "colony of heaven". . . . Small in number, they were big in commitment. . . . By their effort and example they brought an end to such ancient evils as infanticide and gladitorial contests. Perhaps I must turn . . . to the inner spiritual church as the true *ekklesia* and hope of the world. These [ministers who support civil rights] have been the leaven in the lump of the race. Their witness has been the spiritual salt that has preserved the true meaning of the Gospel. . . .[16]

King here eschewed the King James version of the Bible, which he normally used, and followed Fosdick in quoting from the 1922 Moffatt translation of Philippians 3:20 ("We are a colony of heaven").[17] Significantly, the King James translation of this verse— "For our conversation is in heaven"—fails to provide *any* Biblical support for nonconformity. Here King owes a debt not only to Fosdick's lines, but also to Fosdick's choice of a specific scripture *and* a specific translation of that scripture. This translation contrasts substantively not only with the King James edition, but with almost all other available English translations.

Turning to another familiar source, King marshalled his arguments for nonviolence and civil disobedience by refashioning ideas and language from two of Wofford's speeches. He reworded a passage from Wofford that he had used earlier in *Stride:*

WOFFORD: . . . [*Civil* disobedience] involves the highest possible respect for the law. If we secretly violated the law, or tried to evade it, or violently tried to overthrow it, that would be undermining the idea of law, Gandhi argued. But by openly and peacefully disobeying an unjust law and asking for the penalty, we are saying that we so respect the law that when we think it is so unjust that in conscience we cannot obey, then we belong in jail until that law is changed.[18]

KING: In no sense do I advocate evading or defying the law. . . . One who breaks an unjust law must do so openly, lovingly, and with a willingness to accept the penalty. I submit that an individual who breaks a law that conscience tells him is unjust, and who willingly accepts the penalty of imprisonment in order to arouse the conscience of the community over its injustice, is in reality expressing the highest respect for the law.[19]

King also paraphrased Wofford's citation of Socrates, Augustine, and Aquinas as proponents of civil disobedience and Wofford's call for nonviolent gadflies.[20]

For part of his analysis of segregation, King turned to George Kelsey, his professor at Morehouse, whose remarks on segregation proved useful on several occasions. In *Stride*, "A Challenge to Churches and Synagogues," and "Letter," King sometimes reiterated and sometimes adapted passages from Kelsey:

> KELSEY: . . . segregation is itself utterly un-Christian. It is established on pride, fear, and falsehood. . . . It is unbrotherly, impersonal, a complete denial of the *"I–Thou"* relationship, and a complete expression of the *"I–It"* relation. Two segregated souls never meet in God.[21]

Compare King's statement in "A Challenge to the Churches and Synagogues":

> . . . segregation is morally wrong and sinful. It is established on pride, hatred, and falsehood. It is unbrotherly and impersonal. Two segregated souls never meet in God. . . . To use the words of Martin Buber, segregation substitutes an "I–it" relationship for the "I–thou" relationship and ends up relegating persons to the status of things.[22]

King distilled this analysis in "Letter":

> Segregation, to use the terminology of . . . Martin Buber, substitutes an "I–it" relationship for an "I–thou" relationship and ends up relegating persons to the status of things.[23]

For his affirmation of interdependence, King borrowed another passage from Fosdick. Fosdick's "We are intermeshed in an inescapable mutuality" became King's "We are caught in an inescapable network of mutuality."[24]

The black church originally supplied King with ideas about nonconformity, nonviolence, segregation, interdependence, and other themes trumpeted in "Letter." Invoking sacred time, he compared himself to the prophets and Paul and talked about Jesus, Martin Luther, John Bunyan, Lincoln, and Jefferson as though they shared his cell block in Birmingham. Wielding his customary argument from authority, he also cited Socrates, Augustine, Aquinas, Tillich, Niebuhr, T.S. Eliot, and three Old Testament heroes.[25] He skillfully wove each of these references into the fabric of an astute analysis of segregation and civil disobedience in Birmingham.

While King drew on familiar sources for the content of "Letter," the intricate structure of his argument reflects his exposure to famous Euro-American philosophers, whose works offer many precedents of fine-spun philosophical persuasion. *Christian Century* and black and white sermons provide far fewer examples of the carefully layered appeals that structure "Letter."

King's essay can be seen as an exemplary, modern version of an oration from ancient Greece or Rome.[26] Basically "Letter" follows the steps of a typical classical speech: introduction, proposition, division, confirmation, refutation, and peroration. His tendency to move his argument forward through skillful digressions is a standard classical strategy. Offering a modest variation of classical form, he packed the bulk of his argument into his refutation, effectively refuting both major and minor premises of the eight clergymen's implicit syllogisms.[27] He practiced "multipremise refutation" by expressing disappointment at being labelled an extremist, then folding that argument into a vigorous defense of certain forms of extremism.[28] His "tone of sadness and compulsion" and expert understatement (e.g., "I cannot join you in your praise of the Birmingham police department") also enjoy precedents in classical rhetoric.[29] By registering his humility, his understatements paradoxically buttress his claims instead of undermining them.

Layered philosophical argument is just as crucial to "Letter" as the black conception of religious roles that made it possible in the first place. *Christian Century*, white sermons, and black folk religion also inform King's essay in powerful ways. "Letter" masterfully interlaces themes of Fosdick, Wofford, Crane, and Kelsey; invokes multiple authorities; reinvigorates the sacred time of the folk pulpit; and supplies rich Pauline allusions and other Biblical echoes. King carefully subsumed each of these appeals within a larger inductive argument consisting of box-within-a-box, multipremise refutation —an argument as lucid as it is intricate. His keen awareness of the readership of *Christian Century* enabled him to choose truisms from appropriate authorities (including Tillich, Niebuhr, and Martin Buber) that would fit suitably into his larger scheme.

King's study of philosophy and theology during his years at Crozer and Boston accounts for the classical argument that structures his essay. Classical rhetoric directly or indirectly influenced every masterpiece of Western philosophy and theology that King's professors assigned him to read. Though he often expressed the major themes of "Letter"—sometimes with remarkably similar wording—at no other time did he ever summon its rigorously ordered, predominantly inductive logic and controlled understatement.

The uniqueness of the essay results primarily from his decision to go to jail, which reflects Biblical and African-American precedents for combining the roles of preacher, theologian, and agitator. His isolation in Birmingham jail—an isolation he never again experienced—enabled him to translate into popular terms the kind of argument he learned in the academy.

NINE

BECOMING MOSES

K ing balanced the Pauline qualities of "Letter from Birmingham Jail" with the slaves' vision of Exodus. Not only in "Death of Evil," but throughout the freedom struggle, he and his colleagues identified black Americans with the Hebrews enslaved in Egypt.[1] According to King, African Americans would languish in the Egypt of segregation until their protests could loosen the grip of Southern Pharaohs. Participating in sacred time, mid-century blacks joined their slave foreparents in yearning for a new savior, a Moses/Jesus figure who would hasten their liberation. In fact, the slaves' vision of deliverance became the overriding theme of the 1960s struggle for racial equality.

Civil rights songleaders, for example, renewed "Go Down, Moses" by taking the lyrics of the spiritual—

Go down Moses, way down in Egypt land.
Tell old Pharaoh to let my people go.

and adapting them typologically to their own circumstance:

Go down Kennedy, way down in Georgia land.
Tell old [Sheriff] Pritchett to let my people go.[2]

Fannie Lou Hamer, who epitomized courageous grassroots activism, adapted these lyrics by inserting the name of Robert Moses, a Mississippi organizer:

Go down, Bob Moses, way down in Egypt land.
Tell old Pharaoh to let my people go.

Birmingham leader Wyatt Walker cites "Go Down, Moses" and other spirituals as "the most suitable music" for the struggle and regards "Go Down, Moses" as offering "universal appeal for all oppressed people."[3] Agreeing with Walker, organizers of the March on Washington distributed song sheets for "Go Down, Moses" and other spirituals. Mahalia Jackson regarded the March as another Exodus: ". . . here was a nation of people marching together. It was like the vision of Moses that the children of Israel would march into Canaan."[4]

King himself revived slave typology by interpreting the movement within the framework of the Exodus. He repeated "Death of Evil," and frequently enlivened rallies with spirituals by Mahalia Jackson and other soloists. Invariably, he labelled his racist opponents as "Pharaohs." In 1957, wearing his pulpit robes on the steps of the Lincoln Memorial, he observed, "[God] is leading us out of a bewildering Egypt, through a bleak and desolate wilderness, toward a bright and glittering promised land."[5]

Outstanding organizer Septima Clark noted King's ability to mine the story of the Hebrews' escape from Egypt: "As he talked about Moses, and leading the people out, and getting the people into the place where the Red Sea would cover them, he would just make you see them. You believed it."[6] Andrew Young also remarked King's success in reinvigorating the familiar folk pulpit imagery of dry bones and the Exodus when straightforward political appeals had failed.[7]

King interpreted the Exodus as an archetypal human experience, a narrative that reasserted itself throughout history. His final book, *Where Do We Go from Here?*, invokes sacred time to intertwine blacks' fate with that of the Hebrews:

The Bible tells the thrilling story of how Moses stood in Pharaoh's court centuries ago and cried, "Let my people go." This was an opening chapter in a continuing story. The present struggle in the United States is a later chapter in the same story.[8]

If segregationists constituted the new Pharaohs and if blacks reenacted the struggles of the Hebrews, then surely someone must function as Moses. A new Moses would need national recognition, an ability to stir the masses, a balance of militancy and realism, and the correct gender.

There were few strong candidates for the job. Despite his name, Robert Moses was too soft-spoken to achieve a national reputation. Moreover, he, Ella Baker, and other leaders of the Student Nonviolent Coordinating Committee (SNCC) believed in highly democratic, grassroots organizing and disdained the entire notion of a Moses-like leader. While Roy Wilkins and Whitney Young maintained highly visible profiles, they aroused no one with their painstaking gradualism and their plain-vanilla, straightforward speechifying. John Lewis and King's lieutenants Andrew Young, James Bevel, and Jesse Jackson were simply too young. Wyatt Walker, Bevel, and Jackson also lacked the right temperament, as did Hosea Williams, another SCLC official.[9] Missing the polish of a Northern, white education, Ralph Abernathy, a son of the rural South and King's close friend, was too folksy to appeal to whites and too loyal to challenge King's leadership. James Forman and Stokely Carmichael were too stridently militant. Founding CORE and leading the Freedom Rides gave James Farmer excellent credentials for the part of Moses; but Farmer was not a minister, and he did not view the black church as a vital agent of change. In the eyes of many male activists, Rosa Parks, Ella Baker, Fannie Lou Hamer, Septima Clark, and other movement stalwarts automatically failed to qualify as Moses—or even as potential seminarians—simply because they were female.

Unlike these other candidates, King loomed as a potential Moses. Certainly no one, not even the articulate Farmer, could match King's magisterial, yet fiery orations. During and after the Montgomery bus boycott, many people—including prominent white journalists—began to designate King as a black Moses. As early as June 1956—roughly halfway through the Montgomery campaign—the *American Negro* magazine titled an essay: "Rev. M.L. King: Alabama Moses."[10] *Jet* magazine also heralded King as "'Alabama's Modern Moses.'"[11] The young John Lewis, who became a major civil rights leader, was initially so mesmerized by King that he regarded his hero as "a Moses."[12]

While King did not directly claim to be Moses during the early 1960s, his use of the Moses/Pharaoh model in "Death of Evil" and elsewhere invited his listeners and readers to ask, "Who, then, is our Moses?" and to fill in the name themselves. Actively promoting the Moses image was King's alter ego, Ralph Abernathy. At a rally in Birmingham, Abernathy spoke of God, Moses, and other Biblical figures before introducing King: "He is the leader! He is the Moses!"[13]

King's followers adopted other Biblical images as well. For example, after the Birmingham campaign, Duke Ellington celebrated its success by composing "King Fit the Battle of Alabam," a variation of "Joshua Fit the Battle of Jericho."

King himself invoked typology to explain his life. For example, in 1960, reflecting on a stabbing from a would-be assassin, he wrote, "So like the Apostle Paul I can now humbly yet proudly say, 'I bear in my body the marks of the Lord Jesus.'"[14] He again compared himself to Paul in "Letter from Birmingham Jail." He telescoped distance and evoked sacred time by declaring, "[Jesus] said all men are created equal."[15] By placing Jefferson's assertion on the lips of Jesus, this statement makes Jesus and Jefferson contemporaries. It also interprets each of these figures as the type for the other. King related Fosdick's typological story about a black woman who held her child aloft to see Lincoln's coffin. She told the child, "He died for you"—a common Christian explanation of Jesus's death on the cross.[16]

One comparison, however, was more startling than any of these. Just as slaves sometimes collapsed Moses and Jesus into a single liberator, so did some movement workers. At times the conflation occurred subtly. For example, Fannie Lou Hamer combined the lyrics of the spiritual "Go Tell It on the Mountain" with the lyrics of "Go Down, Moses." In her hands the original lyrics of the spiritual "Go Tell It on the Mountain"—

Go tell it on the mountain that Jesus Christ is born.

became

> *Go tell it on the mountain to let my people go.*[17]

Because Moses's liberating words to the Pharaoh—"Let my people go"—substitute for the event of liberation—"Jesus Christ is born"—Hamer's line subtly fuses Moses and Jesus.

Others lacked Hamer's subtlety and directly compared King to Jesus. As early as the Montgomery bus boycott, some boycott supporters dubbed their leader "Little Lord Jesus."[18] When a reporter in Montgomery observed a group cheering King, he observed, "They think he's a Messiah."[19] As King left a courtroom, followers shouted, "Behold the King!" Soon afterward he was introduced as someone who had been "nailed to the cross" for their sake.[20] Several years later, in a ceremony honoring his work, another speaker likened him to Jesus.[21]

The comparison recurred in subsequent years. In 1961, after hearing King calm an unruly crowd, the president of the Atlanta Chamber of Commerce remarked, "I had heard him called 'Little Jesus' in the black community. Now I understood why."[22] In 1963 members of one church sang "Come Thou Almighty King" before King spoke. An observer saw this gesture as "an obvious effort to honor King and to identify him with Jesus Christ."[23] During the Selma crusade Stokely Carmichael commented that rural blacks regarded King "like a God."[24] Coretta King observed that, during his sojourn to Chicago the following year, ghetto dwellers regarded her husband "almost like a Messiah."[25]

Abernathy also made the comparison. Once he "lamented the assassination of President Kennedy but explained that Dr. King was protected by 'invisible bodyguards.'"[26] Introducing King for "How Long?", he characterized his friend as "conceived by God."[27] While this comment might seem embarrassingly ham-handed, King occasionally proffered the same comparison. When Freedom Riders pleaded with him to join their protest, he replied, "I think I should choose the time and place of my Golgotha."[28] On other occasions he spoke of "bearing the cross" of undeserved suffering.[29] In Albany he again reflected on the possibility of martyrdom: "It may get me crucified. I may die. But I want it said even if I die in the struggle that 'He died to make men free.' "[30] In King's sentence, the pronoun "He," which in "The Battle Hymn of the Republic" refers to Christ, obviously designates King as well.

During the Birmingham protest King chose to be arrested on Good Friday. As Coretta King tells the story, he rose to the pulpit to explain his desire "to be a good servant of his Lord and Master."[31] When he left, one person yelled, "There he goes, just like Jesus," and many left the church to join his demonstration.[32] Later he collapsed Moses, Jesus, and himself into a single figure, explaining that blacks' hopes "to cross the Red Sea of injustice" caused him to be arrested on Good Friday.[33] In this sentence the narratives of Moses, Jesus, and King form a single story.

King's frequent discussions of his possible martyrdom did nothing to discourage the Jesus parallel. In *Stride* he analyzed at some length the bombings of his home and other buildings associated with the Montgomery bus boycott.[34] Throughout his career, he often meditated aloud on subsequent death threats and assassination attempts, including the nearly fatal stabbing in Harlem and the bombing of his hotel room in Birmingham. In his final speech, "Mountaintop," he seemed to anticipate his own assassination.

Over the years King came more and more to anticipate a violent death and freely discussed the possibility with his family and friends. His calm attitude made him appear even more like a Christian martyr. He had fully explained the nature of his martyrdom before it ever occurred, and in "Drum Major Instinct" indicated what he wanted said at his funeral. No actual eulogist could possibly have summarized the meaning of his life more satisfactorily than King did in these instructions.

First-rate journalists also described King as a potential martyr and sometimes likened him to Jesus. David Halberstam, for example, published "The Second Coming of Martin Luther King" in a 1967 issue of *Harper's* magazine. Some Freedom Riders and SNCC activists, however, resented King's ability to monopolize the news media. Because poor blacks seemed to wait for a Messiah instead of enacting their own liberation, SNCC workers often regarded King's charisma as counterproductive. They disdained the entire King/Jesus equation. However, even as they scorned the comparison by mocking King as "De Lawd," their nickname reiterated the same parallel.[35]

Although King himself occasionally identified himself with Jesus, he balked at the Messianic expectations placed on him and declared truthfully, "I'm no messiah, and I don't have a messiah complex."[36] He frankly recognized his own limitations and often discussed with friends and staff members the gap between his decidedly larger-than-life image and the imperfect human being he knew he was.[37]

During the last two years of King's life these limitations seemed greater. An avalanche of criticism fell on him from both left and right, and his political difficulties mounted in the wake of widespread riots, an escalating war in Vietnam, and a campaign of harassment mounted by the director of the FBI. As the prospect for political victories declined, he sometimes struggled with bouts of depression.[38] His superhuman image may have contributed to his anxiety; for, while he recognized the value of his image, he also knew that no one could live up to it.

King and other activists applied Biblical models persuasively because, with a few exceptions, they used them suggestively, not literally. No proponent of civil rights insisted that the March on Washington was a reincarnation of the Exodus. Almost all Biblical references could be viewed as straightforward literary allusions and nothing more. But oppressed blacks could easily take hope from prophetic and eschatological assurances that their movement formed a sequel to God's narrative of Exodus and Resurrection.

One of the most suggestive uses of typology involved the name "Martin Luther King, Jr.," which does not appear on King's birth certificate. When King was born, his father's name was Michael King, Sr., and his name was Michael King, Jr. A few years later, when the elder King changed his name to "Martin Luther King, Sr.," his son officially became "Martin Luther King, Jr."

During the younger King's years of growing up, his family and friends dubbed him "M.L." or "Mike." Well into the middle and late 1950s, friends continued to call him "Mike" and to greet him in letters as "Dear Mike." His family, however, preferred the name "M.L." In April 1968, when King, Sr., walked up to his son's casket, he shouted "M.L.! Answer me, M.L."[39] And, writing about King, Jr., years after his assassination, his father and sister continued to talk about "M.L."[40] During his years at Morehouse, friends often labelled him "Tweedie," in honor of his tweed suits. Coretta King preferred the name "Martin." So did Abernathy. But King's staff members often designated him as "Doc."

Thus the full name "Martin Luther King, Jr.," had virtually no meaning for King before he became a public figure. None of the people he knew well ever called him "Martin Luther" or "Martin Luther King, Jr." Some liked "Martin," but no one used the name "Luther" with or without "Martin." Although King's name was officially changed to "Martin Luther," this name is essentially a public name, not a private one. It can almost be called a title.

King did not choose this full name independently; instead he had it literally thrust upon him. Granting King his conditions for accepting a pulpit in Montgomery, the committee chair addressed his letter to "Rev. M.L. King, Jr."[41] When Rosa Parks wrote him four months before her famous arrest, she mailed her letter to "Rev. M.L. King, Jr."[42] Early newsletters of the organization sponsoring the boycott (MIA) listed its president as "M.L. King, Jr." As the boycott continued in earnest, the *MIA Newsletter* bandied the names "M.L. King, Jr.," "Martin L. King, Jr.," and "Martin Luther King, Jr.," interchangeably.[43]

During 1956, the year of the boycott, most of his voluminous correspondence was addressed to "Dr. Martin Luther King, Jr.," or "Rev. Martin Luther King, Jr." But, despite his correspondents' preference for his full name, he closed most of his own letters with the typed name of "M.L. King, Jr." Occasionally he had his secretary type "Martin L. King, Jr." as his sign-off. Only on rare occasions that year did he conclude letters with "Martin Luther King, Jr." Throughout 1956 and 1957 he continued to close most letters with "M.L. King, Jr."

In 1958 and 1959, however, this practice began to change. He ended his correspondence with "M.L. King, Jr." far less often than before, preferring either "Martin L. King, Jr." or his entire name, "Martin Luther King, Jr." He frequently used these two names in 1958 and 1959 and into the early months of 1960.

However, by late 1960 and early 1961, he closed virtually all letters with "Martin Luther King, Jr." He even used his full name when answering mail addressed to "M.L. King, Jr." or to "Martin L. King, Jr." For the remainder of his life, he continued to end his correspondence with "Martin Luther King, Jr." If he knew the correspondent, he would often actually sign the letter "Martin," but he would sign it above the typed name "Martin Luther King, Jr."[44]

Thus, it seems clear that King's followers and the public did not care for "M.L. King, Jr.," the name he initially favored. Certainly it did little to distinguish him from eighteen other reverends on the MIA Executive Board who used only a set of initials and a last name (e.g., Rev. S.S. Seay, Rev. B.J. Simms, etc.).[45] Gradually the significance of the name "Martin Luther" and its popularity among the public swayed King to adopt it, even when correspondents preferred "M.L." or "Martin L." In short, civil rights supporters and the news media—not King himself—created the public name of "Martin Luther King, Jr." King slowly but completely adopted the name that his community had selected for him.

The media certainly played a major role in popularizing the longer name. Journalists almost always trumpeted the complete "Martin Luther King," with or without "Jr.," despite their normal practice in naming prominent public figures. In headlines and elsewhere, Eisenhower became "Ike," Eugene McCarthy shrank to "Gene," Robert Kennedy narrowed to "Bob" or "Bobby," and Edward Kennedy contracted to "Ted" or "Teddy." Headline writers often substituted acronyms for proper names: "JFK" indicated John Fitzgerald Kennedy, "RFK" stood for Robert Francis Kennedy, and "LBJ" meant Lyndon Baines Johnson. Though "MLK" appeared occasionally, headline writers usually preferred "King," which fit just as easily into a headline.[46] The inability of King's family and friends to agree on a single name may have encouraged the media to adopt "Martin Luther King" (with or without "Jr."). But, for whatever reason, the press did indeed expand King's name beyond the names favored by everyone who knew him well.

Even King's strongest critics and most bitter enemies helped solidify the use of his full name. Harlem congressman Adam Clayton Powell ridiculed him as "Martin Loser King."[47] Diehard racists and Ku Klux Klansmen taunted him as "Martin Luther Coon" and "Martin Luther Kink."[48] Although Powell's phrase is insulting and the Klan appellations are abhorrent, these puns nevertheless served as variations of "Martin Luther King" and thus reiterated and validated the longer name, which became accepted universally.

"Martin Luther," the name of the nonviolent founder of Protestantism, was an eminently appropriate name for a Protestant minister directing a massive political protest. Obviously "King" betokens powerful leadership, either of a monarch or of Jesus, the

"King of Kings." "Jr." adds a slight qualification to the name—
which might otherwise sound a trifle grandiose—without altering
it significantly. Certainly "Martin Luther King" distinguished King
from other civil rights leaders whose names—"A. Philip Randolph," "John Lewis," "James Lawson," "James Farmer," and
"James Forman"—proved far less memorable and sometimes
confusingly alike.

Unlike these other names, "Martin Luther King" evoked the
memory of the leader who sparked a revolution in Christendom.
On one conspicuous occasion King strongly associated his name
with that memory. In 1966 he led thousands of protestors along the
streets of downtown Chicago until they arrived at City Hall.
Imitating Martin Luther's nailing of ninety-five theses onto the
doors of a German church, King taped his version of ninety-five
theses onto the doors of City Hall. He clearly capitalized on the
rhetorical value of "Martin Luther King"—a name that aided his
process of composing a heroic public self.

King certainly enhanced this heroic self through his final
speech, "I've Been to the Mountaintop." There he interpreted the
Moses/Pharaoh archetypes more masterfully than he or anyone
else had ever done before.[49] The incandescent brilliance of the
address stems from his wholehearted, highly imaginative adaptation of the slaves' theology of liberation. While the King of "Death
of Evil" remained outside the Biblical narrative, the King of
"Mountaintop" enlisted his followers in a new performance of the
Exodus drama. He located their struggle within the cosmos of the
slaves, which blurs distinctions of space and time and of heavenly
and earthly deliverance.

When King delivered "Mountaintop" to a rally of striking
garbage workers, their situation was grim. The city of Memphis had
adamantly rejected their demands and refused to negotiate; the
national press also ignored their plight. Calling attention to their
cause, King had led a group of marchers who ignored his teachings
and degenerated into a frenzied, destructive mob. As a result of
their riot, one young man lost his life. Returning to Memphis, King
determined to salvage nonviolence by instituting a successful,
peaceable campaign.

With a tempest bellowing outside and rain drumming stead-
ily upon the roof, King began "Mountaintop" by mentioning
Abernathy's complimentary introduction. Calling Abernathy his

"best friend," King started with the "I" of his everyday self—a straightforward "I."[50] He immediately enlarged the "I" by adapting the slaves' sense of sacred time that erases all historical and geographical barriers. He fantasized a grand tour of world history beginning with the Exodus. After witnessing the Hebrews' escape from bondage, he overheard a conversation among the outstanding thinkers of ancient Greece. He then observed the culture of ancient Rome and the Renaissance. Extending his magical trip through time and space, he gazed at "the man for whom I'm named" as Luther nailed his theses to a church door in Wittenberg. He then spied a hesitant Lincoln signing the Emancipation Proclamation and listened to Franklin Roosevelt console a devastated nation.[51] Several of these events—notably Luther's protest and Lincoln's declaration—were world-changing expressions of the great historical movement from oppression to freedom. Essentially they recapitulated the Exodus.

However, scanning these majestic sights does not satisfy the time traveller, who asks God to continue his odyssey into the twentieth century. He wants to witness a political awakening across Africa and the United States, where "the cry [of the oppressed] is always the same: 'We want to be free.' "[52] The American awakening occurs despite a national atmosphere of crisis. Applying the apocalyptic imagery of Biblical prophecy and the folk pulpit, he declares, "The nation is sick. Trouble is in the land. Confusion all around."[53]

This dire situation necessitates solidarity. Reinterpreting the Exodus, King remarks, ". . . whenever Pharaoh wanted to prolong the period of slavery in Egypt" he "kept the slaves fighting among themselves."[54] To frustrate the Pharaoh's strategy, King calls for mutual support: "When the slaves get together, that's the beginning of getting out of slavery. Now let us maintain unity."[55] The "us" are King's listeners, the garbage workers and their allies, but the "us" are also the Hebrews enslaved by the Pharaoh. Here garbage workers in Memphis strain against the yoke of a new Pharaoh governing a new Egypt.

After analyzing the struggle in Memphis, he recapitulates the movement's shining moment in Birmingham when nonviolent protestors defied police dogs and fire hoses. Bull Connor, sheriff of the city, failed to realize that demonstrators possessed "a certain kind of fire that no water could put out"—a sanctified, holy fire largely responsible for the Civil Rights Act of 1964.[56] As they confronted dogs and hoses, King states, demonstrators sang, "Over my head I see freedom in the air."[57] Adapted from a spiritual, this brief lyric effectively merges the two strands of the slaves' dual theme of redemption. Freedom is not simply in the air at eye level or below. It is above them in heaven. Singers testified that freedom and deliverance in the next world were immanent in this world. When activists and King repeat the lyric, sacred and secular worlds blend and heaven comes down to earth.

Freedom did arrive, King explains, for ". . . we won our struggle in Birmingham."[58] Clearly the achievement of Birmingham replicates the grand struggles that King had cited before—the Exodus, the Reformation, the Emancipation Proclamation, and Africa's emergence from colonialism. Birmingham exemplifies the contemporary African and American struggle he had chosen as the last stops of his historical journey. In effect, he refuses to conclude this sojourn before arriving in Birmingham.

Referring to that city, King declares, "Now we've got to go on to Memphis just like that."[59] With this phrase he extends his historical odyssey from Birmingham to Memphis, which offers an opportunity for another event of international importance akin to the Exodus and Lincoln's freeing of the slaves. Preachers should support the garbage strike in Memphis because "Somehow the preacher must be an Amos and say, 'Let justice roll down like waters and righteousness like a mighty stream.' Somehow the preacher must say with Jesus, '. . . the Lord . . . hath anointed me to deal with the problems of the poor.'"[60] Undergirding these assertions is the assumption that contemporary ministers can and should leapfrog time, becoming Amos and accepting Jesus's two-thousand-year-old mission to the poor. In this religious system the needs of the poor are paramount and are essentially identical in the ages of Amos, Jesus, and twentieth-century America.

King warns ministers not to focus primarily on heaven. Citing black pulpit imagery of "long white robes over yonder," he insists that pastors who evoke "the new Jerusalem" must also portray "the new Memphis, Tennessee."[61] Here he again blurs heavenly and earthly salvation. The "new Memphis" is the "new Jerusalem" come down to earth.

After calling for local boycotts, he analyzes the good Samaritan and tells listeners to treat sanitation workers as the Samaritan treated the roadside victim.[62] He then remembers a woman who stabbed him in the chest, wounding him so gravely that he would have died had he simply sneezed. Sneezing would have prevented him from savoring the landmark events in civil rights: the 1960 lunch-counter sit-ins, Albany, Birmingham, "I Have a Dream," Selma, and Memphis.

Extending the time travel that opened "Mountaintop," this autobiographical narrative enumerates further examples of the American political awakening that King had hailed earlier. He arranges the undeniably noteworthy events of the current struggle within the context of the most important events of Western history. The "I" who avoided sneezing also zoomed through time, pausing to witness epochal moments in the quest for freedom. Through this self-making he affirms that the meaning of Memphis is quite comparable, if not identical, to the meaning of the Hebrews' triumph over Pharaoh, Luther's reform of a corrupt church, and Lincoln's Proclamation. Like previous episodes of the movement, the drama of the garbage workers allows for a successful reproduction of the Exodus. Human identity remains stable in his updated rendition of the inclusive, typological universe of slaves, who cried for Moses to appear in the Egypt of Mississippi and Alabama.

Concluding "Mountaintop," King remarks his pilot's extra safety precautions, threats on his life, and his possible assassination. His ominous tone builds upon the atmosphere of crisis he had strongly evoked just after the imaginary journey through time. He had exclaimed, ". . . the world is all messed up. The nation is sick."[63] By recounting the nearly fatal stabbing incident and recent death threats, he intensifies the climate of crisis and evokes the looming possibility of tragedy. All this dark imagery reflects and modifies the vision of impending doom and Satanic hellfire common in Baptist revival meetings, including those conducted at Ebenezer Baptist Church. He simply applies a political, this-worldly twist to a stock theme of evangelical sermonizing.

But King is not content to situate the movement within the drama of crisis and typology. Perhaps sensing the near-inevitability of his assassination, he ignores the risk of showboating and concludes his address by dramatically installing himself at the head of the typological procession. He boldly equates himself with Moses at the end of the Hebrews' forty-year trek through the wilderness. At this point God directed Moses to climb to the top of a mountain, where he could gaze at the Promised Land that he could not enter:

> I just want to do God's will. And He's allowed me to go up to the mountain. And I've looked over. And I've seen the Promised Land. I may not get there with you. But I want you to know tonight that we as a people will get to the Promised Land. And I'm happy tonight. I'm not worried about anything, I'm not fearing any man. Mine eyes have seen the glory of the coming of the Lord![64]

King's final sentence is the first line of "The Battle Hymn of the Republic." Union soldiers sang these lyrics as they walked into the Civil War, and churchgoers often sing them as well. "Mine eyes" are the eyes of the narrator of the hymn. "Mine eyes" are also the eyes of Moses, the prototype in the Old Testament, who sees the glory of the coming of Christ the Lord, the fulfillment of the type in the New Testament. Of course, "Mine eyes" are also the eyes of King, the speaker, the "I" of the speech—King the friend of Abernathy; King the theologian who propounds typology by insisting that the preacher "must be an Amos"; King the black preacher who blurs this-worldly and otherworldly deliverance; King the activist who aligns Memphis garbage workers with the victim in Jesus's greatest parable; King the time traveller who observes the panorama of the Exodus, the Reformation, and the Emancipation Proclamation; King the sojourner who magically completes his time travel by witnessing the sit-ins, Birmingham, Selma, and Memphis; and King the leader who repeatedly risks martyrdom. All these selves—the narrative voice of "Battle Hymn," Moses, and King in his multiple, yet cohesive identities— merge together in King's extraordinary act of self-making.

Rejecting a linear, European view of history, King involves himself and his audience in a single process of self-discovery and persuasion within a universe of sacred time. This cosmos unites heaven and earth; collapses Egypt and Alabama; and merges Memphis, the capital of ancient Egypt, with Memphis, Tennessee. The current scene in Memphis recalls the greatest personalities and events of the Bible and Western history, which unfold in a seamless fabric of time that includes the civil rights movement. These mighty deeds of the movement culminate in the humble but heroic efforts

of the Memphis garbage workers and their supporters, who struggle to reproduce the Exodus as their leader—King—directs them
against a recalcitrant Egyptian mayor. Struggling against Almighty
God, the mayor will surely fail. Though King expects to die himself,
the strikers and their sympathizers will escape Pharaoh, survive the
wilderness, and actually reach the Promised Land.

The typological theology and process of self-definition undertaken in "Mountaintop" represent the consummate expression of
the distinctive theology and system of knowledge found in slave
religion. Throughout his career, and especially in "Mountaintop,"
King's oratory illuminates the American landscape because, like the
slaves, he testifies that the road African Americans walked was, as
one spiritual attests, the same "rough, rocky road what Moses done
travel."[65]

King's death the next day seemed to confirm his interpretation of
his life. After the assassination many civil rights partisans embraced
typological imagery to explain his death, which occurred near
Easter. On the Sunday following the murder, Abernathy compared
King to Moses and called the murder "a crucifixion." He spoke of
staff members as King's "disciples," who now looked for the Holy
Ghost to descend among them.[66] Later that year SCLC held its
long-scheduled Poor People's Campaign in Washington, D.C., a
program that King had advocated for months (and one that featured
C.L. Franklin as a speaker). The organization christened its tent
encampment "Resurrection City," which Abernathy thought "had
just the right touch" for a city that would serve as "a new founding,
the creation of a model for the just society."[67]

Four days after King's death, Coretta King explained the loss as
an event "which to me represents the Crucifixion, on toward the
resurrection and the redemption of the spirit."[68] In her autobiography the following year, she repeatedly compared her husband to
Jesus. When he and his staff agonized over a crisis in Albany, the
experience reminded her of Jesus and his disciples in the Garden of
Gethsemane.[69] When he finished "I Have a Dream," she felt that
"the Kingdom of God seemed to have come on earth."[70] The lyrics
of "Sweet Little Jesus Boy" reminded her of "Martin's own life
experience."[71]

On the first federal holiday honoring King, Harry Belafonte,

King's friend and fundraiser, continued the Jesus typology by singing "Black Prince of Peace" on a primetime television extravaganza. Abernathy's recent autobiography often depicts King and the movement through typological imagery. His title, *And the Walls Came Tumbling Down,* comes from the spiritual "Joshua Fit the Battle of Jericho," portions of which he quotes as a headnote. The lyrics refer to his own role as Joshua, who won the battle of Jericho after Moses had led the Hebrews to the brink of the Promised Land.

When slaves collapsed Moses and Jesus into one powerful deliverer, little did they realize that more than a hundred years later journalists and scholars—most of whom were white—would conflate Moses and Jesus into a liberating figure named "King." But that is exactly what happened. A year after King's murder, *Look* magazine published "Dr. King, One Year After: He Lives, Man!" In 1986 *Ebony* offered an entire issue devoted to King, emblazoning its cover with the phrase "The Living King."

Biographers and historians mapped the same typological terrain, offering narratives that at many points compare King to Moses and Jesus. In his 1969 biography, William Miller observes that King's affirmation of hope expressed "an optimism of the cross." Miller concludes by celebrating King's "vision, his faith, and the power of the Resurrection."[72] Merely to scan other scholars' titles is to see King's life plotted according to a familiar set of Biblical coordinates. Consider *Let the Trumpet Sound,* the Biblical title of Stephen Oates's 1982 King biography, and *To Redeem the Soul of America,* the messianic title of Adam Fairclough's 1987 account of King and his organization. Coming directly to the point are two Pulitzer Prize-winning works—David Garrow's 1986 biography, whose title *Bearing the Cross* compares King to Jesus, and Taylor Branch's 1988 narrative, whose title *Parting the Waters* compares King to Moses. In his 1981 study, *The Kennedy Imprisonment,* hard-headed historian Garry Wills debunks the brothers Kennedy but concludes that King "never died."

When Abernathy implied that King committed adultery the night before his death, this "revelation" stirred a huge controversy, for it challenged our strong tendency to identify King with sacred figures. Abernathy disturbed the sanctity of the Moses/Jesus/King typology and violated the image of King as a holy, Christ-like martyr and saint. A Christ-like figure is not supposed to commit sin on the eve of his sacrificial death.

But, since King's triumphs led to Christ-like expectations, to blame King for not being Christ is to make him a victim of his own success. Now, more than twenty years after his death, we can choose to regard King not as a new messiah, but as an extraordinary political pragmatist who persuaded a nation to legalize equality and thereby kept Jefferson's dream alive.

TEN

ALCHEMIZING IRON INTO GOLD

Directing a peaceful army, King transformed Montgomery into Lexington and Concord and thereby launched the Second American Revolution. But the peaceful uprising stalled after the triumphal Selma march of 1965. In 1966 he tried but failed to export the nonviolent insurrection from the South to the North, specifically to Chicago. Riots in Los Angeles, Detroit, Newark, and many other cities tarnished the revolution, altering the prevailing image of blacks from petitioners to criminals. While the Vietnam War raged, he and other anti-war dissidents were denounced and ostracized. Even the SCLC board and his staff resisted his plans for a massive Poor People's Campaign that could offer a last-ditch alternative to riots.

These gigantic political problems took their toll on King. During the last two years of his life, a Buddha-like mask often substituted for his natural ebullience. The simpler days of love, sit-ins, and landmark victories seemed over. As fire-breathing separatists seized the spotlight, nonviolence and integration appeared ineffectual and hopelessly dated. And his own view of

American culture grew more skeptical than ever. He now believed that the entire fabric of American life required radical change.

When King entered the pulpit of the National Cathedral in 1968, he was not the same man who had preached "Death of Evil" at its sister church, the Cathedral of St. John, twelve years earlier. However, his rhetoric changed less than one might expect. Launching a favorite sermon—"Sleeping through a Revolution"—he began it as he always did: with an illustration about Washington Irving's character Rip Van Winkle. Not only did Van Winkle sleep for many years, he also slept through a revolution. He awoke dumbfounded to find a portrait of King George III replaced by one of George Washington. King urged his listeners to participate in social upheavals, not snore through them. He borrowed the Van Winkle analogy from Halford Luccock's "Sleeping through a Revolution."[1] Repeating a portion of his own sermon "Dives and Lazarus," he again echoed Buttrick's analysis of wealth and poverty.[2] And he concluded with Victorian commonplaces beloved in the liberal pulpit—Parker's "The arc of the moral universe is long," Carlyle's "No lie can live forever," Bryant's "Truth crushed to earth will rise again," and Lowell's "Truth forever on the scaffold." For the ten-thousandth time, he affirmed the possibility of a beloved community. Though much of the nation had, like the mob in Memphis, spun into a maelstrom of violence, the peaceful warrior clung to his course, proselytizing for nonviolence in American streets and the jungles of Vietnam.

This sermon was King's last. Four days later an assassin's bullet killed him in Memphis.

Eighteen years after his death the nation honored King by commemorating his birthday as a national holiday. Almost all states followed suit. Most Americans joined Congress in proudly acknowledging his exemplary statesmanship, heroic sacrifice, and monumental achievements.[3] In twentieth-century America, only the contributions of Franklin Roosevelt rival those of the minister of Ebenezer Church. The greatest orator of our century, King exposed, confronted, and tackled racial oppression—always America's most grievous and most intractable dilemma. He emerged as the leader bold enough to slice the Gordian knot of racial inequity that Reconstruction had left hopelessly entangled and unresolved. As the unofficial president of an oppressed people, he undertook his own Emancipation Proclamation. Enacted by nonviolence instead of the extremely bloody civil war waged a century earlier, the Proclamation of Equality issued by King, James Farmer, and Fannie Lou Hamer proved at least as effective as Lincoln's declaration. Their movement pushed the brothers Kennedy off the fence of indifference and shoved them into history as exponents and martyrs for civil rights. By eliminating racism as official public policy everywhere in the U.S., civil rights protest accomplished what absolutely no one in 1953 thought possible by 1968.

Yet, far from pausing to savor his victories and his fame, King continued to labor tirelessly against hunger and war. Seldom hesitating to wade into controversy, he castigated American warmaking in Vietnam, prompting a hostile rejection by a once-friendly president, public repudiation by moderate allies, and vilification from a formerly sympathetic press. He then lost his life while supporting a small group of garbage workers in Memphis.

Black culture made possible King's enormous success. He was born into a community that treated language as a treasure that everyone created, everyone shared, and no one owned. Folk preachers ignored "the rules and requirements of the majority culture," revelling in their common legacy of sermons and songs that had nurtured their parents and slave ancestors.[4] They also demanded and expected deliverance in both this world and the next. Expounding their dual theme of deliverance, they merged voices and crafted authoritative selves through their highly imaginative and formidable system of knowledge and persuasion. Providing hope for a brutalized and exploited race, this system sustained huge numbers of people who might otherwise have been crushed.

Like King's sermons, the ubiquitous anthem of the movement, "We Shall Overcome," exemplifies this system of knowledge and persuasion. "I Will Overcome" (sometimes titled "I'll Be All Right") began before the turn of the century as part of the sacred repertoire of the black church.[5] In the 1940s a black union in Charleston adopted it, changing its title to "We Will Overcome."[6] Because the tune and some of the lyrics remained unaltered, the spiritual associations of the hymn carried over to the union anthem. Then Pete Seeger and others at the Highlander Folk Center heard the song, injected new lyrics, and rechristened it "We Shall

Overcome."[7] Soon the song acquired associations with the civil rights struggle to add to its earlier sacred and secular meanings.

"I Will Overcome"/"We Shall Overcome" succeeded in all its incarnations because it manages to be paradoxically soothing and militant, religious and political, otherworldly and this-worldly. The "we" of the lyrics merges the narrative voice of the hymn, unionists in Charleston, singers at Highlander, and virtually everyone remotely associated with the civil rights movement. Now hymned from Beijing to Berlin, Johannesburg to Prague, and Budapest to Moscow, "We Shall Overcome" enables dissidents around the world to create themselves in part by merging their identities with those of civil rights activists.

While whites may admire black music, they have usually dismissed black folk preachers as illiterate souls directing emotionally frenzied services. Whites have systematically refused to understand and respect black preachers, their rhetorical system, and their sublime message of deliverance. Similarly, liberal intellectuals—black and white—have rarely regarded the folk pulpit as a source of theology and ideas. During King's lifetime, white academics systemically excluded black religion and black curricula from their curricula.

Given white unfamiliarity with folk religion, King could not possibly have triumphed by fastidiously emulating his father, C.L. Franklin, and other folk preachers. Instead he had to adapt for white audiences the message of deliverance and procedures of self-making that he learned while growing up. He accomplished this feat by synthesizing the strengths of black and white sermons while eliminating their weaknesses.

The assets of white preaching were notable. By the time King entered seminary, progressive white ministers articulated a well-established theology and a cohesive worldview. Social concerns—including a rejection of war—comprised an unassailably important part of their theology, which had begun to include the quest for racial justice. Through their extensive network of journals, presses, and pulpit circuit, they energetically spread their intellectually respectable Christianity to millions of Americans.

Yet, despite these prodigious strengths, the white pulpit suffered the appalling weakness of political impotence. By correcting the utopian naïveté of Gladden and Rauschenbusch, Fosdick and his compatriots rescued the social gospel from the dustbin of history. Yet, like the message of Rauschenbusch, Fosdick's social gospel was rapidly losing momentum. It stalled at a political dead end similar to the impasse reached by the utopian social gospel that it replaced. By the time of the Montgomery bus boycott, Fosdick, Buttrick, Luccock, and other preachers could point to few political accomplishments. Their thousands of earnest sermons raised moral awareness but failed to influence national decisions. Political victories are eventually necessary or one's political/theological worldview will surrender both its meaning and its adherents.

Victories proved elusive because, for all their concern for social ethics, liberal homilists remained politically disengaged. Rarely venturing to union halls, they addressed middle-class and upper-crust churchgoers. Instead of clamoring for a strike or a sit-in, their listeners bathed in the rich sonorities of Bach's music and in rainbow-colored light streaming from heavenly windows. Their parishioners generally resided in respectable neighborhoods of New York City, Detroit, and Chicago—not working-class communities or Southern slums. Furthermore, they were not politically organized. Although Fosdick propounded pacifism, racial justice, and women's rights, he never led a demonstration for any of those causes. Unlike black unionist A. Philip Randolph, Buttrick had no notion whatever of leading his audiences to demonstrate *en masse* at FDR's doorstep.[8] And Hamilton never thought of directing a car caravan from his "drive-in" church to protest at the state capitol. In short, Fosdick and his colleagues never intended to mount a political campaign.

Enter King. Leaving graduate school, he undoubtedly realized that most Christians never enjoyed puzzling over Tillich's *Systematic Theology*. And he understood that the brittle ivory-tower idiom prized by the academy would never ignite a mass movement. As a result, when he finished his dissertation, he quickly dropped his professors' wooden formalism in favor of something better.

As a teenager, King learned that millions of Protestants listened enthusiastically to the national radio pulpits of Fosdick and Sockman. The same audience bought and read literally millions of copies of sermons by Fosdick, Sockman, Hamilton, Luccock, McCracken, Kennedy, and a host of others. And tens of thousands listened avidly when these same favored preachers appeared in person on the pulpit circuit.

King also learned that the well-entrenched white view of language as personal property made little difference to the practice of many white preachers. Indeed, thousands of workaday white ministers leaned heavily on the printed sermons of others. And even the most renowned preachers often expounded similar or identical verses of scripture, themes, illustrations, quotations, arrangements, and other material—just as black preachers did.

King may have also sensed that, for Fosdick and many others, the notion of plagiarizing sermons had as much meaning as the notion of stealing air. Homilists typically did not regard a set of sermons as the expression of an idiosyncratic, personal vision, an expression that copyright laws assume every book to be. Instead of erecting barbed wire fences and "No Trespassing" signs around their texts, preachers shared and proclaimed a common gospel, the religion of Jesus and Paul and of millions of Christians around the globe. Although homileticians fulminated about "plagiarism" in the pulpit, twentieth-century preachers could hardly plagiarize from each other when they did not view sermons as commodities in the first place.[9] They copyrighted their published sermons mainly from obedience to convention, not for any other reason.

Facing the task of translating black orality into print, King, like many others, began borrowing sermons early in his career. Adopting a text from nineteenth-century preacher Phillips Brooks helped him land the pulpit of one of the finest black churches in Alabama. Beginning his political career, King continued to borrow sermons. From Northern white liberals and moderates, he received nothing but accolades. When he travelled to the Cathedral of St. John, the Chicago Sunday Evening Club, Riverside Church, and the National Cathedral, congregations applauded his sermons on nonconformity, fear, and an array of other extremely familiar topics. No one groaned when he wielded quotations from Khayyam, Bowring, Shakespeare, Swinburne, Lowell, and others that many had heard before. On the contrary, white churchgoers almost invariably greeted him not merely with approbation, but with an overwhelming adulation reserved for no one else in Protestantism. African Americans also thrilled to King's addresses.

Nor did preachers complain when King borrowed their sermons. Warmly welcoming him to Riverside Church, McCracken repeatedly negotiated a spot on King's jammed schedule and always expressed exuberant pleasure at King's appearance.[10] He did so after King borrowed his sermon about Communism and published much of it in both "Pilgrimage" and *Strength*. Buttrick served as an editorial associate for *Pulpit* the year before King published there a sermon based on Buttrick's explication of a parable.[11] There is no record that Buttrick ever complained about King's sermon. Hamilton's widow, Florence Hamilton, declares that her husband "had great respect and admiration for King."[12] Archibald Carey continued his friendship with King after King had adapted a portion of Carey's speech for "I Have a Dream." The non-minister Harris Wofford may speak for several of King's sources when he states that he would be "complimented" if King borrowed his lines.[13]

King's language impressed whites not in spite of his borrowing but because of it. Much of his material resonated with white Protestants precisely because they had heard it before. Repetition aids memory: if people hear a tune often enough, they will begin humming it themselves. Listeners remember lines from folk sermons partly because preachers keep repeating their best lines. King's listeners retained his ideas and phrases more easily because the familiar strains of his sermons made them more memorable.[14]

King also validated himself by offering forms of argument that whites had already internalized and by propounding themes that they already understood and respected. He routinely supplied surefire, doctrinally sound sermons with recipe-perfect proportions of Biblical exegesis, application, quotations, illustrations, and the like. Borrowing enabled him to foolproof his sermons against theological error, weak themes, faulty structure, and other mistakes. Had he instead supplied sermons with profoundly original content, he would never have legitimized his radical tactic of civil disobedience and his radical goals of ending racism, poverty, and war. Much too strange and much too radical to gain acceptance, he would have been dismissed as a black Eugene Debs, a black Norman Thomas, or another W.E.B. DuBois or Malcolm X.

Borrowing also let King escape the restrictions of the clock and therein become a Houdini of time. This Houdini could elude the straitjacket of twenty-four-hour days by undertaking a variety of activities at the same moment. He could simultaneously lead demonstrations; administer a large organization; raise tens of thousands of dollars; tell presidents what to do; serve time in jail;

maintain a huge correspondence; and publish scores of essays as well as several books. While enchanting listeners in Cleveland, he could simultaneously direct a world famous march from Selma. He could mediate a crisis with the mayor in Chicago while confronting "Black Power" on a Mississippi highway. This ubiquitous leader could magically advise senators, write a column, publish an essay, rally voters, placate unruly staffers, preach a sermon, and comfort a church janitor—all in a single day.

Barnstorming the nation as a Houdini of time became possible only because King consulted sources and thereby foolproofed his discourse. No one can consistently compose flawless sermons without spending a gargantuan amount of time doing so. If forced to construct sermons entirely from scratch, he would have had no choice but to spend far more time writing and far less time engaged in other vital activities.

King's most grueling endeavor was a dramatic oratorical marathon that can only be compared to a non-stop, never-ending presidential campaign. Speaking on two or three hundred occasions each year, he reached hundreds of thousands of listeners in the flesh. He dedicated himself to this nostalgically old-fashioned, person-to-person communication because it was the best way to enlist support. Had he chosen not to borrow sermons, he would have communicated in person to far fewer people, seriously diluting the impact of his message.

Moreover, when King abandoned his sources, his words often fell flat. His frequently ghostwritten policy speeches—such as "A Time to Break Silence"—resemble the speechifying of Hubert Humphrey, George McGovern, and other liberal Democrats. Like them, he filled his policy statements with detailed political analysis, which he omitted from his sermons and sermonic speeches. Just as the oratory of Humphrey and McGovern failed to seduce voters, his policy addresses never received the enthusiasm commanded by his sermonic oratory.[15] By contrast, his sermons always succeeded. So did almost all of his sermonic speeches, only small portions of which were ghostwritten. For that reason, he mainly cycled and recycled sermonic material—not ghostwritten language—as he conducted his marathon speaking tour over a twelve-year period.

Merging black and white homiletics, he subordinated Fosdick's entire worldview to the slaves' grand theme of deliverance. He did so by radically changing the context of borrowed themes. Unlike others, he was never content merely to preach to well-dressed Northern liberals gazing at Biblical stories frozen in sculptured stone and dazzling stained glass. Instead, he baptized the huge congregation commanded by Fosdick and Hamilton into the massive political movement imagined by W.E.B. DuBois and A. Philip Randolph. Releasing energy from the cozy, closeted sanctuaries of Northern churches, he electrified the tense streets of Alabama. Through the folk procedures of voice merging and self-making, he simultaneously propelled, intensified, and interpreted a huge national drama that Fosdick, Hamilton, and Buttrick could never have staged. Like the spirituals and gospel songs whose lyrics he wove into his oratory, he offered balm to soothe and lightning to energize both participants and spectators of that drama. No one could have predicted that a group of liberal, white sermons would help trigger a Second Reconstruction. By directing a large-scale assault on segregation, he transformed each of his sermons into a powerful political act—something that could never be said about Fosdick, Buttrick, or Hamilton. He turned their iron ore into gold.

Through skillfully choreographed political confrontations, King repeatedly tested the clichés of Jefferson ("All men are created equal"), the Bible ("You shall reap what you sow"), and progressive pulpits ("Truth crushed to earth will rise again") against the billy clubs of Southern police and the hatred of recalcitrant governors. He essentially argued that, should Bull Connor and George Wallace win, they would expose noble American truths as sheer sentimentality. In that event, the Revolution of 1776 (with its "unalienable rights"), America ("sweet land of liberty"), Christ's *agape* ("Love your enemies"), and the Christian law of history ("Unearned suffering is redemptive") would be entirely refuted, and injustice would reign forever and ever.

Similarly King tested dust and divinity, Jesus's parables, antidotes to fear, and an entire array of other orthodox and standard themes. If racists prevailed, they would disprove an entire Christian perspective, exposing a widely shared world picture as an expression of utter naïveté. By tossing boilerplate sermons into a cauldron of disruptive confrontation, King measured an entire worldview against the bomb on his porch, the hoses and dogs of Bull Connor, and the dynamite that killed four girls in Birmingham. He thereby brought to life a language that had never before spoken decisively to power brokers and presidents.

King's borrowing made it difficult for audiences to reject his leadership without also rejecting a nostalgic universe not yet shattered by Darwin, Freud, and Einstein. By tracing a vision of love and justice shared by millions, he established himself as the exponent of order and stigmatized his adversaries as promoters of chaos. They had overturned God's justice by institutionalizing racial oppression. For this reason, in King's rhetorical universe, cosmic justice necessitated disruption, and only a revolution could achieve true stability.

King adapted material in a highly creative way. No matter what he borrowed or how often, after leaving Boston University, he managed never to sound stilted or artificial. Instead, he paradoxically, but invariably, sounded exactly like himself. His long training in the folk pulpit accounts for his extraordinary ability to use others' language to become himself. This training also explains why his audiences never objected to his borrowing and why an entire generation of scholars failed to guess that he mined sources frequently. His skill in transporting procedures of folk preaching into print ensured that his borrowed lines fit his persona more closely than did the words of ghostwriters.

King's achievements are awesome. Borrowed sermons gave white Americans their best—and probably last—chance to solve what had always been the nation's worst problem. Not only did voice merging keep Jefferson's dream alive, it also helped compel the White House to withdraw from the nightmare of Vietnam. Then in the wake of his movement came the second wave of American feminism, the campaign for gay rights, and the crusade to save the environment.[16] Constantly invoking King's name, thousands of grassroots dissenters routinely emulated his tactics.

But the triumphs of American protest mark just the beginning of King's immensely potent social gospel. Americans are not the only ones to sing "We Shall Overcome." So do courageous nonconformists at Soweto, Tiananmen Square, the Berlin Wall, the Gdansk shipyards, the machine-gunned churches in El Salvador, and the striped, onion domes of the Kremlin. Lech Walesa, Oscar Romero, Desmond Tutu, and many other international liberators repeatedly cite King as the moral exemplar and authority for their demonstrations, boycotts, and civil disobedience. Like American activists they do so for the simple reason that better nonviolent strategies are yet to be found and probably do not exist.

Paradoxically King became himself by reviving and politicizing the words of others as he choreographed a grand protest against the indescribable horror, brutality, and tragedy of segregation. Borrowing beloved sermonic themes meant defining the current struggle as a drama that God would satisfactorily resolve in his reliable, beneficent universe. Borrowing also helped King emerge as an authoritative public intellectual who could simultaneously participate in the political fray and stand philosophically above it. Foolproofing his discourse enabled him to articulate the overarching principles of the movement while towering above its day-to-day frustrations. His magisterial public persona helped valorize the struggle.

Whoever would condemn King's borrowing necessarily assumes that King would have persuaded whites just as easily had he originated every word out of his mouth. But the original, sublime eloquence of Frederick Douglass, DuBois, Farmer, Hamer, and a host of other blacks long before and throughout the civil rights struggle never changed white people's minds. Had King composed original language, as they did, there is no evidence that he would have been any more persuasive than they were. Certainly he thought he had found the most persuasive words available. Indeed, had he stopped borrowing, black America would have surrendered the best method it ever devised for unstopping the ears of whites to the demand for freedom. Had he stopped borrowing, he would have helped extend the life of an abhorrent racial system that exploited and brutalized tens of millions of people.

For his role in ameliorating oppression, King certainly earned the status of a national hero. But he was too great a man for us to treat him as a god. We do not honor him by creating a walking marble statue or by fantasizing an implausible black champion lacking intellectual and rhetorical roots in his own community. Nor do we honor him by ignoring his borrowing. Ignoring his borrowing means bypassing his original, highly imaginative act of yoking black orality and print culture. And bypassing this act means refusing to fathom how social change actually occurs.

We honor King through celebrations, parades, and speeches. But we honor him best simply by understanding him. We honor him by probing his ability to revitalize white texts as he fit them into the slaves' sublime narrative of the Exodus. We honor him by realizing how, immersed in the folk pulpit, he reached millions by marshalling its grand theme of deliverance, formidable system of knowledge, and imaginative sense of sacred time. We honor him by understanding his powerfully creative act of rhetorical self-making.

KEY FIGURES WHO SHAPED KING'S LANGUAGE AND THOUGHT

AUSTIN, EUGENE—White preacher who spoke at the commencement ceremony when King graduated from seminary. King later borrowed portions of that address, which champions nonconformity and lambastes Joseph McCarthy.

BORDERS, WILLIAM HOLMES—Highly successful black preacher whom King heard as a child and adolescent in Atlanta. King followed Borders's example of going North to a liberal white seminary.

BRIGHTMAN, EDGAR—White exponent of Boston Personalism, a theology that emphasized the personal, fatherly nature of God. By reiterating that familiar concept, Brightman attracted King to a PhD program at Boston University.

BROOKS, PHILLIPS—Well-known, white abolitionist preacher from Boston. King borrowed Brooks's orthodox Protestant themes and part of his sermon on the Exodus.

BROWN, CHARLES REYNOLDS—White preacher, professor, and advocate of the social gospel. King borrowed Brown's well-known sermon on the good Samaritan.

BUTTRICK, GEORGE—Well-known white preacher and scholarly editor of the widely used, multi-volume *Interpreter's Bible*. While composing sermons on the parables, King often borrowed from Buttrick's classic *Parables of Jesus* (1928).

CAREY, ARCHIBALD—Leading black minister in Chicago and an acquaintance of

199

King. In "I Have a Dream," King borrowed and refined part of Carey's speech at the 1952 Republican Convention.

DeWolf, L. Harold—White professor who directed King's dissertation at Boston University. DeWolf encouraged its highly stilted, academic prose and overlooked King's plagiarism.

Edwards, J.H.—King's third-grade Sunday School teacher who later served on the committee that ordained him for the ministry. Edwards was one of the many supportive members of Ebenezer Church who shaped King's early life.

Enslin, Morton—King's white professor of the New Testament. King rejected Enslin's "demythologizing" approach to the Bible in favor of the slaves' view of Biblical events as recurring acts in history.

Farmer, James—Black civil rights leader. In 1942 Farmer sponsored the first Gandhian protests on behalf of black equality. Like King, his mentors included Howard Thurman and Benjamin Mays. By shifting the nation's attention to race, he and other activists helped create a massive audience for King.

Fosdick, Harry Emerson—Pacifist dean of liberal white preachers. Fosdick's weekly radio pulpit commanded an audience of over two million. King borrowed explanations of nonviolence, fear, and nonconformity from his early collection of sermons, *Hope of the World* (1933).

Franklin, C.L.—The most popular of all black folk preachers. During the 1950s and 1960s Franklin's "whooping" delivery captivated crowds around the nation; dozens of his recorded sermons sold well on blues labels. Admired by King, he typified a tradition of folk sermonizing that King adapted for white audiences.

Hamilton, J. Wallace—Eloquent white preacher whose congregation in Florida overflowed the sanctuary and listened to his sermons from their cars. King borrowed an explanation of nonviolence and many other themes from Hamilton's popular sermonic collection *Horns and Halos in Human Nature* (1954).

Johns, Vernon—Learned black preacher whose eccentric personality strongly resembled that of an Old Testament prophet. Johns prepared churchgoers in Montgomery to accept King's leadership and participate in a bus boycott. Although he exerted only a minor influence on the early King, he offered a precedent for the later King's unpopular, prophetic stances.

Johnson, Mordecai—Black president of Howard University and noted lecturer. Johnson's speech about nonviolence helped spark King's interest in Gandhi.

Jones, E. Stanley—Longtime white missionary to India who knew Gandhi and who sermonized on the American pulpit circuit. King often reiterated Jones's analysis of nonviolence.

Keighton, Robert—White professor of homiletics at King's seminary. Offering several courses that King took, Keighton taught his students useful methods of structuring sermons for liberal white audiences.

KELSEY, GEORGE—Black professor of religion at Morehouse College who helped inspire King to become a minister. King later borrowed Kelsey's analyses of love and segregation.

KENNEDY, GERALD—Popular white preacher who warned ministers against borrowing from each others' sermons, yet who nevertheless published a collection of homiletic illustrations for preachers to draw from. Kennedy thus exemplified the ambivalent attitude toward homiletic borrowing found in white seminaries. King used his standard illustrations and his theme of a balanced Christian life.

KING, ALBERTA—King's mother. By playing the organ and organizing a church choir, Alberta King inspired her children's affinity with music, an affinity reflected in King's melodic, rolling phrases.

KING, MARTIN LUTHER, SR.—King's father. A folk preacher, King, Sr., was by far the most important influence on King, Jr.'s language, ideas, and politics.

LUCCOCK, HALFORD—White professor of homiletics at Yale. Luccock's *Marching off the Map* (1952) is the source for King's "Sleeping through a Revolution."

MAYS, BENJAMIN—Skillful black president of Morehouse College and close friend of King's father. During the 1940s Mays travelled to India to discuss nonviolence with Gandhi. By facilitating King's enrollment in a liberal white seminary, he provided the crucial connection between King and a large Protestant audience. He was King's most important academic mentor.

McCRACKEN, ROBERT—White successor to Fosdick who regularly welcomed King to Riverside Church and who never complained when King borrowed his themes. Ignoring anti-Communist hysteria during the early 1950s, McCracken offered a balanced response to Communism that King adopted in the 1960s.

MORRISON, C.C.—Ardent white pacifist. Founder of the *Christian Century*, Morrison created a significant forum (and a loyal readership) for King's important essays, including "Letter from Birmingham Jail."

NELSON, WILLIAM STUART—Black dean of the School of Religion at Howard University and teacher of the first American course in nonviolence. King borrowed part of Nelson's essay about Gandhian nonviolence.

NIEBUHR, REINHOLD—Important white theologian who advocated "neo-orthodoxy" and condemned pacifism. King rejected many of Niebuhr's ideas, including his blanket condemnation of Communism and his claim that violent and nonviolent protest were almost morally identical.

PRITCHARD, JAMES—King's white professor of the Old Testament, who suggested that Moses may not have existed. Resisting Pritchard's "demythologizing" approach, King insisted not only that Moses existed, but that new incarnations of Moses continued to lead oppressed people.

RAUSCHENBUSCH, WALTER—White advocate of a utopian social gospel who attempted to cure the ills of poverty and war while ignoring segregation. Railing against poverty, violence, and racism, King explained that these "triple evils" were inseparably related.

THURMAN, HOWARD—Renowned black mystic whose contemplative, poetic language enraptured white audiences. Journeying to India in 1935, Thurman heard Gandhi predict that American blacks would perfect Gandhian nonviolence. King heard him at Boston University and used his *Deep River* (1955) as a source for meditations about slavery.

TILLICH, PAUL—Famous white theologian who concentrated on metaphysics. King's dissertation rejects Tillich's conception of God as a vague and distant "Ground of Being."

WEATHERHEAD, LESLIE—Britain's most famous preacher. Weatherhead embraced pacifism until Hitler made him change his mind. King borrowed his analysis of frustration.

WIEMAN, HENRY NELSON—White theologian who taught Mays. King's dissertation rejects Wieman's conception of God as an impersonal creative force.

WOFFORD, HARRIS—First white male to graduate from Howard University Law School. Wofford advised King during the late 1950s, and his discussion of nonviolence served as an important source for King's *Stride toward Freedom* and "Letter from Birmingham Jail." He also prompted John Kennedy's attention to King, which brought Kennedy the black vote during the presidential election of 1960.

PRECEDENTS FOR TITLES OF KING'S SERMONS

B elow I list titles of King's sermons (and one book) alongside parallel titles of sermons (or passages in sermons) from other preachers. Some of the King titles I discuss in this book and some I do not. Unless otherwise noted, all King sermons are unpublished and available at the Martin Luther King, Jr., Center, in Atlanta. I add an asterisk to sources that King used directly. He may or may not have read the other texts.

KING'S SERMON TITLES (AND ONE BOOK TITLE)	PREVIOUS TITLE, AUTHOR, AND BOOK
"Desirability of Being Maladjusted"	"The sacredest obligation of the Christian is to be maladjusted." *Harry Emerson Fosdick. *Hope of the World.*[1]
"The Dimensions of a Complete Life"	"The Dimensions of the Christian Life." Elmer Homrighausen. *American Pulpit Series.*[2]
"Discerning the Signs of the Times"	*Discerning the Signs of the Times.* Reinhold Niebuhr.

"Drum Major Instinct"	"Drum-Major Instincts." *J. Wallace Hamilton. *Ride the Wild Horses!*
"Hope of the World"	*Hope of the World.* Fosdick.
	"Jesus-The Hope of the World." William Holmes Borders. *Seven Minutes.*
"Interruptions"	"Interruptions." *Hamilton. *Ride the Wild Horses!*
"Is the Universe Friendly?"	"Is the Universe Friendly to Man?" John Sutherland Bonnell. (Fosdick, Charles Reynolds Brown, Leslie Weatherhead, E.F. Tittle, and Vernon Johns also ask this question.[3]
"Making the Best of a Bad Mess"	"Making the Best of a Bad Mess." *Fosdick. *Hope of the World.*
"Merits of Maladjustment"	"The sacredest obligation of the Christian is to be maladjusted." *Fosdick. *Hope of the World.*
"The Most Durable Power"	"The Most Durable Power in the World" Fosdick. *Successful Christian Living.*
"Our God is Able"	"Our God is Able." John Ferguson. *Our God is Able.*
	"Our God is Able." Basil Miller. *American Pulpit Series.*
"Remember Who You Are"	"Remember Who You Are." *Hamilton. *Horns and Halos in Human Nature*
"Shattered Dreams" (*Strength to Love*)	"Shattered Dreams." *Hamilton. *Horns and Halos in Human Nature*
"Sleeping through a Revolution"	"Sleeping through a Revolution." *Halford Luccock. *Marching off the Map.*
"Standing by the Best in an Evil Time"[4]	"Standing by the Best in an Evil Time." *Fosdick. *On Being Fit to Live With.*
"This Is a Great Time to Be Alive"[5]	*A Great Time to Be Alive.* Fosdick.
"Three Dimensions of a Complete Life"	"Three Dimensions of Love." L.E. Barton. *Three Dimensions of Love and Other Sermons.*

"To Serve the Present Age"	"To Serve the Present Age." Luccock. *Communicating the Gospel.*
"What Is Man?"	"What Is Man?" Many precedents.
Where Do We Go from Here?	"Where Do We Go from Here?" Charles Reynolds Brown. *The Gospel for Main Street.* "Where Do We Go from Here?" James Pike. *Pulpit Digest.*

ACKNOWLEDGMENTS

When I visited Nashville in 1979, I had no idea that a large project lay in wait. There my friend Bob Hill (now a pastor in Kansas City) was attending Vanderbilt Divinity School, where he took a class from Rev. Kelly Miller Smith, a civil rights activist and friend of Martin Luther King, Jr. Hill told me about a paper he wrote for Professor Smith in which he argued that King probably borrowed much of his sermon "Drum Major Instinct" from a text by J. Wallace Hamilton. According to Hill, Smith was surprised by this discovery. So was I. Hill's paper provided the spark for the dissertation I began several years later, for several subsequent essays, and for this book.

I have many others to thank for help with this project. My father, Ernest Miller, is a retired Disciples of Christ minister who attended a liberal white seminary at the same time that King attended a similar institution. Because my father studied a curriculum similar to King's, he could provide invaluable information (and books) about the state of liberal Protestantism during the late 1940s and early 1950s. Along with my father, my mother, Doris Miller, supplied unflagging support throughout this entire effort. In 1966 they had the wisdom to drive their sons three hundred miles to hear King give a speech—a decision for which I am profoundly grateful. I also thank Steve Miller, Diane Miller, Faith Miller, Andrew Miller, Kirk Miller, (another) Diane Miller, Jessica Miller, Katie Miller, Joyce Nettles, and Paul Nettles.

Jim Corder and Gary Tate, who co-directed my dissertation at Texas Christian University, also deserve my thanks, as do committee members Betsy Colquitt, David Vanderwerken, and James Derry. At various stages of this project, many professional colleagues acted as sounding boards, providing encouragement, ideas, and criticism. They include Karen Adams, Fred Antczak, Phil Arrington, Hunter Beckelhymer, Dale Billingsley, Linda Billingsley, Brenda Jo Brueggemann, Paul Boller, Jr., Marilyn Brady, Cheree Carlson, Kelton Cobb, Frank Coffin (and his fellow basketball stars), Ed Corbett, Sharon Crowley, John Doebler, Ann Dobyns, Ken Donelson, Diane Dowdey, Don Dowdey, Suellynn Duffey, Sara Garnes, Henry Louis Gates, Jr., Sally Harrold, Susan Helgeson, Randy Helms, Joe Herring, Jean Krupko, Deborah Kuhlmann, Mary Kuhner, Rebecca Lehman, Harold Lawrence, Timo Lepisto, Bret Lott, Ralph Luker, Andrea Lunsford, Bob Mayberry, Moses Moore, Kate Motoyama, Quin Meyers, Frank O'Hare, Bethyl Pearson, Martin Rosenberg, Laura Ross, Marsha Ryan, Delores Schriner, Fran Shapiro, Linda Skillman, Denise Stephenson, Jack Suggs, Patricia Sullivan, Tilly Warnock, Bob Welker, Donna Haisty Winchell, Mindy Wright, and Susan Wyche-Smith. Those who supplied especially useful advice include Jim Baumlin, Frank D'Angelo, Lisa McClure, Pat Naulty, John Ramage, David Schwalm, and Candadai Sesachari. The former chair of my department, Gretchen Bataille, also encouraged my research, as did my current chair, Wendy Wilkins. And Nick Salerno gave me a job when no one else would.

Along with other members of the King Holiday Committee at Arizona State University, John Doebler, Walter Harris, Amalia Lopez, Nancy Russo, and Bob Shafer expressed confidence in my work by asking me to speak at the 1989, 1990, and 1991 King Holiday festivities celebrated at Arizona State. I appreciate those invitations.

Many of my students at Texas Christian University, Ohio State University, and Arizona State University also gave useful tips and critiques. I especially thank students in my classes in Contemporary Rhetorical Theory, History and Theory of Rhetoric, Literature of the 1960s, and Literature of Today. Susan Davis, Susan Gassman, Cynthia Jeney, Suzanne Mark, Sharma Martineau, Randy Sandmeyer, Jennifer Scoutten, JoAnn Stockwell, and Barbara Urrea made particularly helpful suggestions.

Editorial criticism also benefitted this project. Editors of several professional journals and scholarly collections supported my research and suggested new avenues and possibilities. They include John Kronik of *PMLA*, Jim Raymond of *College English*, David Thelen of *Journal of American History*, George Yoos of *Rhetoric Society Quarterly*, and book editors Jim Baumlin, Tita Baumlin, Carolyn Calloway-Thomas, and John Lucaites. Earlier versions of portions of this book appeared or will appear in the following essays: "Martin Luther King, Jr., Borrows a Revolution." *College English* 48 (1986): 249–265; "Epistemology of a Drum Major: Martin Luther King, Jr., and the Black Folk Pulpit." *Rhetoric Society Quarterly* 18 (1988): 225–238; "Voice Merging and Self-Making: The Epistemology of 'I Have a Dream.'" *Rhetoric Society Quarterly* 19 (1989): 23–32; "Composing Martin Luther King, Jr." *PMLA* 105 (1990): 70–81; "Taking a Ride on the Old Ship of Zion: Self-Making in Black Folk Religion." *Ethos.* Eds. James Baumlin and Tita Baumlin (Dallas: Southern Methodist University Press, forthcoming); "Alabama as Egypt: Martin Luther King, Jr. and the Religion of Slaves." *The Power of Oratory.* Eds. Carolyn Calloway-Thomas and John Lucaites (University, Al: University of Alabama Press, forthcoming); "Martin Luther King, Jr., and the Black Folk Pulpit" *Journal of American History.* Forthcoming.

Sponsors of professional conferences gave me opportunities to present preliminary reports of my research and to hear feedback that aided my revisions. These meetings include the Conference of College Composition and Communication, Discourses of Power, Oratory of Dr. Martin Luther King, Jr., (cosponsored by the Speech Communication Association and the King Center), National Association of Ethnic Studies, Penn State Conference of Rhetoric and Composition, Rhetoric Society of America, and the Wyoming Conference on English.

I pour a libation for the encouragement and criticism offered by friends outside the academy: Cindy Archer, Pat Archer, Dave Barboza, Jeff Bartow, Brenda Buren, Truett Burke, Lon Burnam, Jan

Cain, Ted Coonfield, Janis Checchia, Jean Douglas and her family, Phyllis Fetzer, Susan Helms, Bob Hill, Joshua Horwitt, Nehoma Horwitt, Benjamine Hughes, Maria Odezynskyj, Elizabeth Riggs, Erma Roesch, the late Tom Shaw, Sandy Sterrett, Steve Sterrett, Joe Wallis, Kerry Wyche, and Marilyn Welker. My thanks go as well to Tina Calos, who criticized the manuscript.

Jackie Alper taught me much about the folk music of the 1960s and the life and times of Pete Seeger and the Old Left. Few can match her knowledge of American folk music.

Not only did Pam Buchek, Phil Buchek, Brij Singh, Frances Singh, Steve Wright, and Sue Wright serve as sounding boards and critics, they also put me up in their homes during my research expeditions to their cities. Without their hospitality and aid, those expeditions would not have been possible. I thank them.

A number of ministers provided assistance and information, often sharing their libraries with me. They include Gene Brink, Lou Buckalew, Weldon Gaddy, John Keeny, Mike Pearson, and Gordon Roesch. David Buttrick, who studied at Union Theological Seminary during the heyday of Fosdick and Niebuhr, offered an invaluable perspective on homiletics and theology during that era. He also corrected several of my errors when he read and criticized the entire manuscript. Florence Hamilton generously mailed several of J. Wallace Hamilton's privately printed sermons as well as booklets and other materials pertaining to his ministry. She also responded at length to my queries about her husband. Frederick Maser answered questions about twentieth-century Methodism, and Barry Goldwater explained his current (largely unchanged) view of the civil rights movement.

For their encouragement I thank the good people of Community of Hope Lutheran Church (Fort Worth, Texas); Summit United Methodist Church (Columbus, Ohio); Dove of the Desert United Methodist Church (Glendale, Arizona); and First Unitarian Church (Phoenix).

Of course, a number of Martin Luther King, Jr.'s friends, family members, mentors, and colleagues deserve special gratitude for their willingness to converse with or be interviewed by a stranger. They include Juanita Abernathy, William Holmes Borders, James Farmer, Major Jones, George Kelsey, the late Martin Luther King, Sr., the late Benjamin Mays, Gardner Taylor, Larry Williams, and Harris Wofford. Melvin Watson granted an interview and also criticized the entire manuscript. Longtime members of Ebenezer Church were extremely gracious and gave informative interviews. These members include Rev. J.H. Edwards, Jethro English, Arthur Henderson, Laura Henderson, Fannie Lou Heard, James Kemp, and Sarah Reed. Rev. Edwards kindly drove me around Atlanta to meet other members of his church. I value his friendship. Joseph Roberts, current pastor of the Ebenezer congregation, also shared his ideas about homiletics.

My research assistants Cynthia Kleinman, Carol Roark, and Barbara Urrea contributed greatly to the project. Elizabeth Vander Lei conscientiously spent dozens of hours rechecking books and nailing down endnotes. Margaret Walters helped in many ways, especially with the index. And Peter Lafford rescued my computer from the jaws of death.

For their assistance, I thank librarians and archivists at the following institutions: Archive of American Folk Culture, a division of Library of Congress; Arizona State University; Burnett Library of Texas Christian University (especially Rosalie Dowdey and Wendy Gottlieb); Archives of the Martin Luther King, Jr., Center (especially Danny Bellinger, Cynthia Lewis, and Diane Ware); Fort Worth Public Library; Library of Congress; Main Library, Ohio State University; Methodist Theological Seminary; Moorland-Spingarn Library of Howard University (especially Karen Jefferson); Mugar Library of Boston University; Recorded Sound Division, Library of Congress; Schlesinger Library of Radcliffe College; Schomburg Center for the Study of Black Culture, a division of the New York City Public Library; State Library of Ohio; Trinity Lutheran Seminary; and Vanderbilt Divinity School. Vicki Endres, Roberta Rosenburg, and others at the Interlibrary Loan office of Arizona State University logged many hours coordinating my book orders, and I acknowledge their help.

All King scholars owe a large debt to D. Louise Cook, who organized the King Center Archives in an exemplary fashion. She also oriented me to the universe of King studies.

Arizona State University provided generous research support for this project in the form of a Faculty Grant-in-Aid, a College of Liberal Arts and Sciences Grant, and a Faculty Mini-Grant. I appreciate the financial support of my institution.

I also acknowledge the guidance of Joyce Seltzer, my editor at the Free Press. Her many suggestions have vastly improved this book.

Upon reading one of my essays, David Garrow called me to welcome me as a colleague. He subsequently introduced me to James Cone and offered valuable criticism and counsel. I especially appreciate Garrow's eagerness to help someone he had never met.

I toast everyone who offered assistance, including the bus driver in Atlanta who gave me a ride when I had no fare, and others whose names I never knew or have managed to overlook. Thank you—all of you.

A NOTE ON SOURCES

The King Collection at Boston University and the King Papers at the King Center of Atlanta are rich repositories of thousands of speeches, sermons, essays, book manuscripts, letters, and other materials of Martin Luther King, Jr. A number of other archives and libraries also contain many valuable documents related to King, SCLC, and the civil rights movement. Thousands of pages of transcripts of FBI-recorded conversations involving King and his associates are now available through the Freedom of Information Act. The sum total of all this material is so vast that it would seem to satisfy almost any scholar's curiosity about King.

Yet, despite this mountain of historical data, problems exist for anyone studying King's intellectual development, his ideas, and his language. One major obstacle is that King's personal library is not available for study and has never been examined by any King scholar. Indeed, no one has ever compiled a list of the books in his library. For that reason—with a very few exceptions that I have noted along the way—I located King's sources largely through internal evidence. That is, in many cases, passages from certain texts by other authors correspond to King's discourse so closely that one can only conclude that King used those texts as his direct sources. In other cases, I state or imply that King may have borrowed a passage from any one of several books. I fully expect that when and if the King family makes his library available for study, a more exact and more complete analysis of King's printed sources will be possible. When that happens, someone can correct whatever errors lurk in this book. And King's (or someone else's) library may contain new sources that I have failed to locate while researching a book that is not definitive.

If new sources are uncovered, some of them may be ones that Ralph Abernathy alludes to in his autobiography. Abernathy observes that King traveled with collections of sermons from eighteenth- and nineteenth-century preachers and that he often borrowed from those texts. I have located no preachers from the eighteenth century and only a single preacher from the nineteenth century, Phillips Brooks, whose texts served as direct sources for King. However, I confess that I am more familiar with twentieth-century homiletics than I am with earlier traditions. King may have consulted eighteenth- and nineteenth-century homilies that have escaped my attention.

According to Abernathy, King also borrowed sermons that Benjamin Mays delivered at Morehouse Chapel. Mays's overall influence on King is certainly huge—greater than that of Fosdick or any other white preacher—and I note one or two of Mays's texts that King may have consulted. However, after examining the standard Mays works and much of the large Mays Collection at the Moorland-Spingarn Research Center of Howard University, I have failed to locate textual evidence to support Abernathy's claim. Still, Abernathy may be right. I would be anything but surprised if someone were to uncover additional Mays texts that King used. (Unfortunately Abernathy died before I could interview him.)

Furthermore, Taylor Branch maintains that King borrowed several sermons from Vernon Johns. I can neither corroborate nor refute this claim. I simply do not know whether King borrowed from Johns. I suspect that King may have done so had he been able to locate copies of Johns's largely unpublished sermons.

In addition to the unavailability of King's library, further obstacles complicate the study of his homiletic roots. Determining the precise relationship between his sermons and those of his father and grandfather is made difficult by the almost complete unavailability of their sermons. When I talked to King, Sr., in 1983, he explained that he was in the process of collecting his sermons for a book. Sadly he died before he could bring this project to fruition. Apart from members of the King family, no one knows how many tapes, notes, outlines, or manuscripts of his sermons exist or what their condition happens to be. Nor is it clear whether any of the elder King's extant homiletic material dates back to the boyhood— or even the lifetime—of King, Jr. The King family retains this material and has never allowed anyone to examine it.

The situation of A.D. Williams's sermons is even murkier. Only members of the King family know whether any manuscripts, outlines, or notes of Williams's sermons exist. If they do exist, they are in the possession of the King family, who have not permitted anyone else to examine them.

Obviously when and if manuscripts, outlines, and notes of sermons by King, Sr., (and, possibly, A.D. Williams) become available, then a much more complete and detailed picture of King's homiletic heritage will emerge.

One undertaking that should shed much light on King's life and discourse is the Martin Luther King, Jr., Papers Project. Edited by Clayborne Carson, the first volume of this project should appear in 1992. Treating King's boyhood, adolescent, and college years, the first volume should add extensively to our knowledge of the Williams and King families and of the origins and evolution of King's ideas and language.

However, despite the promise of the King Papers Project and other future research, I seriously doubt that new discoveries will substantially alter my general picture of King's sources. I strongly suspect that future scholarship will confirm that the most important, formative influence on King was the black folk pulpit of his father and grandfather. I also predict that scholars will confirm that King borrowed texts by Fosdick, Buttrick, Hamilton, and other twentieth century preachers far more often than he relied on sermons published before 1900 or on formal treatises of Euro-American philosophy and theology.

GUIDE TO ABBREVIATIONS

AFC LC   Archive of Folk Culture, Library of Congress

BEM M-S   Benjamin E. Mays Collection, Moorland-Spingarn Library, Howard University

KC A   Martin Luther King, Jr., Center, Atlanta

KC BU   King Collection, Mugar Library, Boston University

LC   Library of Congress

MJC M-S   Mordecai Johnson Collection, Moorland-Spingarn Library, Howard University

M-S   Moorland-Spingarn Library, Howard University

OHC KC A   Oral History Collection, King Center, Atlanta

RSD LC   Recorded Sound Division, Library of Congress

SC   Schomburg Center for the Study of Black Culture, a division of the New York City Public Library

NOTES

INTRODUCTION

1. Edwards Interviews.

2. Laura Henderson Interview.

3. Edwards Interviews and J.H. Edwards, Letter to author, 15 Feb. 1991. Author's files.

4. See Stephen Oates 495.

5. Conversation with Edwards, 6 Jan. 1991.

6. See Oates 497.

7. See Hamilton's pamphlet *Drum-Major Instincts*. Hamilton included a revised version of the sermon in his homiletic collection, *Ride the Wild Horses!* According to both the pamphlet version of the sermon and Hamilton's widow, Florence Hamilton, Hamilton first preached the sermon on 6 Mar. 1949 (when King was a twenty-year old student in seminary). Mrs. Hamilton indicates that her husband initially discussed the subject with her as early as 1929 or 1930 and that they talked about it several times before he finally composed and delivered the sermon. Florence Hamilton, Letter to author, 20 Mar. 1983. Author's files.

8. Appearing in *Ride!*, the 1952 version of Hamilton's "Drum-Major Instincts" served as the direct source for King's "Drum Major Instinct." King's text resembles the 1952 Hamilton sermon more closely than it does Hamilton's earlier version. King also borrowed "Interruptions," another Hamilton sermon from *Ride!* In addition, King's "Shattered Dreams" may have been influenced by "Fruitful Frustrations," another sermon in *Ride!*

9. Hamilton, *Ride* 26–27.

10. Hamilton, *Ride* 27–28.

11. King, Jr., "Drum Major Instinct" 260.

12. Compare Hamilton, *Ride* 28–29, 31–32 and King, Jr., "Drum Major Instinct" 260–261.

13. Compare Hamilton, *Ride* 32 and King, Jr., "Drum Major Instinct" 263.

14. Compare Hamilton, *Ride* 32 and King, Jr., "Drum Major Instinct" 264.

15. King, Jr., "Drum Major Instinct" 264–265.

16. King, Jr., "Drum Major Instinct" 265. See Psalms 46:10. Folk preachers used the Psalmist's phrase. See Hughes and Bontemps 252.

17. Compare Hamilton, *Ride* 33 and King, Jr., "Drum Major Instinct" 265.

18. King, Jr., "Drum Major Instinct" 265. See Mark 10:43.

19. King, Jr., "Drum Major Instinct" 265.

20. Bosley served as pastor of Mount Vernon Place Church in Baltimore and First Methodist Church in Evanston, IL.

21. Bosley, *Firm Faith* 56. Bosley attributes this passage to an anonymous author. King may have borrowed the statement from Bosley or another source.

22. King, Jr., "Drum Major Instinct" 266.

23. King, Jr., "Drum Major Instinct" 267. See Matthew 25:36–37.

24. Compare Alma Androzzo, and King, Jr., "Drum Major Instinct" 267.

25. When King received the Nobel Peace Prize, he delivered several speeches in Oslo, including a briefer "Nobel Prize Acceptance Speech," which is not to be confused with his more substantial "Nobel Prize Lecture."

26. For the analogy, compare Hamilton, *Thunder* 140 and King, Jr., "Nobel Prize Lecture" 22–23. For the discussion of international resources, compare Hamilton, *Horns and Halos* 117, 125–126 and King, Jr., "Nobel Prize Lecture" 15–16, which seems to paraphrase the main argument of *Thunder*.

Published in 1964, *Thunder* is Hamilton's brilliantly original set of sermons about a political awakening occurring throughout the Third World. Although the astuteness of Hamilton's analysis matches Niebuhr at his best, *Thunder* owes nothing to Niebuhr. It anticipates many points liberals later raised against the war in Vietnam and Reagan's policies in Central America.

27. Hamilton, *Horns and Halos* 72–73.

28. King, Jr., "Nobel Prize Lecture" 24–25. King replays the metaphor of the world house in his final book, *Where?* 167. Hamilton probably located the metaphor in either Halford Luccock's *Marching* 63–64 or Gerald Kennedy's *Reader's Notebook*. Luccock apparently originated the anecdote; he also identified the novelist as F. Scott Fitzgerald. Elsewhere in *Horns and Halos*, Hamilton quotes Luccock by name. Another preacher brought the analogy to the Chicago Sunday Evening Club. See Paul Robinson, 182.

29. See, for example, John Ansbro; Donald Smith; Kenneth Smith and Ira Zepp; Taylor Branch 69–105; Oates 25–26, 34–35; William Miller 27–28, 32–33; Frederick Downing 155–159; and Martin Marty 441.

30. Donald Smith 43.

31. My argument about King's roots expands and elaborates an interpretation that David Garrow and James Cone make in essays. I also build on Zepp's 1971

dissertation, which identifies two of King's unacknowledged sources, and books by William Watley and Lewis Baldwin.

32. For example, the Library of Congress owns only a fraction of the recorded sermons of C.L. Franklin, the most famous of all African-American folk preachers.

33. For example, Bruce Rosenberg's award-winning work, *Art of the American Folk Preacher* (recently reissued as *Can These Bones Live?*) completely ignores segregation and the fact that folk preachers responded to segregation.

34. I thank David Buttrick for this observation.

35. See Garrow's *Bearing* for an account of Wilkins.

36. King listened patiently to many different points of view, from the go-slow moderates in the Kennedy Administration (including the brothers Kennedy) to fire-eating militants such as Stokely Carmichael. However, while he took some women seriously—such as Marian Logan, who served as a member of the SCLC board—he often failed to listen carefully to Ella Baker and other female activists.

37. See Meier and Rudwick 221–223.

38. Juanita Abernathy Interview.

39. Juanita Abernathy Interview.

40. I thank David Schwalm and Jennifer Scoutten for help with this Introduction.

CHAPTER ONE: EXODUS

1. King, Jr., "Death of Evil," Unpublished.

2. Brooks, "Egyptians Dead" 105.

3. King, Jr., "Death of Evil," Unpublished 2. King's later, published version of "Death of Evil" contains other passages from Brooks. Many similarities connect the Brooks and King sermons, most notably the tendency to list evils as dead Egyptians (or Egyptians about to die) and the optimism that God will eventually vanquish every evil. Compare Brooks, "Egyptians Dead Upon the Seashore" 105–115 to King, Jr., *Strength* 58–65.

4. Compare Buttrick, *Parables* 65–66 to King, Jr., "Death of Evil," Unpublished, 1.

5. Fosdick, "How Believe in a Good God in a World Like This?" *Living Under Tension* 216; in Fosdick, *Riverside Sermons* 250.

6. King, Jr., "Death of Evil," Unpublished 2.

7. Compare Fosdick, *On Being Fit* 94 and King, Jr., "Death of Evil," Unpublished 3.

8. King, Jr., "Death of Evil," Unpublished 3.

9. "President's Annual Address [to National Baptist Convention of 1898]."

10. Fosdick, *Living Under Tension* 247. Ralph Sockman also comforted listeners with Bryant's line. See Sockman, *Paradoxes* 191–192.

11. Keighton 82.

12. See Francis Grimke, 77.

13. See Fosdick, "How Believe in a Good God in a World Like This?" *Living Under Tension* 220; rpt. in Fosdick, *Riverside Sermons* 253; Fosdick, *Riverside Sermons* 99; Fosdick, *On Being Fit* 94; Fosdick, *Successful* 223. For the other book that King read, see E. Stanley Jones, *Mahatma Gandhi* 88. See also Sockman, *Paradoxes* 192

(which quotes half the lines); Hamilton, *Who Goes There?* 111, 121; Paul Robinson 184; Laurence Howe, 119; and William Sangster, *He Is Able* 49 (which cites half the lines). King's copy of Jones's *Mahatma Gandhi* has been exhibited at KC A. Rauschenbusch also cited this poem (*Rauschenbusch Reader* 18).

14. Compare Buttrick, *Parables* 65–66 and King, Jr., *Strength* 58. Compare Fosdick, *On Being Fit* 94 and King, Jr., *Strength* 60.

15. See Fosdick, "How Believe in a Good God in a World Like This?" *Living Under Tension* 58; rpt. in Fosdick, *Riverside Sermons* 253; Fosdick, *On Being Fit* 94; Thurman, *Meditations of the Heart* 92. Compare to King, Jr., *Strength* 60.

16. Fosdick, *On Being Fit* 94; Buttrick, *Prayer* 61; Buttrick, *So We Believe* 174; Sockman, *Date* 13; and Tittle, *World* 108. Compare to King, Jr., *Strength* 60.

17. For Arnold's chestnut, see Fosdick, *Successful* 67; Tittle, *World* 7; Tittle, *Religion* 241; Hamilton, *Who Goes There* 13. Compare to King, Jr., *Strength* 65.

18. For Beard's lessons, see Fosdick, *Riverside Sermons* 156; Sockman, *Highway* 218; Kennedy, "Creation by Explosion" 67; Tittle, *What Must* 21. Compare to King, Jr., *Strength* 63. Tittle offers no attribution for his lesson. For the homiletician's comment, see H. Grady Davis, *Design* 244.

19. Borders, *World Unity* 44. Borders offers no attribution for the lesson.

20. See Genovese 258, 267, 270.

21. Genovese 283. For the larger argument, see Genovese 159–284.

22. See Douglass 159–160. See also Raboteau 246–251 and Genovese 248–251. Fisher strongly emphasizes the spirituals' theme of earthly liberation.

23. Genovese 252. See also Cone, *Spirituals* and V.P. Franklin.

24. See Clifton Johnson.

25. See John Lovell 228.

26. Cone, *Spirituals* 69–70.

27. The others include "My Army Cross Over," "O the Dying Lamb," "Leaning on the Lord," "O It's Gonna Be a Mighty Day," and "Wheel in a Wheel." For "My Army" and "Dying Lamb," see Higginson 85–86, 88; for the others, see Lovell 229–255.

28. Absalom Jones 13.

29. Molefe Asante 89.

30. See Levine 30–80.

31. See Levine 38. Stuckey regards the ring shout as an extremely important expression of slave culture.

32. See Genovese 252.

33. See Levine 50 and Genovese 252.

34. See Lovell 234.

35. Genovese 254.

36. Tutu 56–57.

37. See Landau 40.

38. Typology affords a much stronger form of argument than the extremely common strategy of arguing from analogy. Chaim Perelman and Lucie Olbrechts-Tyteca correctly maintain that analogy functions as "an unstable means of argument" (393) and that refutation of an analogy by extension is "nearly always possible" (387). In an analogy, either set of terms is susceptible to challenge; by contrast, in typology, the first set of terms may not be challenged because it is

Biblical and therefore undeniably true. Furthermore, believers view Biblical truth
as necessarily applying to the present. In a typological universe the Christian's task
is simply to understand how contemporary circumstances fit into a set of Biblical
coordinates. Next to typology, analogy serves as a makeshift and almost random
form of argument.

39. Taylor Interview.

40. See Wilmore 106.

41. Levine's contention that the slaves' sacred world was later "shattered"
(158) is simply wrong with respect to the folk pulpit.

42. See Pipes 111.

43. Arthur Raper, qtd. in Pipes 141.

44. Mitchell, *Recovery* 36.

45. Pipes 80.

46. "Dry Bones."

47. Ben Palmer.

48. Coppin 39.

49. Louis Lomax 47.

50. For the unavailability of Williams' and King, Sr.'s sermons, see A Note on
Sources.

51. Shortly before the 1963 March on Washington, Franklin joined King in
leading a major civil rights march and rally in Detroit where King rehearsed "I
Have a Dream" before tens of thousands of listeners. Franklin supported candi-
dates Coleman Young and John Conyers, who became, respectively, Mayor of
Detroit and U.S. Congressman. The best source of information on Franklin is
Titon. For Franklin's rejection of black nationalism, see Breitman 3.

52. See Baldwin 299.

53. C.L. Franklin, "Moses" *Give Me* 107–108.

54. See Franklin, "Dry Bones," *Give Me* 81.

55. See Rosenberg, *Art* 28, 155–162, 200–208; Cleveland, "Dry Bones";
Cleveland, "Eagle"; Gates, *Eagle;* Spillers, 14–15; Moody 71; Gerald Davis
136–142; Franklin, "Eagle"; Franklin, *Eagle;* Franklin, "Dry Bones"; "Dry Bones";
Holt 201–204. For the origin of "Eagle" during the 1860s, see Lyell 135–136. For
the origin of "Dry Bones" during slavery, see White 54.

56. See Branch 384.

57. For Franklin's use of "Dry Bones," see Jackson, "Foreword" vii. For
Jackson's use of "Dry Bones," see Holt 201–204.

58. See Rosenberg 105.

59. See Ong, *Orality* 33–36, 131; and Ong, *Interfaces* 284.

60. Mitchell 13.

61. See Rosenberg 105.

62. See Mays and Nicholson 279.

63. See Lincoln 6.

64. DuBois 141. For King's reading of this book, see Branch 747.

CHAPTER 2: THEY CAN'T OUTTALK HISTORY

1. Edwards Interviews.

2. King, Jr., "Autobiography" 3.

3. Confusion exists over this change in names. For King, Sr.'s explanation of the name change, see King, Sr., *Daddy King* 87–88. For an earlier version of the story, see Reddick 43, 48, 50–51. Branch, however, disputes these accounts and offers his own (44–47).

4. King, Sr., *Daddy King* 28–35, 39–44.

5. King, Sr., *Daddy King* 61.

6. King, Sr., *Daddy King* 61–62.

7. See King, Sr., *Daddy King* 75–77, 87.

8. King, Sr., *Daddy King* 84.

9. King, Sr., *Daddy King* 85; Watson Interview (Luker).

10. See Branch 27–30.

11. See King, Sr., *Daddy King* 89.

12. See Watson Interview (Miller).

13. See *Daddy King* 85–87, 100–101; Donald Smith 21; Watson Interviews.

14. See Branch 33.

15. See King, Sr., *Daddy King* 93. However, Rev. Edwards repeatedly insists, "The doors of Ebenezer were never padlocked." See Edwards Interview, Aug. 1990.

16. For "giant," see Andrew Young 12.

17. See Henderson and Henderson Interview. See also Andrew Young 10.

18. I base this observation on my own interviews with church members.

19. See Farris 56, Henderson Interview, and Juanita Abernathy Interview.

20. King, Jr., "Autobiography" 3, 4.

21. King, Jr., "Autobiography" 2–3, 6.

22. King, Jr., "Autobiography" 1.

23. King, Jr., "Autobiography" 7–8.

24. King, Jr., "Autobiography" 6. Throughout his life King, Jr., retained the close ties that bound him to his family of origin. Those ties brought him back to co-pastor Ebenezer Church with his father the last eight years of his life. They also led his brother A.D. to work closely with him in Birmingham, brought his entire family to Sweden when he won the Nobel Prize, and prompted him and A.D. to play a telephone joke on their mother the last day of his life.

25. For both stories, see Coretta King 83.

26. King, Jr., "Autobiography" 12.

27. King, Jr., "Autobiography" 13.

28. King, Sr., *Daddy King* 74.

29. King's devotion to nonviolence apparently came more from his mother than his father. See Henderson Interview and Baldwin 123–124.

30. See Williams Interview.

31. Borders remembers that, as a child, King, Jr., listened to his sermons both in person and over an outdoor loudspeaker (Borders Interview). Larry Williams testifies that he and King often heard Borders when King was a teenager (Williams Interview). See also Baldwin 276–277 and Branch 64, 66.

32. However, Larry Williams believes that King did not hear Gates's sermons either in person or on record.

33. Heilbut 301.

34. See Henderson and Henderson Interview and Kemp Interview. However, King may have been at Crozer or Boston at the time Franklin visited Ebenezer Church.

35. I have reconstructed King, Sr.'s sermons to the extent that I reasonably can, based on his autobiography, interviews with ministers who knew him (including Taylor, Watson, Mays, Borders, and Larry Williams), interviews with older members of his church, a brief interview with him, and other sources.

36. See King, Sr., *Daddy King* 23, 45, 61.

37. King, Sr., *Daddy King* 27. As for the power of his memory, King, Sr., reports that he "could sing nearly any song after hearing it just a few times" (27).

38. King, Sr., *Daddy King* 62.

39. See Branch 267 and Baldwin 31.

40. Rosenberg describes these features of borrowing in the folk pulpit. When I interviewed King, Sr., in 1983, he denied borrowing sermons. The black folk preachers Rosenberg studied also denied borrowing sermons, even when confronted with incontrovertible evidence.

41. See Taylor Interview, Williams Interview, Edwards Interviews, Kemp Interview, English Interview, and Henderson and Henderson Interview.

42. See Taylor Interview.

43. King, Sr., *Daddy King* 98–101, 104–107, 122–124, 132–133. Older members of Ebenezer Church also recall these protests.

44. See King, Sr., *Daddy King* 125–126.

45. King, Sr., *Daddy King* 96, 154–155.

46. King, Sr., *Daddy King* 123.

47. See Kemp Interview.

48. See James English 56–58.

49. Borders, *Seven Minutes* 16.

50. See Williams Interview.

51. See James English 74.

52. See James English.

53. Watson Interview (Luker).

54. A church loyalist made this remark at a 1983 anniversary celebration of Ebenezer Church—an observance that I attended. King, Sr., laughed when he heard this comment.

55. King, Sr., *Daddy King* 82. For the traditional tendency, see Henry Young 13.

56. For the Pulitzer-Prize winner's description, see Branch 41, 58, 62–63. See also Oates 3 and Baldwin 278. Juanita Abernathy, George Kelsey, and older members of the Ebenezer congregation insist, however, that King, Sr., was not a fundamentalist.

Despite King, Jr.'s own characterization of Ebenezer Church as "fundamentalistic," such was not the case. What separates white fundamentalists from liberal white Protestants is the issue of the literal truth of scripture. But, despite the clash between J.H. Jackson and Gardner Taylor, black Protestants have never found the issue of Biblical literalism to be paramount or divisive. In fact, Biblical literalism is essentially a non-issue among black Protestants. Throughout his public career King never publicly stated whether he believed the Bible to be literally true. Nor in hundreds of interviews and press conferences was he ever asked to do so. The entire question did not matter to him, his followers, or other blacks. But it is the most important issue dividing fundamentalist and liberal white Protestants.

Branch also portrays King, Sr., as a less-than-courageous man who refused to agitate regularly because of his fear of whites and desire not to offend them. This view is unfair. In an era when whites murdered blacks and never went to jail, many blacks understandably did not vigorously protest racism. Some of them remembered the Atlanta race riot of 1906 that resulted in the murders of fifty African Americans. During the 1940s two separate incidents involving the murder of blacks occurred in rural Georgia not far from Atlanta. In this context, where a complete political timidity would hardly qualify as cowardice, the protests of A.D. Williams, King, Sr., and Borders displayed considerable courage. If the elder King saw certain times as more suitable for racial agitation than others, so did King, Jr., who staged no protests between 1956 and 1960. If the elder King were actually the theologically benighted and fearful man that Branch describes, he could not possibly have raised a son like King, Jr., or have co-pastored a church with him for eight years.

Branch's interpretation of King, Sr., is not unusual, for King specialists frequently assume that the religion of Ebenezer Church was anti-intellectual and fundamentalist. Branch actually demonstrates more respect for the elder King than do many King scholars, who dismiss him by almost entirely ignoring him.

57. See Kelsey Interview.

58. Information about the Johnson's visit to Ebenezer Church is available in KC BU. For Mays's visits, see Reed Interview. H.H. Crane, a leading liberal white preacher from Detroit, also served as a guest preacher at Ebenezer Church.

59. Reed Interview.

60. Farmer, *Lay Bare* 33.

61. Farmer emphasizes the rebellion of many "PKs."

62. Downing theorizes that King's willful rebellion against FBI Director J. Edgar Hoover amounted to a displacement of his earlier rebellion against the puritanism of another stern disciplinarian, his father (237–243).

63. See Garrow, *Bearing* 141, 151, 367, 425–426.

64. See Abernathy, *And the Walls* 479.

65. King, Jr., "Autobiography" 9.

66. See Branch 79–80.

67. King, Jr., "Autobiography" 10.

68. See Edwards Interviews. Edwards explains that the examining committee consisted of "about six pastors with churches in the city." Letter to author, 15 Feb. 1991. Author's files.

69. Andrew Young 12.

70. King, Jr., "Autobiography" 11.

CHAPTER THREE: THE BIGGEST PROBLEM FACING THE WORLD

1. King, Jr., qtd. in King, Sr., *Daddy King* 140.

2. See Mays Interviews.

3. The best sources of information about Mays's life are his autobiographies *Born* and *Lord*.

4. See Branch 56.

5. King, Jr., *Stride* 145.

6. See Mays Interviews.

7. See Mays, *Lord* 35, 44.

8. Kelsey Interview.

9. See Ronald Stone 109.

10. Mays, "Christian Youth" 370.

11. See Martin Duberman 324.

12. Mays, *The Christian in Race Relations* 2, 5, 13. Although this pamphlet bears no date, Mays delivered the lecture in April 1952.

13. Qtd. in Duberman 255, 267.

14. See Mays Interviews.

15. The best place to study Mays's career is the Moorland–Spingarn Library. Mays donated many boxes of written materials that are now catalogued as the Benjamin E. Mays Collection. Other Mays materials are available in the library's Mordecai Johnson Collection.

16. See Williams Interview and Branch 66. Because King greatly admired Borders's wife, Julia Pate Borders, his eighth-grade English teacher, he may have felt a closer affinity with Borders as a teenager than he had as a child. He later praised Mrs. Borders for having "a keen mind, a beautiful spirit, and a warm heart" ("Statement: Death of Julia Pate Borders.")

17. Qtd. in Robert Handy, *Christian America* 137.

18. Rauschenbusch, *Rauschenbusch Reader* 28. Rauschenbusch used the phrase in his *Christianity and the Social Crisis*, which first appeared in 1907.

19. Handy, *Christian America* 151–158, 157.

20. Gladden, "Remarks" 204.

21. For "for the man," see Kelsey Interview. Kelsey does not fault Rauschenbusch for ignoring race.

22. For an overview of the social gospel, see Handy, *Christian America* 134–158.

23. Grimke, *The Negro* 13, 23.

24. "Brotherhood of Man" 36–41. This address was delivered by a leader of the National Baptist Convention.

25. The best source of information about Fosdick is Robert Miller.

26. Fosdick, "Christianity and War" 4.

27. Luccock's column appeared under the pseudonym "Simeon Stylites."

28. Mays Interviews.

29. For Mays's pacifism, see his "Inescapable."

30. Niebuhr, *Beyond Tragedy* 59.

31. See Fox 291. Fox provides the best account of Niebuhr's life and contributions. For a discussion of Niebuhr's break with pacifism, see Harland 214–224. For a useful selection of Niebuhr's prolific writings, see Niebuhr, *Essential* 33.

32. For example, Tillich's vague definitions of the supreme being as "God above God" and the "Ground of Being" categorically did not appeal to preachers,

who almost never mention them. Instead they celebrated the same fatherly God that King's grandfather and father extolled from the Ebenezer pulpit.

33. Luccock, *East Window* 141.

34. Niebuhr, *Beyond Tragedy* 231.

35. For Weatherhead's reflections on the horror of World War I, his pacifism after World War I, and his acceptance of a just war theory following the failure of the League of Nations, see Weatherhead, *Thinking Aloud.*

36. See David Buttrick Interview. David Buttrick is the son of George Buttrick.

37. David Buttrick Interview.

38. Hamilton, *Horns and Halos* 63, 102. King borrowed extensively from this work.

39. Niebuhr, *Moral Man* 253.

40. Fosdick, *Hope* 34. For Fosdick's position on race, see Robert Miller 449–463.

41. See E. Stanley Jones, *Victorious Living* 163–164; E. Stanley Jones, *Way to Power and Poise* 134–135; Hamilton, "Unwilling Missionaries" 96.

42. Fosdick, *Great Time* 152.

43. For official pronouncements about race made by the Federal Council of Churches and other ecclesiastical bodies, see Richardson, "What Can the Church Do?" (1947) and "Protestantism on Justice and Integration" (1958). For records of other church statements about race, see Soper (1947) 220–246 and Bosley's *Doing* (1960) 63–73; also note Haselden's *Racial Problem* (1959).

44. For these leaders' appearances at the Chicago Sunday Evening Club, see Motter's two volumes. As dean of the School of Religion at Howard University, Mays worked under Mordecai Johnson and was succeeded as dean by Nelson. Mays's eulogy at Johnson's funeral is available in MJC M-S. Vernon Johns also preached before white listeners at least occasionally.

45. See advertisements for the Detroit Series in KC BU.

46. See *New York Journal American.* See also Robert Miller, *Harry Emerson Fosdick* 461.

47. See David Buttrick, Letter to author, 10 Feb. 1991, Author's files. In this letter David Buttrick also describes George Buttrick's friendships with Thurman and Gardner Taylor. Major Jones, one of King's classmates at Boston University, also attests to the Buttrick/Thurman pulpit exchange. Conversation with Major Jones, June 1983.

48. See Butler's nine sets of *Best Sermons.* Vernon Johns also published his sermon "Transfigured Moments" in Newton's *Best Sermons: 1926.* Newton's *Best Sermons: 1924* includes texts by Fosdick, Luccock, Sockman, and Tittle.

49. For Mays's relationship with Nelson, see Kelsey Interview.

50. Niebuhr did, however, occasionally editorialize about race relations in *Christian Century* and other journals.

51. See Thurman, *With Head* 131–132.

52. See Fosdick, *Great Time* 148–149.

53. See Rayford Logan 544.

54. See Kelsey Interview.

55. See McCall Interview.

56. Farmer Interview. See also Farmer, *Lay Bare* 135–136, 142–143.

57. See Meier and Rudwick 3–39.

58. The early version of "Pilgrimage" appeared as a chapter in King, Jr., *Stride.* For the later version, see King, Jr., "Pilgrimage," *Testament.*

59. In this chapter, I treat three major themes of the essay—the social gospel, Niebuhr's realism, and love—and three minor themes—Hegel's theory of history, Personalism, and interrelatedness. In Chapter 5, I explore the two remaining major themes—nonviolence and Communism.

60. For example, as evidence for what King supposedly learned from Rauschenbusch, a number of scholars cite a statement that King actually borrowed from Fosdick. See Oates 26; Ansbro 169–170; Donald Smith 33; Smith and Zepp 33; and William Miller 28.

61. Fosdick, *Hope* 25.

62. Fosdick, *Hope* 38.

63. King, Jr., "Pilgrimage," *Stride* 91.

64. King, Jr., "Pilgrimage," *Testament* 37–38.

65. King, Jr., "Pilgrimage," *Stride* 98–99.

66. See Robert Miller 449–463.

67. The social gospel of Gladden and Rauschenbusch was hardly a complex theology requiring years of study. After all, they attempted to Christianize the entire nation. Their social gospel was decidedly *less* complex than the religion of A. D. Williams, King, Sr., Borders, Mays, and Johns. Gladden and Rauschenbusch oversimplified social problems by ignoring the crucial relationship between poverty and racial injustice. By contrast, the African-American ministers in and around Ebenezer Church recognized this connection quickly and explained it repeatedly.

68. King, Jr., "Pilgrimage," *Stride* 98–99.

69. King, Jr., "Pilgrimage," *Stride* 99.

70. King, Jr., "Pilgrimage," *Testament* 35. King's use of the label "fundamentalistic" to describe his earlier training reflects his professors' and other white archliberals' tendency to stereotype all Protestantism that *seemed* more conservative than their own as "fundamentalistic."

71. Compare Nelson, "Satyagraha" 17–18 to King, Jr., "Pilgrimage," *Stride* 102–104. Compare Kelsey, "Christian Way" 40 to King, Jr., "Pilgrimage," *Stride* 104. Compare Paul Ramsey, *Basic Christian Ethics* 92–99. to King, Jr., "Pilgrimage," *Stride* 104–105.

Elsewhere in *Stride,* King also borrows from Kelsey. Compare Kelsey, "Christian Way" 29, 44, 47–48 to King, Jr., *Stride* 205, 206, 210. In his analysis, Kelsey distills Nygren's thought and quotes Nygren. Because King borrows from Kelsey's summary of Nygren, some King scholars have decided that King borrowed directly from Nygren. This conclusion is a mistake. Because *all* of King's ideas and phrases that *seem* to mirror Nygren are found in Kelsey and because King also borrows other passages from Kelsey unrelated to Nygren, there is no reason to suppose that King borrowed from Nygren at all. Nygren did influence King—but only indirectly, by way of Kelsey's analysis and quotation.

72. Fosdick, *On Being Fit* 6–7.

73. King, Jr., "Pilgrimage," *Stride* 104.

74. See, for example, Sockman, *Man's First* 22–23 and Hickerson, "Can We Love" 68–72.

75. King, Jr., "Pilgrimage," *Stride* 100.

76. David Buttrick Interview.

77. See Martin Luther King, Jr., Papers Project, "Martin Luther King, Jr.'s Student Papers," *Journal of American History*, forthcoming.

78. King, Jr., "Pilgrimage," *Stride* 100.

79. King, Jr., "Pilgrimage," *Stride* 100.

80. King, Jr., "Pilgrimage," *Stride* 101.

81. King, Jr., "Pilgrimage," *Stride* 106.

82. King, Jr., "Pilgrimage," *Stride* 107.

83. Henry Young 106.

84. King, Jr., *Why* 61.

CHAPTER 4: DUST AND DIVINITY

1. See two volumes edited by Alton Motter; Motter, "Foreword." For Hamilton's appearances, see his *What* 101.

2. See Motter, "Foreword" 14.

3. During the years that King preached in the Detroit Lenten Series, Mays, Buttrick, Sockman, Crane, Bosley, and Gardner Taylor preached at least once in the series. See Detroit Lenten Series programs in KC BU. For King's sermons in Crane's church, see Mervyn Warren 10. See also correspondence between King, Jr., and his secretary Dora McDonald with Crane and James Laird of Central Methodist Church of Detroit, KC BU. See also Central Methodist Church worship programs, KC BU. When co-pastoring Ebenezer Church, King welcomed Crane as guest preacher at Ebenezer.

4. During these years Buttrick, Mays, Thurman, Kennedy, Sockman, Tillich, Bosley, and E. Stanley Jones all preached at the Chicago Sunday Evening Club at least once. See Chicago Sunday Evening Club program schedules for 1958–1959, 1960, and 1962–1963, and the club service program for 19 April 1959, KC BU. See also many letters between club organizer Joseph Hanson and King and between Hanson and King's secretaries Maude Ballou and Dora McDonald, letters between Mrs. Elmer Crane and King, and Maude Ballou's letter to C.E. Randall, KC BU.

5. See correspondence between King and McCracken. KC BU.

6. The company began as Harper and Brothers, then changed its name to Harper and Row.

7. By my count, Harper issued one work by Buttrick, eight by Thurman, four by Luccock, two by McCracken, ten by Kennedy, four by Bosley, three by Morrison, one by Niebuhr, four by Tillich, three by Brown, six by Bonnell, and two posthumous collections by Rauschenbusch.

8. See two volumes edited by Motter.

9. In 1959 Harper issued *The Racial Problem in Christian Perspective* by Kyle Haselden, an editor of *Christian Century.*

10. Of course, part of his system of knowledge came from black folk preaching, but not from philosophy or theology.

11. King habitually borrowed from himself, replaying passages in literally

hundreds of orations, including scores that I do not mention in this book. Because much of the reiterated material came from unacknowledged sources, I claim that most of his discourse includes segments derived from sources. This observation applies to works that King himself composed, not to discourse that his ghostwriters wrote for him. The best examination of his use of ghostwriters appears in Garrow, *Bearing*.

12. For Hamilton's preaching at Riverside Church, see Margaret Babbage.

13. Although I consider Hamilton theologically and politically liberal, his widow, Florence Hamilton, thinks of her husband more as a moderate than a liberal. She explains, "He always kept the *redemptive note*"—more so than certain other liberal preachers. See Hamilton, Florence, Letter to author, 23 Nov. 1990, Author's files.

14. Joseph Hanson letter to King, 13 Jan. 1958, KC BU.

15. King, Jr., "What Is Man?" Unpublished.

16. Compare Hamilton, *Horns and Halos* 46–55 to King, Jr., *Strength* 87–92. For a further discussion of the relationship between King's "What Is Man?" and the Hamilton sermons, see Keith Miller, "Influence" 68–71. Borrowing from Hamilton, King also preached a sermon titled "Remember Who You Are."

17. Compare Fosdick, *Hope* 25 and King, Jr., "What Is Man?" Unpublished.

18. See Fosdick, *Successful Christian* 265–266; Kennedy, *Reader's Notebook* 128; Bonnell, *What Are You* 36–37. For *Christian Century* readers who sought to banish this illustration, see Sweazey 198.

19. Compare Charles Brown, *Finding Ourselves* 122 and King, Jr., "What Is Man?" Unpublished.

20. See Tittle, *Word That Cannot* 18–29; Bonnell, *What Are You* 37.

21. Compare Bonnell, *What Are You* 45 and King, Jr., "What Is Man?" Unpublished 1. King also uses the definition in the *Strength* edition of the sermon (87).

22. Compare Fosdick, *Successful Christian* 39; Fosdick, *As I* 74; and King, Jr., "What Is Man?" Unpublished 1–2.

23. See Hamilton, *Horns and Halos* 60; Bosley, *Firm Faith* 136; Mays, "Knowledge Alone" 83; Bonnell, *What Are You* 37; George Truett, *Who Is Jesus?* 89–90; and H. Grady Davis, *Design* 226. For the pamphlet, see Harrington 15. Compare all these to King, Jr., "What Is Man?" Unpublished 1. King included the Harrington pamphlet in the papers he donated to Boston University.

Someone might argue that I have demonstrated nothing by citing this quotation from Shakespeare and other familiar citations. That person might claim that these quotations are so well-known that I have not established a homiletic lineage for King's use of them. Or a critic might argue that the familiarity of the quotations means that the homiletic lineage is not important since King could have gotten them from anywhere. Such criticism would be misguided, for many famous literary quotations are absent both in King's texts and in those of other preachers. This absence is not merely a coincidence. Like other liberal preachers, King rarely quoted from Cervantes, Flaubert, Samuel Johnson, Blake, Coleridge, Hardy, Dickens, Twain, Melville, Hawthorne, Poe, Shaw, Yeats, Gide, Pound, Joyce, Faulkner, Hemingway, Camus, Sartre, Beckett, Kafka, O'Neill, Arthur Miller, Wallace Stevens, William Carlos Williams, Tennessee Williams, and many other prominent literary figures. King eschewed these literary masters precisely because other liberal preachers also ignored them. The lineage of the considerable majority of King's quotations—including familiar quotations—lies largely in popular, liberal sermons. Like other parts of King's sermons, his familiar and less familiar quotations cannot be understood apart from that lineage.

24. Compare Chalmers, *Constant Fire* 104 and *High Wind* 76–77 to King, Jr., "What Is Man?" Unpublished 3.

25. Compare Hamilton, *Horns and Halos* 17, 51 and King, Jr., *Strength* 90, 91. "What Is Man?" appears in the first edition of *Strength* but not in later editions. King also preached this sermon under the title "Who Are We?"

26. See A. Binga, Jr.

27. See Thomson.

28. See E.F. Tittle, "What Is Man?" and Tittle, "The Church of the Living God."

29. See Robert Calhoun.

30. See Borders, "What Is Man?" 13.

31. See H. I. Loutitt.

32. See Hamilton, *Horns and Halos* 46–55 and Hamilton, *Who Goes There?* 72–82.

33. See Tillich *Eternal Now* 66–80; Bosley, *Firm Faith* 135–152; Loutitt; Paul Robinson; Babbage, "Man the Enigma" 64–68; and Harrington.

34. See Taylor, "Some Comments" 189–190 and Weatherhead, *That Immortal Sea* 130.

35. King, Jr. "What Is Man?" Unpublished 1.

36. Compare Fosdick, *Hope* 25; King, Jr., "What Is Man?" Unpublished 1; and King, Jr., *Strength* 89, 97.

37. See King, Jr., "What Is Man?" Unpublished 3; King, Jr., "What Is Man?" *Strength* 91–92.

38. See King, Jr., "What Is Man?" Unpublished 1; King, Jr., "What Is Man?" *Strength* 89.

39. See Revelations 21:16. King sometimes preached the sermon under the title "The Dimensions of a Complete Life."

40. See Coretta King 59.

41. See Coretta King 59; Warren 71; and Inventory of the King Center Archives.

42. See Brooks, "Symmetry" 195–206. Warren asked King whether Brooks's "Symmetry" served as a model for "Three Dimensions." King replied that it had and that Brooks had influenced several of his other sermons as well. See Warren 71.

43. Compare Brooks, "The Symmetry" 202 and King, Jr., *Strength* 74.

44. Compare Fosdick, *On Being Fit* 45–46 and King, Jr., *Strength* 68.

45. Five of Mays's achievers make King's list as well. Compare Mays, *Seeking* 13–14 and King, Jr., *Strength* 70.

46. See Matthew 10:16.

47. King published this sermon in both *Pulpit* and *Strength*. The first sentence of "Tough Mind" comes from E. Stanley Jones, *Mahatma Gandhi* 17. Hamilton and Niebuhr preceded King in citing H.G. Wells's characterization of God as a kind but

helpless figure. See Niebuhr, *Discerning* 150; Hamilton, *Horns and Halos* 149; Hamilton, *Who* 140; King, Jr., *Strength* 7. In *Horns and Halos* 68–69 Hamilton also anticipated King's point that some Israelites preferred servitude in Egypt to the rigors of traversing the wilderness.

48. King, Jr., *Strength* 4.

49. Compare Buttrick, *Parables* 137–146 to King, Jr., "Dives and Lazarus"; Buttrick, *Parables* 127–135 to King, Jr., "Man Who Was a Fool," *Strength* 51–57; and Buttrick, *Parables* 149–156 to King, Jr., "On Being," *Strength* 16–24. For other preachers who borrowed from Buttrick's *Parables*, compare, for example, Buttrick, *Parables* 127–135, 149–156 to Weatherhead, *In Quest* 140–160, 173–182; and Buttrick, *Parables* 127–135 to Stamm 55–60. Weatherhead's text *appears* indebted to Buttrick's at several points. Undoubtedly Stamm's text derives in part from Buttrick. Neither Weatherhead nor Stamm acknowledges Buttrick. In *Parables He Told* Redding announces his debt to Buttrick, and much of his book reiterates ideas and phrases from Buttrick. Compare, for example, Buttrick, *Parables* 127–135, 149–156 to Redding 127–131, 118–124.

50. I thank Barbara Urrea and Susan Gassman for clarifying this point for me.

51. For more information about Buttrick, see Joseph Sittler, "Dr. George A. Buttrick"; Frank Cross et al., "George Buttrick," *Harvard Gazette* 15 (April 1983): 7, 15, Author's files.

52. Buttrick, *Parables* 149; King, Jr., *Strength* 17.

53. Buttrick, *Parables* 150; King, Jr., *Strength* 17.

54. Buttrick, *Parables* 151; King, Jr., *Strength* 17.

55. Buttrick, *Parables* 150.

56. King, Jr., *Strength* 20.

57. Buttrick, *Parables* 152–53; King, Jr., *Strength* 17.

58. Buttrick, *Parables of Jesus* 150, 152–153; King, Jr., *Strength* 17–18.

Buttrick's and King's texts overlap at other points as well. Both writers speculate that the Levite and priest preferred an institutional solution to the problem of highway thievery. Both conjecture that the Levite and priest viewed the man not primarily as a human being but as someone unlike themselves. Both apply the lesson to the present, suggesting that we also fit people into categories of race and religion instead of treating them as neighbors. King echoes Buttrick's praise of the Samaritan's unselfishness and modifies Buttrick's discussion of organized philanthropy. See Buttrick, *Parables* 151–155 and King, Jr., *Strength* 19, 21–22.

59. In Brown's version, the robber's actions express the philosophy of " 'What's yours is mine, I'll take it' "; the priest and Levite embody the philosophy of " 'What's mine is my own—I'll keep it' "; and the Samaritan represents the principle of " 'What's mine is ours—we'll share it.' " Of course, both Brown and King emphasize that the Samaritan's philosophy is the Christ-like approach that Christians need to emulate. Like Brown, King explains the social gospel implications of each philosophy—including complex, legal forms of robbery. See Brown, "What Value Has the Right Motive" 88–129. With minor changes, this text also appears as Brown, "Jericho Road" 32–47.

60. King's earlier interpretation of this parable also came from Hamilton. Compare Hamilton, *Horns and Halos* 17 and King, Jr., *Strength* 91.

61. Hamilton, *Horns and Halos* 59, 60.

62. King, Jr., "Prodigal Son" 5.

63. Hamilton, *Horns and Halos* 59; King, Jr., "Prodigal Son" 5. Other features of King's sermon also come from sources. *Horns and Halos* (29) supplied King's quotations of three partial quatrains of Omar Khayyam ("Come, fill the Cup . . . ," "Take the cash . . . ," and "A Book of Verses . . ."). (Sockman also quoted one of these poems [*Live for Tomorrow* 12].) Buttrick's *Parables* (viii) provided King's metaphors "the tang of the human and the glow of the divine" ("Prodigal Son" 1). King's quotation from George Murray ("Prodigal Son" 1) could stem from either Buttrick's *Parables* (189) or *Horns and Halos* (163).

64. Buttrick, *Parables* 192.

65. See Charles Heimsath 134.

66. See Fosdick, *Great Time* 88.

67. C.L. Franklin, *Give Me* 56.

68. King sometimes delivered this sermon under the title "Mastering Our Fears."

69. Significantly, Tillich's volume originated as a series of lectures, not a theological tome.

70. King warned of the "frittering road" of drink and promiscuity (*Strength* 108). Liebman decried the "frittering path of Don-Juanism" (86). King's catalogue of fears concludes with "phobiaphobia" or "the fear of fear itself" (*Strength* 108). Fosdick admonished readers to avoid "phobophobia" or "the fear of fear" ("Conquest of Fear" 61). (Hamilton's "Make a Friend of Your Fear" (105) also warns of "phobiaphobia.") King's warning about nuclear catastrophe (*Strength* 109, 116) came from Buttrick ("Anxiety and Faith" 37, 42–43) and was anticipated by McCracken ("What to Do with Our Fears?" 122). King's metaphorical definition —"Fear is the elemental alarm system of the human organism . . ." (*Strength* 109)—came from Fosdick ("Conquest of Fear" 59) and parallels lines from McCracken, Hamilton, and Thurman. Consider McCracken: "Natural fear, like pain, is one of the sentinels of life" ("What to Do with Our Fears" 124); Hamilton: "Fear is God-given. . . ." ("Make a Friend" 102); and Thurman: "Fear, then, becomes the safety device. . . ." (*Jesus and the Disinherited* 40).

Following Liebman (84), King embraced Freud's distinction between normal and abnormal fears (*Strength* 109–110). Without mentioning Freud, McCracken proposed the same contrast ("What to Do with Our Fears" 124). Fosdick ("Conquest of Fear" 61) supplied King's quotation from Emerson (*Strength* 109). Another of King's quotations (*Strength* 109) emerged earlier in Fosdick's *On Being Fit* (125) and Charles Wallis's collection of illustrations (124), which King consulted.

71. See McCracken, "What to Do with Our Fears" 125–126. E. Stanley Jones also urged readers to confront fear. See Jones, *Growing Spiritually* 39. Buttrick, however, dismisses this solution ("Anxiety and Faith" 38–39).

72. Tillich, *Courage* 22, 34, 36, 66; King, Jr., *Strength* 111.

73. Anticipating King, McCracken also advocated courage as a remedy for fear. Compare McCracken ("What to Do with Our Fears" 127–128) and King, Jr., *Strength* 110–112. In "What to Do with Our Fears" (129) McCracken also quotes

another preacher's metaphor—"this strange medley of life"—that King recirculates in the courage section of his sermon (*Strength* 111).

74. See Fosdick, "Conquest of Fear" 66; Buttrick, "Anxiety and Faith" 41–43; and King, Jr., *Strength* 112–115. King's analysis of love also incorporates Fosdick's passage about nonviolence. Compare Fosdick, "Conquest of Fear" 66–67 to King, Jr., *Strength* 112.

75. Compare Fosdick, "Conquest of Fear" 65–66; Buttrick, "Anxiety and Faith"; McCracken, "What to Do with Our Fears" 128–129; Liebman 102–104; and King, Jr., *Strength* 114–117. Buttrick's "Anxiety and Faith" (43) also closes with the same brief poem that King uses to conclude "Antidotes" (*Strength* 117).

76. McCracken, *Making* 89.

77. Stephen Peabody, "Managing Our Fears" 12.

78. Beecher, "Through Fear" 451–463.

79. The outpouring began as a trickle in the 1930s. See Tittle's "Overcoming Fear" 147–169 and Truett's "Conquest of Fear," which appeared in the same year (1933) as Fosdick's text of the same title.

During the 1940s and 1950s the topic magnetized an array of writers and preachers. *Pulpit* printed Harold Ruopp's "You Can Master Fear," Richard Wolff's "Mastering Our Fears," Stephen Peabody's "Managing Our Fears and Anxieties," and A.J. Muste's "Overcoming Fear." In the same decades, Fosdick explained "Constructive Use of Fear" and "Dealing with Fear and Anxiety"; Hamilton counseled "Make a Friend of Your Fear"; Thurman added "Fear" as a chapter in *Jesus and the Disinherited;* Weatherhead provided a *Prescription for Anxiety: How You Can Overcome Fear and Despair;* Sockman ventured, "Fears May Be Liars"; E. Stanley Jones communicated "Mastery of Fear," twice uncovered "The Basis of These Fears," and supplied two sets of "Steps Out of Fear"; Liebman announced, "Fear Wears Many Masks"; Bonnell recommended, "Never Strike a Flag to Fear"; Fulton Sheen anatomized "Fears and Anxieties"; James Pike included "Fear" in his *Beyond Anxiety;* an entire book, *Conquest of Fear,* dissected this topic; and yet another preacher proposed solutions in "Fear" and "Getting the Best of Fear." (See Macartney, *Facing Life.*)

In addition to the homilies of Beecher and Tittle, seven other texts also harness the scripture that King used—"Perfect love casts out fear." See Buttrick "Anxiety and Faith"; Jones, "Basis of These Fears" (*Victorious*); Jones, "Basis of These Fears" (*Growing*); Jones, "Steps Out of Fear" (*How to Be*); Jones, "Steps Out of Fear" (*Growing*); Sockman, "Fears May Be Liars"; and Hamilton, "Make a Friend." Inasmuch as thousands of workaday ministers borrowed sermons, one can safely assume that many of them also preached on this topic.

80. The Khayyam quatrains are "Worldly Hope," "Moving Finger . . .", and "Chequer-board." See Thurman, *Inward* 80; Fosdick, *Living Under Tension* 94; Fosdick, *Successful* 235; Hamilton, *Horns and Halos* 29, 31; Buttrick, *So We* 170; Buttrick, *Sermons Preached* 113; Niebuhr, *Beyond Tragedy* 260; Stewart, *A Faith* 61; Stroup 55 and Carrington, *Carry* 58. Each of these authors employs Khayyam's facile pessimism as a counterpoint to Christian hope, just as King does.

81. See Gladden, *Where* 151; Fosdick, *Hope* (77, 99), Fosdick, *On Being Fit* 93; Fosdick, *Riverside Sermons* 254; Fosdick, *Riverside Sermons* 62; Fosdick, *Living under Tension* 221; Fosdick, *Successful* 96; Fosdick, *Dear Mr. Brown* 129, 136; Buttrick,

Christian Fact 234; Hamilton "The First Word" 21; Sockman, *Man's First* 136; Bonnell, *He Speaks* 21; Bonnell, *What Are You* 55; Scherer, *Facts* 174; Harold Walker, *Upper Room* 108; Stewart, *Strong Name* 159; Jenney 37–44, 43; Charles Tindley, *A Book of Sermons* 62; and Macartney, *Macartney's Illustrations* 80.

82. See Fosdick, *Hope* 115; Fosdick, *On Being Fit* 163; Fosdick, *Living under Tension* 52; Fosdick, *Successful* 195; Fosdick, *Riverside Sermons* 151; Weatherhead, *That Immortal Sea* 48; Thurman, *Jesus and the Disinherited* 66; Luccock, *Haunted House* 208; Sockman, *Now to Live!* 75; Tittle, *Mighty Fortress* 105; Chalmers, *High Wind* 153; Johns, *Human* 59; Buttrick, *Christian Fact* 258; and Buttrick, "Gospel" 186–187.

83. See Fosdick, *Living of These Days* 250; Fosdick, *Successful* 160, 161; Fosdick, *Riverside Sermons* 360; Weatherhead, *Key Next Door* 22; Weatherhead, *That Immortal Sea* 90; Weatherhead, *In Quest* 15; Kennedy, *His Word* 152; Kennedy, *With Singleness* 152; Bosley, *Firm Faith* 135; Bosley, *Sermons on Genesis* 129; Buttrick, *Sermons Preached* 178; Luccock, *Christian Faith* 76; Bonnell, "Easter Dawn" 96; Stewart, *Heralds* 15; and Niebuhr, *Nature and Destiny* 3.

84. August Meier, "Conservative Militant."

CHAPTER FIVE: DARKNESS CANNOT DRIVE OUT DARKNESS

1. See Chapter 9.

2. This account of the bombing and the Semon on the Porch is drawn from King, Jr., *Stride* 136–138; Coretta King, *My Life* 127–130; and JoAnn Robinson, *Montgomery* 130–133.

3. For example, Branch contends that Niebuhr served as *the* primary intellectual resource for King (69–104).

4. King, Jr., "Pilgrimage," *Stride* 96.

5. King, Jr., "Pilgrimage," *Stride* 96.

6. Wofford, "Nonviolence and the Law," 32, 34. Wofford delivered this speech at Howard University and elsewhere and published it in *Journal of Religious Thought.* Wofford mailed King a copy of this speech; this copy is now at KC BU.

7. King, Jr., "Pilgrimage," *Stride* 103.

8. Compare Nelson, "Satyagraha" 17, 18 to King, Jr., "Pilgrimage," *Stride* 102, 103–104. Nelson mailed a copy of this essay to King. Reading this copy, King read Nelson's remark, ". . . non-violence is not to be confined to physical action but . . . involves words and even thoughts" (17). In the margin King paraphrased Nelson: "It avoid[s] both external physical and internal violence of spirit." King's rewording of Nelson finds its way into "Pilgrimage": "A fifth point concerning nonviolent resistance is that it avoids not only external physical violence but also internal violence of spirit" (*Stride* 103). King's copy of Nelson's essay is at KC BU.

9. Compare Gregg 75 to King, Jr., "Pilgrimage," *Stride* 102. In 1962 King listed Gregg's *Power of Nonviolence* as one of the ten books that most affected his thinking. See *Christian Century* 79 (1962): 660. King's original list is at KC BU.

10. E. Stanley Jones, *Mahatma Gandhi* 88–89.

11. King, Jr., *Strength* 40.

12. Hamilton, *Horns and Halos* 101.

13. Hamilton, *Horns and Halos* 101–102.

14. Hamilton, *Horns and Halos* 103.

15. King, Jr., *Strength* 37, 39.

16. Fosdick, *Hope* 67.

17. King, Jr., *Strength* 112.

18. These passages are ones that King borrowed *in addition to* those from Wofford that King replayed in "Pilgrimage," which appears as a chapter in *Stride*.

19. Wofford, "Non-violence and the Law," 25–36; King, Jr., *Stride* 213, 216, 220, 223–224.

20. Jones, *Mahatma Gandhi*, 88–89; King, Jr., *Stride* 217.

21. See "A Gandhi Society?"

22. King, Jr., Letter to Fey, 23 June 1962, KC A.

23. While many of these preachers were pure pacifists, others called for nonviolence without necessarily embracing complete pacifism. Hamilton and Sockman, for example, usually remained vague on the question of whether any war ever merited Christian support.

24. For Thurman's 1935 meeting with Gandhi, see Thurman, *With Head* 132; Makechnie 26–31.

25. See Mays, *Born* 155–157; Mays Interview.

26. See Wofford, *Of Kennedys and Kings.*

27. Nelson, "Our Racial Situation" 74–77, 76, M-S; and Nelson, *Bases* 75, 79, M-S.

28. Philip Lenud, King's close friend at Boston, reports that King "loved and respected Thurman" (Baldwin 300–301).

29. See Wofford, *Of Kennedys and Kings* 118.

30. Nelson edited *Journal of Religious Thought.* He published his essay "Satyagraha" and Wofford's "Nonviolence and the Law" in the same issue of the journal.

31. See Fairclough 59–60.

32. Thurman, Fosdick, and King also shared the same publisher—Harper.

33. E. Stanley Jones, "Jesus Comes through Irregular Channels—Mahatma Gandhi's Part" 73–86.

34. For King's explanation, see King, Jr., "Pilgrimage."

35. Niebuhr, *Essential* 166.

36. Niebuhr, *Essential* 167.

37. Niebuhr, *Essential* 173–174, 177, 180.

38. Niebuhr, *Essential* 166.

39. King, Jr., *Stride* 201–202.

40. In his 1940 essay "Why the Christian Church Is Not Pacifist," Niebuhr brushed aside the pacifist tradition that supplied some of King's language about nonviolence (*Essential* 102–119). Niebuhr (107) assailed Richard Gregg's *The Power of Nonviolence*, one of King's sources for "Pilgrimage." In contrast King wrote an approving foreword to the 1959 edition of Gregg's book, praising it as "perceptive" and hoping that it would enjoy a "wide readership." Here and in his use of pacifist passages from Fosdick and Hamilton, King drew upon a tradition that Niebuhr scorned.

41. On the other hand King never accumulated many material possessions. Instead of spending the large sums he earned through speaking, he funneled them into his civil rights organization.

42. Apart from occasional discussions about voluntary poverty, King rarely conversed about Gandhian topics other than nonviolence and civil disobedience. I base this claim on my own interviews and on the King scholarship—especially Garrow's *Bearing* and Branch's *Parting*—that explains in great detail hundreds of conversations that King held during his adult life. Garrow read thousands of pages of transcripts of FBI-recorded conversations among King and his friends and advisors.

43. Henderson Interview; Baldwin 123–124.

44. In *Protest* Garrow convincingly argues that King intentionally provoked violence by police. Ralph Abernathy's *And the Walls* offers strong support for this thesis, if any were needed. Fairclough adds a useful qualification to Garrow's thesis by contending that, while King provoked violence from his adversaries, he elicited their limited, measured violence, eschewing situations where large numbers of people might have lost their lives.

45. McCracken, *Questions* 168.

46. King, Jr., "Pilgrimage," *Stride* 92.

47. McCracken, *Questions* 165–167.

48. King, Jr., "Pilgrimage," *Stride* 93.

49. Compare McCracken, *Questions* 166, 169–170 and King, Jr., "Pilgrimage," *Stride* 92–94.

50. Melvin Watson, Morehouse professor and friend of the King family, also encouraged King's mixed reaction to Marxism. See Branch 80.

51. Hamilton, *Horns and Halos* 44; King, Jr., *Strength* 94.

52. McCracken, *Questions* 166–167; King, Jr., *Strength* 96–97.

53. King, Jr., *Strength* 97.

54. King emphasizes this solution by remarking the zeal of the early Christians, who "out-thought, out-lived, and out-died" their contemporaries (*Strength* 100). This phrase probably comes from Wallis 67.

55. McCracken, *Questions* 170; King, Jr., *Strength* 97–98.

56. While King acknowledges a Yale professor as the source of this observation (Pope 105), it also enlivened a sermon by Gardner Taylor ("They Shall Ask" 15–16), a different sermon by McCracken ("Discrimination" 4), yet another homily (Lunger 100), and Kennedy's collection of illustrations (*Reader's Notebook* 246). Kennedy acknowledges Taylor as the source of the illustration; Taylor states that he originated it (Taylor Interview).

57. See E. Stanley Jones, *Choice* 112, 132, 212. Note Jones's chapter, "A Comparison Between Naziism, Fascism, Communism, and Christianity" 111–135.

58. See E. Stanley Jones, *Way* 137. For more of Jones's view of Christianity and Communism, see his "Why Has Communism Failed" and "Between Individualism and Communism" in *Mastery* 116, 117; and his *Christ's Alternative to Communism*, which appeared in England under the title *Christ and Communism*.

59. See Weatherhead, "Can a Christian Be a Communist?" *When the Lamp* 96–103.

60. John C. Bennett 47.

61. John C. Bennett 20–21, 47.

62. See Mays, *Christian in Race Relations* 13.

63. See Mordecai Johnson, "Heart" 52–58.

64. See King's handwritten manuscript of *Stride* in KC BU.

65. See E. Stanley Jones, *Choice* 132–133, 179; E. Stanley Jones, *How to Be* 336.

66. See Robert Miller 479–486.

67. Hamilton, *Horns and Halos* 73–74.

68. See E. Stanley Jones, *Mastery* 117.

69. See Alan Walker.

70. See also Luccock, *Marching* 71.

71. Several joined McCracken and preceded King in making this argument. See, for example, Mordecai Johnson, "A Pathway"; John C. Bennett 62, 125; and Laubach 7.

72. See Fox 244. Niebuhr delivered two sets of lectures in 1951, which he published a year later as *Irony*.

73. As Fox explains, Niebuhr's harsh anti-Communism is itself ironic because McCarthyites regarded Niebuhr's anti-Communist credentials as suspect and labelled Niebuhr as "un-American." It is hardly to Niebuhr's credit that he failed to denounce McCarthyism altogether. Instead he contributed to the heated, I'm-more-anti-Communist-than-thou climate of the late 1940s and early 1950s, even though he himself was occasionally tarred by those conducting the witch-hunt. For Niebuhr's role during this period, see Fox 224–273.

74. If King read *Irony*, he flatly rejected its argument. However, because King may not have read *Irony*, someone might complain that my points about the book are irrelevant. Such an argument would be short-sighted. King may not have read *Irony*, but that is exactly the point. If he did not read *Irony*, the question is: why not? If Niebuhr were important to King, King certainly would have read Niebuhr's recent work, especially the final book that Niebuhr completed before his stroke. If King avoided reading *Irony*, he did so because he realized that Niebuhr had little to offer.

75. Wofford Interview. The best analysis of this development appears in Garrow's *Bearing* and Cone's *Martin*.

76. Niebuhrians would doubtless claim that Niebuhr resists such labels as "radical" or "conservative" and that his writing is more dialectical than anything else. However, despite the multiple vectors, paradoxes, and tensions of Niebuhr's writings, he began as a radical socialist and pacifist. Plainly his views during the late 1940s and 1950s grew conservative, especially with respect to Communism. Despite its complexities, his political thought unmistakably shifted from the left (during the 1920s) to the right (during the 1950s).

Niebuhr did, however, support the civil rights movement, and joined King and others in opposing the Vietnam War. The ascendency of King and the revived American left *seem* to have influenced Niebuhr's willingness to embrace liberal positions, especially over Vietnam.

A reformer wary of reforms, Niebuhr is a hero neither to the left nor to the right. He advocated civil rights, but because of his forceful and repeated warnings about the perils of reform, King and other activists found little theological comfort and support in his work.

77. They were Bayard Rustin and Stanley Levison.

78. Had McCracken's congregation not warmly received his sermon on Communism, he would probably not have published it.

79. See Fosdick, *Hope* 5. See Matthew 5:13–14; 1 Cor. 5:6–8.

80. Niles published his sermon in both *Christian Century* and in a homiletic collection. See Niles, "Summons," *Christian Century* 1037–1039 and Niles, "Summons," *Preacher's Calling* 127.

81. Compare Niles, "Summons," *Christian Century* 1037 to King, Jr., *Strength* 42, 43, 44.

82. See Fosdick, *Hope* 7; King, Jr., *Strength* 47. Also, King's mockery of ministers' efforts to stabilize people's blood pressure resembles a satiric comment made by Luccock. Compare Luccock, *Marching* 75 to King, Jr., *Strength* 43.

83. Fosdick, *Hope* 6–7.

84. King, Jr., *Strength* 9.

85. Fosdick, *Hope* 112.

86. King, Jr., *Strength* 14.

87. For example, Fosdick and King elucidate the success of the early church in ending Roman baby-killing and gladitorial sports. Both clergy also criticize Americans' infatuation with size, which they term "jumboism." See Fosdick, *Hope* 4, 6; King, Jr., *Strength* 10, 12.

88. A year later Austin published his sermon in *Pulpit*.

89. Austin 13.

90. Austin 14.

91. King, Jr., *Strength* 10.

92. King, Jr., *Strength* 11.

93. Austin 14.

94. King, Jr., *Strength* 11. King also adapts Austin's quotation from Jefferson, his concession about the price of nonconformity, and his long quotation from John Bunyan. See Austin 15; King, Jr., *Strength* 15.

95. McCracken also prefigured King's claim that "a man must be either anvil or hammer." McCracken, however, attributes the anvil-or-hammer metaphor to Voltaire, while King attributes it to Longfellow. See McCracken, "Peril" 20–21; King, Jr., *Strength* 10, 12.

96. King also harnessed James Russell Lowell's eight-line poem, which appeared in a collection of illustrations familiar to King and a volume celebrating a black church in Montgomery. Compare Wallis 248; Dickerson 91; and King, Jr., *Strength* 12–13.

97. See Tillich, *Eternal Now* 135–144.

98. See Johns, *Human* 87 and Lunger 98.

99. See Luccock, *Preaching Values* 297–299.

100. George Webber 49.

101. See Ernest Miller Interview.

102. See Sockman, "Salt" 65–80.

103. Weatherhead, *In Quest* 66.

104. Kennedy, *With Singleness* 29.

105. Kennedy, *Lion* 71.

106. Fosdick, *Dear* 139–148.

107. See Johns, *Human* 98. Johns refers to Barton's *The Man Nobody Knows,* a best-seller from 1925.

108. Luccock, *Preaching Values* 299.

109. See, for example, V.P. Franklin.

CHAPTER SIX: HE WANTED TO BE AN OUTSTANDING PREACHER

1. See Taylor Interview.

2. Obviously speakers also use emotional appeals.

3. See Michael McGee.

4. McGee 197.

5. McGee 197.

6. See Wilder 14–15.

7. Fosdick, *On Being Fit* vii.

8. See Perelman 141.

9. Tillich himself claims this motivation for his preaching. See Tillich, *Shaking,* Preface.

10. Or, in Niebuhr's case, a religious system applied to political affairs.

11. This time included not only the many hours spent writing and delivering addresses, but also the enormous number of hours devoted to related activities. These time-consuming tasks include screening speaking invitations (he received hundreds more invitations than he could possibly accept); arranging his jam-packed speaking schedule and itinerary; dictating many letters of apology when he had to cancel an appearance because of a spur-of-the-moment civil rights emergency; and, on hundreds of occasions, driving to and from airports, waiting for planes, and flying thousands of miles to speak.

12. Those who have tracked King's ghostwriters, particularly Garrow in *Bearing,* point to ghostwritten portions of his books, essays, and speeches—not his sermons. And as far as I can tell, King did not use ghostwriters for sermons. Several of his ghostwriters were not preachers, and those who were did not know white audiences and Fosdick's pulpit tradition nearly as well as King did himself.

13. See Luke 23:34.

14. Fosdick, "Crucified by Stupidity" 222–230; King, Jr., *Strength* 25–33.

15. King, Jr., *Strength* 28.

16. Both preachers argue that the Athenians viewed Socrates as an atheist because his conception of God was superior to their own.

17. See Fosdick, "Crucified by Stupidity" 223.

18. See King, Jr., *Strength* 28–29. In "Love and Forgiveness," a later, revised version of "Love in Action," King mirrors Fosdick by adding Joan of Arc and Galileo to his list of maltreated heroes. See King, Jr., "Love and Forgiveness." "Love and Forgiveness" also relates an account of Lincoln's funeral train that King garnered from Fosdick. Both Fosdick and King interpret Lincoln as one who died for others—a Christ-like leader whose sacrifice helped redeem a nation.

19. Fosdick, "Crucified by Stupidity" 223; King, Jr., *Strength* 29. In "Love in Action" King also describes Jesus's conversation with Peter, who asked whether he should forgive someone seven times and learned to forgive seventy times seven. King's long discussion of this dialogue (*Strength* 26) comes from Hamilton's *Horns*

and Halos (100). A different sermon in Fosdick's *Hope* (33) supplies King's quotation from Shakespeare (*Strength* 31).

20. King borrowed his title from a sermon in Hamilton's *Horns and Halos.* Although Hamilton's "Shattered Dreams" does not address Romans 15:24, Hamilton's 1952 collection *Ride!* contains a sermon based on this scripture (147–159). In their analysis of Romans 15:24, Hamilton and King interpret the verse as an indication of Paul's failure to reach his cherished goal. Both apply Paul's dashed hope to the universal experience of disappointment.

While the frame of King's sermon resembles Hamilton's frame, the content of King's text departs from Hamilton. In his opening paragraph, King describes the personification of hope in a painting by a largely forgotten artist (*Strength* 78). He borrowed this remark from Buttrick's *Sermons Preached* (110).

Hamilton and King were not alone in using Paul's statement as a launching pad for a sermon about facing hardships. According to one midcentury minister, Paul's inability to travel to Spain inspired not only Hamilton and King but also unheralded pastors toiling in ecclesiastical vineyards small and large. See Ernest Miller Interview.

21. King, Jr., *Strength* 79.

22. King organizes the first section of his homily by noting three types of unsatisfactory reactions to adversity: bitterness, withdrawal, and fatalism. Two major sources—Thurman's *Deep River* and Weatherhead's *Key Next Door*—help him explain these reactions. His discussion of bitterness and resentment (*Strength* 79) parallels Weatherhead's points about bitterness (*Key* 50–51) and closely corresponds to Thurman's analysis (*Deep River* 37). His notion that resentment can cause physical ailments (*Strength* 80) echoes Weatherhead's earlier comment (*Key* 50–51). His account of withdrawal (*Strength* 80) paraphrases Thurman's view (*Deep River* 38). His objection to fatalism (*Strength* 80–81) was anticipated by Weatherhead (*Key* 51). Later in "Shattered Dreams," King includes a passage from Jeremiah that serves as the basis for Weatherhead's sermon in *Key.*

23. King, Jr., *Strength* 82.

24. Thurman, *Deep River* 35–36, 39.

25. King, Jr., *Strength* 83.

26. King, Jr., *Strength* 83.

27. King, Jr., *Strength* 61–63.

28. Rosenberg provides several examples of such topic-switching.

29. See Ernest Miller Interview. Luccock has another name for the Key Sermon—the Chase Sermon (*In the Minister's Workshop* 143).

30. See Ernest Miller Interview.

31. For all these forms, see Luccock, *In the Minister's Workshop* 134–147 and Ernest Miller Interview.

32. See Branch 76–77.

33. See Branch 77.

34. For example, classification clearly serves as the major organizational scheme for such King sermons as "Man Who Was a Fool," "On Being," and "Good Samaritan." "Tough Mind," "Love Your Enemies," "Shattered Dreams" and other homilies also feature some form of classification.

35. Compare Brooks, *Sermons Preached* 183–196; Hamilton, *Horns and Halos*

56–67; and King, Jr., *Strength* 118–126. For another example of blended arrangements, consider "How Should a Christian View Communism?" It combines
elements of a Springboard Sermon, a Classification Sermon and a Ladder Sermon.

36. See King, Jr., "Sleeping Through a Revolution," 10 Dec. 1967, 3.

37. Kennedy, *His Word* 124. Kennedy's advice on borrowing, however,
manages to be both vague and self-contradictory. See Kennedy, *His Word* 120–124.

38. James Stewart, *Preaching* 126.

39. Brown, *Art* 73–78.

40. Luccock, *In the Minister's Workshop* 180.

41. John Lambertson 108.

42. As David Buttrick explains, "Most of the teachers then didn't worry too
much about the Illustration books . . . but did discourage outright sermon lifting."
Letter to author, 10 Feb. 1991. Author's files. For an example of this attitude, see
Ilion Jones, *Principles* 144–148. However, on this entire subject, Jones, like
Kennedy, manages to be both vague and self-contradictory.

43. Ilion Jones, *Principles* 145, 146.

44. Every preacher I know admits that preachers often borrow. Some
preachers, however, refuse to admit that they themselves use others' sermons,
preferring to point a finger at another preacher down the street.

45. Robert Miller 337.

46. Robert Miller 337.

47. Robert Miller 338–339.

48. Florence Hamilton, Telephone Interview, 2 Feb. 1983. Sangster also heard
his sermons being preached. See Sangster, *Craft* 200.

49. Weatherhead, *In Quest* 58.

50. Biblical scholars describe this practice as "proof-texting."

51. Robert Keighton 82, 83.

52. Juanita Abernathy Interview.

53. Cleveland, "Eagle." 71.

54. Franklin, *Never Grow Old*. R.E. Winsett wrote "I'm Going Through."

55. The record jacket of *Never Grow Old* does not indicate that the recording of
"I'm Going Through" actually came at the conclusion of a sermon. But, judging
from other published sermons (such as those of Cleveland) that follow this pattern,
my own listening to folk sermons, the reaction of the congregation as recorded in
Never Grow Old, and the lack of any evidence to the contrary, I believe that the
recording of "I'm Going Through" occurred at the conclusion of a sermon.
Whatever is the case, Franklin is still engaging in voice merging through
embedding. For Jesus's remark, see Matthew 16:26 and Luke 9:25.

56. Franklin, *Never Grow Old*.

57. Franklin, *Nothing*.

58. See Branch 69–72.

59. Biblical scholars of the "demythologizing" school, such as King's professors Enslin and Pritchard, attempted to persuade their students and readers to stop
reading the Bible typologically. However, I, for one, have a hard time believing that
Christianity could survive if all vestiges of typology disappeared. By including the
Lord's Prayer and the Last Supper in their worship services, Christians typological-

ly reenact ancient events. And, as Randall Helms and others explain, Biblical writers themselves thought and wrote typologically.

60. Fosdick generally does as well, though not in "Crucified by Stupidity," which King chose as a model for "Love in Action."

61. See Branch 79, 994.

62. Compare Thurman, *Deep River* 35, 55–56 and King, Jr., *Remaining Awake.*

63. King, Jr., "Where Do We Go from Here?" 251.

64. See also King, Jr., "A Christmas Sermon" 258. There King compresses these excerpts from Amos, Micah, and First Isaiah together with another segment from Micah, eschatological imagery from Second Isaiah (who lived more than a generation after First Isaiah) that Jesus repeats; and King's familiar, poetic line from Job. To the self-respecting Biblical scholars who taught King, such preaching would amount to intellectual mayhem and historical mishmash. But King's ensemble never sounds like mishmash. The scriptural passages are Amos 5:24, Micah 6:08, Micah 4:03, Isaiah 11:06 (First Isaiah), Micah 4:04, Isaiah 40:04 (Second Isaiah), Luke 3:05, and Job 38:07.

65. See King's notes on Ropes's *Synoptic Gospels,* KC BU.

66. See Warren 105.

67. For King's use of popular sermon titles, see Appendix II.

68. See Branch 65–66 and Larry Williams Interview.

69. For Scott's experience, see Coretta King 59.

70. Although *Strength* omits concluding hymns, they appear in transcripts of the oral versions of the *Strength* sermons. Since the hymns serve as hymns of invitation, they are more appropriate to delivered sermons than to published sermons. One can only accept a hymn of invitation to join a church while attending church, not while reading a book. For speeches ending with lyrics, see, for example, "Birth," "Give Us," *Remaining Awake,* "If the Negro," "I Have a Dream," "How Long?", "A Time to Break Silence," and "Mountaintop." King scholars often ignore his use of lyrics at the end of his addresses, failing to notice the origin of this practice in the black folk pulpit and sometimes failing to notice that the lyrics are in fact lyrics.

71. In *Bearing* Garrow wisely emphasizes the importance of this experience for King.

72. King, Jr., *In Search.*

73. One editor compiled an entire book of former slaves' accounts of their conversion experiences. See Clifton Johnson.

74. See Mitchell, *Recovery* 38.

75. See King, Jr., "Autobiography."

76. King, Jr., *In Search.*

77. B.B. McKinney wrote "Never Alone."

78. King, Jr., *In Search.*

79. For example, much material from *Strength,* "Nobel Prize Lecture," and "Remaining Awake"—including substantial borrowings from Buttrick, Hamilton, and Luccock—resurfaces in the last chapter of *Where.* See King, Jr., *Where* 165–191.

CHAPTER SEVEN: VOICE MERGING IN WASHINGTON AND MONT-GOMERY

1. See Mahalia Jackson, *Movin'* 198.

2. A brief speech intervened between Jackson's solo and King's address.

3. After an extemporaneous sentence, King began "I Have a Dream" by echoing Lincoln's Gettysburg Address: "Five score years ago . . ." He also incorporated the most memorable lines from the Declaration of Independence: "unalienable rights of life, liberty, and the pursuit of happiness" and ". . . we hold these truths to be self-evident that all men are created equal." King, Jr., "I Have a Dream" 217.

4. King, Jr., "I Have a Dream" 217.

5. King, Jr., "I Have a Dream" 218, 219.

6. King, Jr., "I Have a Dream" 219.

7. King, Jr., "I Have a Dream" 219.

8. King, Jr., "I Have a Dream" 217.

9. In the early 1940s, Carey—a prominent minister in Chicago—functioned as "CORE's patron saint" (Farmer 109). Carey also corresponded with King and offered advice in dealing with the FBI. See the King/Carey correspondence in KC BU, and Garrow, *Bearing* 425, 454, 467.

10. Carey 153–154.

11. King, Jr., "I Have a Dream" 219–220.

12. I thank Suzanne Mark for this observation.

13. King, Jr., "I Have a Dream" 220.

14. See Garrow, *Bearing* 552–553, 711. Garrow reports that most of the speech was written by Vincent Harding and portions by Andrew Young and John Maguire.

15. Moody 338–339.

16. King borrowed "Making the Best of a Bad Mess" from Fosdick's sermon of the same title. Compare Fosdick, *Hope* 117–125; King, Jr., "Making the Best."

17. See Howell Raines.

18. King, Jr., *Stride* 178–179.

19. See King, Jr., "Eulogy" 221.

20. King, Jr., "Eulogy" 221–222.

21. Qtd. in Fager 85–86.

22. King, Jr., "Eulogy" 222.

23. Compare Brooks's "Why Could We Not?" 181–196; Hamilton, *Horns and Halos* 62–63; and King, Jr., *Strength* 118–126. For other parallels, see Mays, *Seeking* 24–32; Sockman, *Unemployed* 92; and E. Stanley Jones, "Christianity and Health" 71.

24. For the Beard quotation, see Fosdick, *Riverside* 156; H. Grady Davis called Beard's observation a "familiar [generalization]" (244). For Carlyle's remark, see Fosdick, *On Being Fit* 94. For the Bryant citation, see Sockman, *Paradoxes* 191–192. Fosdick termed the Bryant statement "a saying" (*Living under Tension* 247). For all or part of Lowell's verse, see Fosdick, *Successful* 223; Fosdick, *On Being Fit* 94; Fosdick, *Riverside* 99, 253; Fosdick, *Living under Tension* 220; Sockman, *Paradoxes* 192; Hamilton, *Who* 111; Sangster, *He Is Able* 49; Paul Robinson 184; and Howe 119. For the line from Shakespeare, see Fosdick, *On Being Fit* 94; Tittle, *World* 108;

Buttrick, *So We* 174; Buttrick, *Prayer* 61; and Sockman, *Date* 13. King usually attributes these quotations to their authors, but invariably fails to attribute "The arc of the moral universe . . ." to Parker or anyone else. He probably got the Parker quotation from an article in *Liberation*. Unlike King, the writer in *Liberation* did attribute the sentence to Parker. See John Haynes Holmes 5. (Articles under King's name occasionally appeared in *Liberation*.)

25. See King, Jr., *Stride* 137, 244. Jesus himself may have borrowed the proverb from a rabbinic source.

26. King, Jr., *Strength* 60, 63; King, Jr., "Mountaintop" 280.

27. For example, see King, Jr., "Facing the Challenge"; King, Jr., "Annual Address"; King, Jr., "Birth of a New Age" Aug. 1956; King, Jr., "Fragment" 13 Jan. 1958; King, Jr., "If the Negro"; King, Jr., "American Dream" 10 Feb. 1963; King, Jr., "Remaining Awake" Aug. 1965; and King, Jr., *Remaining Awake*.

28. King, Jr., "Knock," *Rhetoric* 170–171. In addition King harnessed the lines from Lowell's poem to comfort an NAACP Convention in 1956; New Yorkers who listened to "A Time to Break Silence"; Californians who heard "Transforming," which also included the aphorism from Bryant; and other audiences.

29. King, Jr., "[How Long?]" 227.

30. King, Jr., "[How Long?]" 229.

31. King, Jr., "[How Long?]" 229.

32. King, Jr., "[How Long?]" 230.

33. See Pipes 42, 118. I suspect the listeners may have been spurred partly because the phrase was familiar. Rosenberg explains how the use of formulas in the folk pulpit aids listeners who can more readily shout, clap, or dance when they can anticipate the words of a sermon. It would be difficult for a congregation to respond as gasoline to a match if the preacher's phrases were brand new.

34. King, Jr., *Strength* 64.

35. See Anthony Lewis 183–184.

CHAPTER EIGHT: LETTER FROM JAIL

1. Listen to Carawan, *Birmingham*.

2. For King's oration, listen to *Birmingham*. King distinguishes the three types of love, as delineated by the Greek words *eros, philia,* and *agape*. This discussion has become his standard analysis of love, which he borrowed from Fosdick's *On Being Fit* (6–7) and used in "Pilgrimage," "Loving Your Enemies," and elsewhere. He relied on it so often that "there were few who followed [King's] career who have not heard his favorite discourse on the meaning and significance of *eros, philia,* and *agape*" (David Lewis 44).

3. I thank John Doebler for this observation.

4. See King, Jr., *Strength* 83.

5. For the Pauline qualities of "Letter," see Snow.

6. Kelly Miller Smith 72.

7. Unhappy with what his sermons might look like in print, Niebuhr revised a fairly small number of them into "sermonic essays," which were homilies shaped into miniature theological excursions.

8. Ostensibly "Letter" is King's response to eight moderate clergy, who

wrote not a letter but a statement for a local newspaper, directing their remarks *not* to King, but to "our own white and Negro citizenry" (Snow 321). For that reason, the clergy did not invent the context for "Letter." Together with the editor of *Christian Century,* King invented the context. The comment by the clergy gave King an ostensible context that has been widely mistaken for the real context.

9. King, Jr., Letter to Harold Fey, 30 Mar. 1959, KC BU.

10. See Harold Fey, letter to King, Jr., 11 May 1959, KC BU.

11. Harold Fey, letter to King, Jr., 23 Nov. 1959, KC BU.

12. American Friends Service Committee is an arm of the Quakers.

13. King, Jr., *"Playboy"* 351.

14. Fosdick, *Hope* 5–6.

15. Crane 30, 32, 38.

16. King, Jr., "Letter," *Why* 91, 92.

17. See Moffatt. Preceding Fosdick, who published *Hope* in 1933, Luccock quoted the "colony of heaven" translation in the late 1920s. See Chapter 4. Conceivably, Luccock, Fosdick, and King were drawing on some translation other than Moffatt's, but that seems unlikely, inasmuch as Moffatt's translation appeared shortly before Luccock's book and inasmuch as the "colony of heaven" metaphor represents a decidedly unusual translation of the original passage. I thank Ernest Miller for noticing the importance of the Luccock/Fosdick/King translation from Philippians.

18. Wofford, "Non-violence and the Law" 65–66.

19. King, Jr., "Letter," *Why* 83–84.

20. Compare Wofford, "The Law" 2 and King, Jr., "Letter," *Why* 84; Wofford's "Nonviolence and the Law" 65, 68 and King, Jr., "Letter," *Why* 79, 82.

21. Kelsey, "Christian Way" 44.

22. King, Jr., "Challenge" 158–159.

23. King, Jr., "Letter," *Why* 82. For correspondences between Kelsey's text and King's *Stride* and "Challenge," compare Kelsey, "Christian Way" 29, 40, 44, 47–48; King, Jr., *Stride* 104, 205–206, 210; and King, Jr., "Challenge" 158–159, 168.

24. Compare Fosdick, *Riverside* 251–252 and King, Jr., "Letter," *Why* 77.

25. The heroes were Shadrach, Meshach, and Abednego.

26. Fulkerson makes this argument, which I summarize in this paragraph.

27. See Fulkerson 129.

28. Fulkerson 129.

29. For "tone of sadness," see Fulkerson 126. For "I cannot . . .," see King, Jr., "Letter," *Why* 93.

CHAPTER NINE: BECOMING MOSES

1. My argument in this chapter elaborates Smylie's interpretation.

2. See Lovell 535–536.

3. Wyatt Walker 57, 180.

4. Mahalia Jackson 196. Lawrence Chappell (*Voices*), Kenneth Buford (Norrell 93–94), and Ralph Abernathy (*And the Walls* 195–196) also equated segregated blacks with the Hebrews and powerful white rulers with the Pharaoh.

5. King, Jr., "Give Us" 200.

6. Qtd. in Aldon Morris 98.

7. Qtd. in Charles Hamilton 132–133.

8. King, Jr., *Where?* 170.

9. The egos of Bevel, Williams, and Walker often clashed. See Garrow, *Bearing*.

10. See Silver. KC BU.

11. See Branch 185.

12. Qtd. in Carson 21.

13. Qtd. in Branch 801.

14. King, Jr., "Suffering and Faith."

15. King, Jr., "Testament" 328.

16. Compare Fosdick, "Crucified by Stupidity" 230 to King, Jr., "Love and Forgiveness."

17. Listen to *Voices*.

18. See Oates 80.

19. See Oates 104.

20. See Branch 184.

21. See Branch 270.

22. Oates 171.

23. Donald Smith 254–255.

24. Qtd. in Carson 164.

25. Coretta King 280.

26. See Donald Smith 251.

27. See Oates 363.

28. Qtd. in Farmer, *Lay Bare* 207. Golgotha is the hill where Christ was crucified.

29. See Garrow, *Bearing* 5, 166.

30. Qtd. in Ansbro 97.

31. Qtd. in Coretta King 223.

32. Coretta King 223.

33. King, Jr., *Why* 72–73.

34. King, Jr., *Stride* 132–150.

35. See Farmer, *Lay Bare* 207 and Oates 308.

36. Qtd. in Oates 280.

37. See Garrow, *FBI* 215–219.

38. See Garrow, *Bearing* 431–627.

39. See King, Sr., *Daddy King* 190.

40. See King, Sr., *Daddy King* and Farris.

41. R.D. Nesbitt, Letter to King, 19 Apr. 1954, KC BU.

42. Rosa Parks, Letter to King, 26 Aug. 1955, KC BU.

43. See various issues of *MIA Newsletter*, KC BU.

44. Correspondence reflecting these patterns is included in KC BU.

45. For a list of these board members, see King, Jr., *Stride* 225.

46. I confess that this statement rests on an impression, not on a detailed statistical analysis of headlines.

47. See Wilkins 319.

48. See Oates 357, 412.
49. See Smylie.
50. King, Jr., "Mountaintop" 279.
51. King, Jr., "Mountaintop" 279–280.
52. King, Jr., "Mountaintop" 280.
53. King, Jr., "Mountaintop" 280.
54. King, Jr., "Mountaintop" 280–281.
55. King, Jr., "Mountaintop" 281.
56. King, Jr., "Mountaintop" 281.
57. King, Jr., "Mountaintop" 281.
58. King, Jr., "Mountaintop" 282.
59. King, Jr., "Mountaintop" 282.
60. King, Jr., "Mountaintop" 282.
61. King, Jr., "Mountaintop" 282.
62. King's account of the Jericho road is an adaptation of Buttrick's description that King used before in "On Being."
63. King, Jr., "Mountaintop" 280.
64. King, Jr., "Mountaintop" 286.
65. Qtd. in Levine 51.
66. Abernathy, And the Walls 613–620.
67. Abernathy, And the Walls 501, 503.
68. Coretta King 345.
69. Coretta King 206.
70. Coretta King 240.
71. Coretta King 249.
72. William Miller 314.

CHAPTER TEN: ALCHEMIZING IRON INTO GOLD

1. See Luccock, Marching 129–137. King sometimes preached this sermon under Luccock's title. He also used the Van Winkle illustration in Where? 170–171.
2. See Buttrick, Parables 127–129, 137–146; King, Jr., "Dives and Lazarus"; and King, Jr., "Sleeping."
3. Not everyone has joined the chorus of admiration. As late as 1990, Barry Goldwater stated that he would still vote against the 1964 Civil Rights Act and other major civil rights legislation. See Goldwater Discussion.
4. Mitchell, Black Preaching 13.
5. For the best account of the evolution of "We Shall Overcome," see Reagon, "Songs" 65–71.
6. Reagon, "Songs" 70–75.
7. See Reagon, "Songs" 76–82.
8. Buttrick, however, did not isolate himself from leftist politics. He "lunched weekly with Harlem clergy," and Norman Thomas and A.J. Muste were "fairly frequent visitors" at his home. See Letter to author. David Buttrick, 10 Feb. 1991, Author's files.
9. In this respect, preachers resemble thousands of teachers—including English teachers—who routinely borrow each other's jokes, lectures, syllabi,

assignments, and entire courses while almost never acknowledging their sources. Many of these same teachers violate copyright laws almost daily as they reproduce essays and other materials for their classes, doing so without permission and without paying any copyright fees. Many of these same teachers fail students who plagiarize.

10. See the correspondence between King and McCracken, KC BU.

11. See King, Jr., "Man Who Was a Fool," *Pulpit.*

12. See Hamilton, Florence, Letter to author, 20 Feb. 1983, Author's files; and Florence Hamilton Interview. Hamilton, however, never knew that King borrowed his sermons.

13. Wofford Interview. Carey and Wofford had good reason to be pleased that King borrowed their words. After all, Carey never made a presentation approaching the quality of "I Have a Dream," and Wofford never wrote anything as good as "Letter from Birmingham Jail."

14. I thank Barbara Urrea for this observation.

15. The provocative and radical nature of "A Time to Break Silence" distinguished it from King's other ghostwritten speeches. One policy speech that fell flat was an antiwar address heard by one hundred thousand antiwar protestors. See King, Jr., "Address at U.N. Plaza"; David Halberstam, "When 'Civil Rights'" 187; and Garrow, *Bearing* 556–557.

16. For the impact of the civil rights movement on the growth of feminism, see Mary King and Sara Evans.

APPENDIX TWO: PRECEDENTS FOR TITLES OF KING'S SERMONS

1. See Fosdick, *Hope* 112.

2. Sockman, Jones, Buttrick, Tittle, and Crane all published sermons in this series.

3. See Fosdick, *Meaning of Faith* 51; Brown, *Working Faith* 4–5; Weatherhead, *Why Do Men* 79; Tittle, *Mighty* xxxii; and Johns 73. Fosdick and Brown cite F.W. Myers's use of the phrase.

4. In this sermon King acknowledges Fosdick as the source for his title.

5. Located at KC BU.

WORKS CITED

INTERVIEWS

Abernathy, Juanita. Miller, 21 Aug. 1990, Atlanta.
Borders, William Holmes. Miller, 1 July 1987, Atlanta.
Buttrick, David. Miller, Aug. 1983, Nashville.
Brink, Eugene. Miller, 11 Aug. 1989, Colorado Springs.
Edwards, J.H. Miller, 30 June 1987 and 3 Aug. 1987, Atlanta.
Edwards, J.H. Miller, Aug. 1990, Atlanta.
English, Jethro. Miller, Aug. 1989, Atlanta.
Farmer, James. Miller, 1 June 1985, Columbus, Ohio.
Goldwater, Barry. Miller, 1 March 1990, Class Discussion at Arizona State
    University, Tempe, Arizona.
Hamilton, Florence. Miller, 2 Feb. 1983. St. Petersburg, Florida. Phone.
Heard, Fannie Lou. Miller, March 1983, Atlanta.
Henderson, Arthur and Laura Henderson. Miller, 30 June 1987, Atlanta.
Henderson, Laura. Judy Barton, 10 Dec. 1971, Atlanta. OHC KC A.
Henderson, Laura. Judy Barton, 7 March 1972, Atlanta. OHC KC A.
Kelsey, George. Miller, 28 July 1989, New York City. Phone.
Kemp, James. Miller, Aug. 1989, Atlanta.
King, Sr., Martin Luther. Miller and Candadai Sesachari, 15 March 1983, Atlanta.
Maser, Frederick. Miller, 28 Feb. 1990, Scottsdale, Arizona.
Mays, Benjamin. Miller and Candadai Sesachari, 14 March 1983, Atlanta.
Mays, Benjamin. Miller, Aug. 1983, Atlanta.

McCall, Walter. Herbert Holmes, 31 March 1970, Atlanta. OHC KC A.
Miller, Ernest. Miller, 21 Dec. 1989, McAllen, Texas.
Reed, Sarah. Miller, June 1987, Atlanta.
Roberts, Joseph. Miller, March 1983, Atlanta.
Taylor, Gardner. Miller, Jan. 1987, New York City. Phone.
Watson, Melvin. Ralph Luker, [circa 1986], Atlanta.
Watson, Melvin. Miller, 1 July 1987, Atlanta.
Williams, Larry. Miller, 17 Aug. 1989, Atlanta. Phone.
Wofford, Harris. Miller, 2 Nov. 1988, Harrisburg, Pennsylvania. Phone.

ABERNATHY, RALPH. *And the Walls Came Tumbling Down.* New York: Harper, 1989.

———. "My Last Letter to Martin." *And the Walls.* 613–620.

ALLEN, RICHARD. "An Address to Those Who Keep Slaves. . . ." *The Life Experience and Gospel Labors of the Right Reverend Richard Allen.* New York: Abingdon, 1960. 69–71.

ALVAREZ, ALEXANDRA. "Martin Luther King's 'I Have a Dream': The Speech Event as Metaphor." *Journal of Black Studies* 18 (1988): 337–357.

ANDROZZO, ALMA. *If I Can Help Somebody.* Arr. Kenneth Morris. Chicago: n.p., 1945. RSD LC.

ANSBRO, JOHN. *Martin Luther King, Jr.: The Making of a Mind.* Maryknoll, NY: Orbis Books, 1982.

ASANTE, MOLEFI. *The Afrocentric Idea.* Philadelphia: Temple University Press, 1987.

AUSTIN, EUGENE. "Peril of Conformity." *Pulpit* 23 (1952): 13–15.

BABBAGE, JOHN. "Man the Enigma." Butler, *Best Sermons: 1949–50 Edition.* 64–68.

BABBAGE, MARGARET. "Dr. James Wallace Hamilton." *Golden Jubilee: Our First Half Century.* Ed. William Gillis. St. Petersburg, FL: Pasadena Community Church, 1975. Author's files.

BARTON, L.E. "Three Dimensions of Love." *Three Dimensions of Love and Other Sermons.* Boston: Gorham 1929. 9–18.

BEECHER, HENRY WARD. "Through Fear to Love." *The Original Plymouth Pulpit.* Vol. 9. Boston: Pilgrim, 1873. 451–467.

BENNETT, JOHN C. *Christianity and Communism.* New York: Association, 1948.

BENNETT, LERONE. *What Manner of Man.* Chicago: Johnson, 1964.

BINGA, A. JR. *Sermons on Several Occasions: Volume I.* N.p.: n.p., 1889. LC.

BONNELL, JOHN SUTHERLAND. "Easter Dawn." *Best Sermons: 1947–1948 Edition.* Ed. G. Paul Butler. New York: Harper, 1947. 92–98.

———. *Fifth Avenue Sermons.* New York: Harper, 1936.

———. "Is the Universe Friendly to Man?" *Fifth Avenue Sermons.* 1–12.

———. "Never Strike a Flag to Fear." *Certainties for Uncertain Times.* New York: Harper, 1956. 21–23.

———. *What Are You Living For?* New York: Abingdon-Cokesbury, 1950.

BONNELL, JOHN SUTHERLAND, et al. *He Speaks from the Cross*. Westwood, NJ: Revell, 1963.

BORDERS, WILLIAM HOLMES. "Communism, Capitalism, and Christianity—The Greatest of These Is Which?" *Television Sermons*. Atlanta: OIC Printers, n.d. [c. 1971]. Author's files.

———. *Men Must Live as Brothers*. N.p.: n.p., n.d. [c. 1946] LC.

———. *Seven Minutes at the 'Mike' in the Deep South*. 1943. Atlanta: Arnold's Printing Service, 1980. Author's files.

———. *Television Sermons*. Atlanta: OIC Printers, n.d. [c. 1971]. Author's files.

———. "What Is Man?" *Seven Minutes*. 13–15.

———. *World Unity and 19 Other Sermons*. Atlanta: Morris Brown College Press, n.d. Author's files.

BOSLEY, HAROLD. *The Character of Christ*. New York: Abingdon, 1967.

———. *Doing What Is Christian*. Nashville: Graded, 1960.

———. *A Firm Faith for Today*. New York: Harper, 1950.

———. *Sermons On Genesis*. New York: Abingdon, 1958.

BOSMAJIAN, HAIG. "The Letter from Birmingham Jail." *Martin Luther King, Jr.: A Profile*. Ed. C. Eric Lincoln. New York: Hill, 1984.

BRANCH, TAYLOR. *Parting the Waters: America in the King Years 1954–63*. New York: Simon & Schuster, 1988.

BRATCHER, ALFRED. "The Meaning of the Christian Way and Ideals in International Relations." Bratcher, *Eighty-Three Years*. 49–53.

———. ed. *Eighty-Three Years: The Moving Story of Church Growth*. Montgomery, AL: Paragon, 1950. 49–53. SC.

BREITMAN, GEORGE. HEADNOTE. "Message to the Grassroots." *Malcolm X Speaks*. New York: Grove, 1965.

BROOKS, PHILLIPS. "Egyptians Dead Upon the Seashore." *Selected Sermons*. Ed. William Scarlett. New York: Dutton, 1950. 105–111.

———. "The Symmetry of Life." *Selected Sermons*. 195–206.

———. "Why Could We Not Cast Him Out?" *Sermons Preached in English Churches*. New York: Macmillan, 1906. 181–196.

"The Brotherhood of Man." *Sermons, Addresses and Reminiscences and Important Correspondence*. Ed. E.C. Morris. Nashville: National Baptist Publishing Board, 1901. 36–41. LC.

BROWN, CHARLES REYNOLDS. *Art of Preaching*. New York: Macmillan, 1922.

———. *Finding Ourselves*. New York: Harper, 1935.

———. "The Jericho Road." *Where Do You Live?*. New Haven, CT: Yale University Press, 1926. 32–47.

———. *Social Message of the Modern Pulpit*. New York: Scribner's, 1906.

———. "What Value Has the Right Motive?" *A Working Faith*. Chapel Hill: University of North Carolina Press, 1926. 88–129.

———. "Where Do We Go from Here?" *The Gospel for Main Street.* New York: Century, 1930.

BUTLER, G. PAUL, ed. *Best Sermons: 1944 Selection.* New York: Davis, 1944.

———, ed. *Best Sermons: 1946 Edition.* New York: Harper, 1946.

———, ed. *Best Sermons: 1947–1948 Edition.* New York: Harper, 1947.

———, ed. *Best Sermons: 1949–1950 Edition.* New York: Harper, 1949.

———, ed. *Best Sermons: 1951–1952 Edition.* New York: Macmillan, 1952.

———, ed. *Best Sermons: 1955 Edition.* New York: McGraw-Hill, 1955.

———, ed. *Best Sermons: Vol. 7 1959–1960.* New York: Crowell, 1959.

———, ed. *Best Sermons: Vol. 8 1962.* Princeton, NJ: Van Nostrand, 1962.

———, ed. *Best Sermons: Volume 9 1964 Protestant Edition.* Princeton, N.J.: Van Nostrand, 1964.

BUTTRICK, GEORGE. "Anxiety and Faith." *Sermons Preached at a University Church.* New York: Abingdon, 1959. 37–43.

———. *The Christian Fact and Modern Doubt.* New York: Scribner's, 1934.

———. "Gospel of Immortality." *A Treasury of Great Sermons.* Ed. Daniel Poling. New York: Greenberg, 1944. 186–191.

———, ed. *Interpreter's Bible:* Vols 1–12. New York: Abingdon-Cokesbury, 1951.

———. *Parables of Jesus.* New York: Harper, 1928.

———. *Prayer.* New York: Abingdon-Cokesbury, 1942.

———. *So We Believe, So We Pray.* New York: Abingdon-Cokesbury, 1951.

CALHOUN, ROBERT. *What Is Man?* New York: Association, 1939.

CARAWAN, GUY, AND CANDIE CARAWAN. *Birmingham, Alabama, 1963: Mass Meeting.* Folkways Records 5487.

CAREY, ARCHIBALD. "Address to the Republican National Convention." *Rhetoric of Racial Revolt.* Ed. Roy Hill. Denver: Golden Bell, 1964. 149–54.

CARRINGTON, WILLIAM O. *Carry a Little Honey.* New York: Revell, 1936.

CARSON, CLAYBORNE. *In Struggle: SNCC and the Black Awakening of the 1960s.* Cambridge: Harvard University Press, 1981.

CHALMERS, ALLAN KNIGHT. *Constant Fire.* New York: Scribner's, 1944.

———. *High Wind at Noon.* New York: Scribner's, 1948.

CLEVELAND, E.O.S. "Dry Bones in the Valley." *The Eagle Stirring Her Nest.* N.p.: n.p., 1946. 31–37. SC.

———. "The Eagle Stirring Her Nest." *The Eagle Stirring Her Nest.* 63–71.

CONE, JAMES. *Martin and Malcolm and America.* Maryknoll, NY: Orbis, 1991.

———. "Martin Luther King, Jr., Black Theology—Black Church." *Theology Today* 40 (1984): 409–420.

———. *The Spirituals and the Blues.* New York: Seabury, 1972.

———. "The Theology of Martin Luther King, Jr." *Union Seminary Quarterly Review* 40 (1986): 21–39.

COPPIN, L.J. *Fifty Years of Religious Progress: An Emancipation Sermon.* Philadelphia: African Methodist Episcopal Book Co., 1913. SC.

CRANE, H.H. "Thermometers Versus Thermostats." Motter, *Great Preaching Today.* 30–39.

CROSS, FRANK, et al. "George Buttrick." *Harvard Gazette* 15 April 1983: 7, 15. Author's files.

DAVIS, H. GRADY. *Design For Preaching.* Philadelphia: Muhlenberg, 1958.

DAVIS, GERALD. *I Got the Word in Me and I Can Sing It, You Know.* Philadelphia: University of Pennsylvania Press, 1985.

DICKERSON, MAHALA. "The Task of Christian Citizenship." Bratcher, *Eighty-Three Years.* 89–93.

DOUGLASS, FREDERICK. *The Life and Times of Frederick Douglass.* 1892. London: Collier-Macmillan, 1962.

DOWNING, FREDERICK. *To See the Promised Land.* Macon, GA: Mercer University Press, 1986.

"Dr. George A. Buttrick, 87, Renowned Preacher, Scholar." *Boston Globe* 3 Feb. 1980: 53.

"Dry Bones." Tennessee. 1942. Tape 6685 B, 6686 B, 6687 A-D, 6688 A, B. (Possibly recorded by John Henry Falk.) AFC LC.

DUBERMAN, MARTIN. *Paul Robeson: A Biography.* New York: Ballantine, 1989.

DUBOIS, W.E.B., ed. *The Negro Church.* Atlanta: Atlanta University Press, 1903.

———. *The Souls of Black Folk.* 1903. Greenwich, CT: Fawcett, 1961.

ELLISON, JOHN. "The More Excellent Way." Butler, *Best Sermons: 1949–1950.* 258–265.

ENGLISH, JAMES. *The Prophet of Wheat Street: The Story of William Holmes Borders, a Man Who Refused to Fail.* 1967. Elgin, IL: Cook, 1973. (Also published as *Handyman of the Lord.*)

EVANS, SARA. *Personal Politics.* New York: Random House, 1979.

FAGER, CHARLES. *Selma 1965.* New York: Scribner's, 1974.

FAIRCLOUGH, ADAM. *To Redeem the Soul of America: The Southern Christian Leadership Conference and Martin Luther King., Jr.* Athens: University of Georgia Press, 1987.

FARRIS, CHRISTINE KING. "The Young Martin: From Childhood through College." *Ebony* 41 (1986): 56–58.

FARMER, JAMES. *Lay Bare the Heart: An Autobiography of the Civil Rights Movement.* New York: Arbor House, 1985.

FERGUSON, JOHN. "Our God Is Able." *Our God Is Able.* Nashville: Men's Club, Belmont Methodist Church, 1951. 9–21.

FISHER, MILES MARK. *Negro Slave Songs in the United States*. 1953. New York: Citadel, 1969.

FOSDICK, HARRY EMERSON. *Adventurous Religion*. New York: Grossett, 1946.

———. *As I See Religion*. New York: Harper, 1932. (Also published by Grossett).

———. "Christianity and War." *Best Sermons, 1926*. Ed. Joseph Fort Newton. New York: Harcourt, 1926. 1–18.

———. "Christianity's Stake in the Social Situation." *Hope of the World*. 21–29.

———. "Constructive Use of Fear." *On Being Fit*. 125–133.

———. "Conquest of Fear." *Hope of the World*. 59–68.

———. "The Cross and the Ordinary Man." *Successful Christian Living*. 200–219.

———. "Crucified by Stupidity." *Hope of the World*. 222–230.

———. "Dealing with Fear and Anxiety." *On Being a Real Person*. New York: Harper, 1943. 108–132.

———. *Dear Mr. Brown: Letters to a Person Perplexed About Religion*. New York: Harper, 1961.

———. *A Great Time to Be Alive: Sermons on Christianity in Wartime*. New York: Harper, 1944.

———. *Hope of the World*. New York: Harper, 1933.

———. "How Believe in a Good God in a World Like This?" *Living under Tension*. 213–221.

———. *The Living of These Days*. New York: Harper, 1936.

———. *Living under Tension*. New York: Harper, 1941.

———. *The Meaning of Faith*. New York: Abingdon, 1917.

———. *On Being Fit to Live With*. New York: Harper, 1946.

———. *Riverside Sermons*. New York: Harper, 1958.

———. *Successful Christian Living*. New York: Harper, 1937.

———. "Through the Social Gospel into Personal Religion." *Hope of the World*. 30–38.

———. *What Is Vital in Religion*. New York: Harper, 1955.

FOX, RICHARD. *Reinhold Niebuhr: A Biography*. New York: Pantheon, 1985.

FRANCIS, JAMES ALLEN. *Christ Is All*. Philadelphia: Judson, 1928.

FRANKLIN, C.L. "Dry Bones in the Valley." *Give Me This Mountain*. 80–88.

———. *The Eagle Stirs Her Nest*. Jewel LPS 0083, 1973. Author's Collection.

———. *The Eagle Stirring Her Nest*. Chess, 61, 62, 63. Deutch; DLC 85 1363–1369. Author's Collection.

———. *Give Me This Mountain*. Ed. Jeff Todd Titon. Urbana: University of Illinois Press, 1989.

———. *Moses at the Red Sea*. Chess 19, ca. mid-1950s. Author's Collection.

———. "Moses at the Red Sea." *Give Me This Mountain*. 107–113.

——. *Never Grow Old.* Checker 10083, n.d.; Chess 9145, 1984. Author's Collection.

——. *Nothing Shall Separate Me from the Love of God.* Chess CH 9154, n.d. Author's Collection.

FRANKLIN, V.P. *Black Self-Determination.* Westport, CT: Hill, 1984.

FULKERSON, RICHARD. "The Public Letter as a Rhetorical Form: Structure, Logic, and Style in King's 'Letter from Birmingham Jail.'" *Quarterly Journal of Speech* 65 (1979): 121–136.

"A Gandhi Society?" *Christian Century* 79 (1962): 735–736.

GARROW, DAVID. *Bearing the Cross: Martin Luther King, Jr., and the Southern Christian Leadership Conference.* New York: Morrow, 1986.

——. *The FBI and Martin Luther King, Jr.* New York: Norton, 1981.

——. "The Intellectual Development of Martin Luther King, Jr.: Influences and Commentaries." *Union Seminary Quarterly Review* 40 (1986): 5–20.

——. *Protest at Selma.* New Haven, CT: Yale University Press, 1978.

GATES, J. M. *Dry Bones in the Valley.* Victor I, 35810-A, DLC 0242/1549, n.d. RSD LC.

——. *The Eagle Stirs Her Nest.* Matrix, 400302-B, Okeh 8582. 22 Feb. 1928. RSD LC.

——. *Moses in the Wilderness.* Matrix, 3649-1, Vi 20421. 2 Dec. 1926. RSD LC.

GENOVESE, EUGENE. *Roll, Jordan, Roll.* New York: Vintage, 1976.

GLADDEN, WASHINGTON. "Remarks of Washington Gladden." *The Negro Church.* Ed. W.E.B. DuBois. Atlanta: Atlanta UP, 1903. 204–207.

——. *Where Does the Sky Begin?* Boston: Houghton. 1904.

GREGG, RICHARD. *The Power of Nonviolence.* Nyack, NY: Fellowship, 1959.

GRIMKE, FRANCIS. *The Negro: His Rights and Wrongs.* Washington, D.C.: n.p., 1898. SC.

HALBERSTAM, DAVID. "Second Coming of Martin Luther King." *Harper's* 1967. Rpt. as "When 'Civil Rights' and 'Peace' Join Forces" in Lincoln, *Martin Luther King, Jr.* 187–211.

HALLOCK, G.B.F. *New Sermon Illustrations for All Occasions.* Westwood, NJ: Revell, 1953.

HAMILTON, CHARLES. *The Black Preacher in America.* New York: Morrow, 1972.

HAMILTON, J. WALLACE. *Drum-Major Instincts.* St. Petersburg, FL: Sermon Publication Committee of Pasadena Community Church, 1949. Author's files.

——. "Drum-Major Instincts." *Ride the Wild Horses!* 26–38.

——. "The First Word." Bonnell, et al. *He Speaks from the Cross.* 11–23.

——. *Horns and Halos in Human Nature.* Westwood, NJ: Revell, 1954.

——. "Make a Friend of Your Fear." *Ride the Wild Horses!* 101–111.

——. "Remember Who You Are." *Horns and Halos.* 46–55.

——. *Ride the Wild Horses!* Westwood, NJ: Revell, 1952.

———. *The Thunder of Bare Feet.* Westwood, NJ: Revell, 1964.

———. "Unwilling Missionaries." *American Pulpit Series.* Vol. 9. New York: Abingdon-Cokesbury, 1946. 87–102.

———. *What About Tomorrow?* Ed. Florence Hamilton. Old Tappan, NJ: Revell, 1972.

———. *Who Goes There? What and Where Is God?* Westwood, NJ: Revell, 1958.

HANDY, ROBERT. *Christian America: Protestant Hopes and Historical Realities.* New York: Oxford University Press, 1984.

HARLAND, GORDON. *The Thought of Reinhold Niebuhr.* New York: Oxford University Press, 1960.

HARRINGTON, DONALD. *What Religious Liberals Believe about Man.* New York: Community Church, n.d. [circa 1956]. KC BU.

HASELDEN, KYLE. *The Racial Problem in Christian Perspective.* New York: Harper, 1959.

HEILBUT, TONY. *The Gospel Sound.* New York: Simon and Schuster: 1971.

HEIMSATH, CHARLES. *Sermons on the Inner Life.* Nashville: Cokesbury, 1940.

HELMS, RANDEL. *Gospel Fictions.* Buffalo, NY: Prometheus, 1988.

HICKERSON, CLYDE. "Can We Love Our Enemies Now?" *American Pulpit Series.* Vol. 5. New York: Abingdon-Cokesbury, 1945. 68–72.

HOLMES, JOHN HAYNES. "Salute to Montgomery." *Liberation* Dec. 1956. 5.

HOLT, GRACE. "Stylin' Outta the Black Pulpit." *Rappin' and Stylin' Out: Communication in Urban Black America.* Ed. Thomas Kochman. Urbana: University of Illinois Press, 1972. 189–204.

HOMRIGHAUSEN, E.G. "The Dimensions of the Christian Life." *American Pulpit Series.* Vol. 5. New York: Abingdon-Cokesbury, 1945. 78–99.

HOWE, LAURENCE. "As We Behold His Glory." *American Pulpit Series.* Vol. 5. New York: Abingdon-Cokesbury, 1945. 110–124.

HUGHES, LANGSTON AND ARNA BONTEMPS. *The Book of Negro Folklore.* New York: Dodd, 1958.

JACKSON, JESSE. Foreword. Franklin, *Give Me This Mountain.* vii–viii.

JACKSON, MAHALIA (WITH EVAN WYLIE). *Movin' on Up.* New York: Hawthorn, 1966.

"James Wallace Hamilton —May 4, 1900–Oct. 7, 1968." *Parish Visitor* 7 (Oct.– Nov. 1968): 1, 3. Author's files.

JENNEY, RAY. "God's Unashamed." Butler, *Best Sermons: 1947–1948 Edition.* 37–44.

JOHNS, VERNON. *Human Possibilities: A Vernon Johns Reader.* Ed. Samuel Gandy. Washington, DC: Hoffman, 1977.

———. "Transfigured Moments." *Best Sermons, 1926.* Ed. Joseph Fort Newton. New York: Harcourt. 1926.

JOHNSON, CLIFTON, ed. *God Struck Me Dead: Religious Conversion Experiences and Autobiographies of Ex-Slaves.* Philadelphia: Pilgrim, 1969.

JOHNSON, MORDECAI. "Heart of the Matter." *Education for Freedom: The Leadership of*

Mordecai Wyatt Johnson Howard University 1926–1960. Washington, DC: Howard University Archives, 1976. 52–58. MJC M-S.

———. "A Pathway to World Peace." *Education for Freedom: The Leadership of Mordecai Wyatt Johnson Howard University 1926–1960.* Washington, DC: Howard University Archives, 1976. MJC M-S.

JONES, ABSALOM. *A Thanksgiving Sermon.* Philadelphia: Fry, 1808. SC.

JONES, E. STANLEY. "Basis of These Fears." *Victorious Living.* New York: Abingdon-Cokesbury, 1936. 213–214.

———. "Between Individualism and Communism—The Kingdom." *Mastery.* 117.

———. *Christ at the Round Table.* New York: Abingdon, 1928.

———. *Christ of the Indian Road.* New York: Abingdon, 1925.

———. *Christ's Alternative to Communism.* New York: Abingdon, 1935. (Also published as *Christ and Communism.*)

———. "Christianity and Health." Motter, *Great Preaching Today.* 71–81.

———. "A Comparison between Naziism, Fascism, Communism, and Christianity." *The Choice Before Us.* New York: Abingdon, 1937.

———. *How to Be a Transformed Person.* New York: Abingdon, 1941.

———. "Jesus Comes Through Irregular Channels—Mahatma Gandhi's Part." *Christ of the Indian Road.* 73–86.

———. *Mahatma Gandhi: An Interpretation.* New York: Abingdon-Cokesbury, 1948.

———. *Mastery.* New York: Abingdon, 1955.

———. "Mastery of Fear." *Mastery.* 152.

———. "Steps Out of Fear." *Growing Spiritually.* New York: Abingdon-Cokesbury, 1953. 39–46.

———. "Steps Out of Fear." *How To Be a Transformed Person.* 162–167.

———. "Steps Out of Fear." *The Way to Power and Poise.* New York: Abingdon, 1949. 225–232.

———. "Why Has Communism Failed?" *Mastery.* 116.

JONES, ILION. *Principles and Practice of Preaching.* New York: Abingdon, 1956.

KEIGHTON, ROBERT E. *The Man Who Would Preach.* New York: Abingdon, 1956.

KELSEY, GEORGE. "The Christian Way in Race Relations." Nelson, *The Christian Way in Race Relations.* 29–50.

KENNEDY, GERALD. *The Christian and His America.* New York: Harper, 1956.

———. "Creation by Explosion." Butler, *Best Sermons: Vol. 8 1962.* 63–72.

———. *His Word Through Preaching.* New York: Harper, 1947.

———. "The Mind and the Heart." *The Lion and the Lamb: Paradoxes of the Christian Faith.* New York: Abingdon-Cokesbury, 1950.

———. *A Reader's Notebook.* New York: Harper, 1953.

———. *While I'm on My Feet.* New York: Abingdon, 1963.

—. *With Singleness of Heart.* New York: Harper, 1951.

KING, BASIL. *The Conquest of Fear.* New York: Doubleday, 1948.

KING, CORETTA. *My Life with Martin Luther King, Jr.* New York: Holt, 1969.

KING, MARTIN, LUTHER, JR. "Address at the U.N. Plaza." New York, NY. 15 April 1967. KC A.

—. "Address to Holt Street Baptist Church." Montgomery, AL. 5 Dec. 1955. KC A.

—. "Annual Address." Montgomery, AL. 3 Dec. 1956. KC A.

—. "American Dream." Brooklyn. 10 Feb. 1963. KC A.

—. "American Dream." 6 June 1961. KC A.

—. "The American Dream: Part II." *The Wisdom of King.* Audiofidelity Enterprises, AFE-3-1, n.d.

—. "Answer to a Perplexing Question." *Strength to Love.* 118–26.

—. "Antidotes for Fear." *Strength to Love.* 108–117.

—. "Autobiography of Religious Development." N.D. [circa 1949]. KC BU. Rpt. in Warren, 269–284.

—. "Beyond Vietnam." New York, NY. 4 April 1967. KC A.

—. "Birth of a New Age." 7 Aug. 1956. KC A.

—. "A Challenge to the Churches and Synagogues." *Race: A Challenge to Religion.* Ed. Matthew Ahmann. Chicago: Regnery, 1963. 155–169.

—. "A Christmas Sermon on Peace." *Testament of Hope.* 253–258.

—. "Death of Evil on the Seashore." New York, NY. 17 May 1956. KC A.

—. "Death of Evil on the Seashore." *Strength to Love.* 58–65.

—. "Discerning the Signs of the Time." Atlanta. 15 Nov. 1964. KC A.

—. "Dimensions of a Complete Life." Chicago. 19 April 1959. KC A.

—. "Desirability of Being Maladjusted." Chicago. 13 April 1958. KC A.

—. "Dives and Lazarus." Atlanta. 10 March 1963. KC A.

—. "Drum Major Instinct." *Testament of Hope.* 259–267.

—. "Eulogy for the Martyred Children." *Testament of Hope.* 221–223.

—. "Facing the Challenge of a New Age." *Phylon* 28 (1957) 25–34. Rpt. in *Testament of Hope.* 135–144.

—. Foreword. Gregg, *Power of Nonviolence.*

—. "Fragment." 9 Feb. 1957. KC A.

—. "Fragment." 13 Jan. 1958. KC A.

—. "Give Us the Ballot." *Testament of Hope.* 197–200.

—. "Good Samaritan." Atlanta. 28 Aug. 1965. KC A.

—. ["How Long?"] *Testament of Hope.* 227–230.

—. "How Should a Christian View Communism?" *Strength to Love.* 93–100.

——. "I Have a Dream." *Testament of Hope.* 217–220.

——. "If the Negro Wins, Labor Wins." *Testament of Hope.* 201–207.

——. *In Search of Freedom.* Mercury Records, SR 1170, n.d.

——. "Interruptions." Atlanta. 21 Jan. 1968. KC A.

——. "Is the Universe Friendly?" Atlanta. 12 Dec. 1965. KC A.

——. "[I've Been to the Mountaintop]." *Testament of Hope,* pp. 279–288.

——. "A Knock at Midnight." *Rhetoric of Christian Socialism.* Ed. Paul Boase. New York: Random, 1969. 162–171.

——. "A Knock at Midnight." *Strength to Love.* 42–50.

——. *Letter from Birmingham City Jail.* Philadelphia: American Friends Service Committee, 1963. Rpt. in *Nonviolence in America: A Documentary History.* Ed. Staughton Lynd. Indianapolis: Bobbs-Merrill, 1966. 461–481.

——. "Letter from Birmingham Jail." *Christian Century* 80 (1963): 767–773.

——. "Letter from Birmingham Jail." *Why We Can't Wait.* 76–95.

——. "Love in Action." *Strength to Love.* 25–33.

——. "Love and Forgiveness." 1966. KC A.

——. "Loving Your Enemies." *Strength to Love.* 34–41.

——. "Making the Best of a Bad Mess." Atlanta. 24 April 1966. KC A.

——. "The Man Who Was a Fool." *Pulpit,* 32 (1961): 4–6

——. "The Man Who Was a Fool." *Strength to Love.* 51–57.

——. "The Meaning of Hope." Montgomery, AL. 10 Dec. 1967. KC A.

——. "Merits of Maladjustment." *New York Amsterdam News.* 19 Jan. 1963. KC A.

——. "The Montgomery Story." San Francisco. 27 June 1956. KC A.

——. "The Most Durable Power." *Christian Century* 74 (1957): 708–709.

——. "Nobel Prize Lecture." Oslo, Norway. 11 Dec. 1964. KC A.

——. "Nonconformist—Julian Bond." Atlanta. 16 Jan. 1966. KC A.

——. "On Being a Good Neighbor." *Strength to Love.* 16–24.

——. "Our God Is Able." *Strength to Love.* 101–107.

——. "Paul's Letter to American Christians." *Strength to Love.* 127–134.

——. "Pilgrimage to Nonviolence." *Stride Toward Freedom.* 90–107.

——. "Pilgrimage to Nonviolence." *Testament of Hope.* 35–40.

——. "*Playboy* Interview." *Testament of Hope.* 340–377.

——. "Prodigal Son." Atlanta. 4 Sept. 1966. KC A.

——. *Remaining Awake through a Great Revolution.* Creed Records, 3024, n.d.

——. "Remember Who You Are." 7 July 1963. Atlanta. KC A.

——. "Shattered Dreams." *Strength to Love.* 78–86.

——. "Sleeping through a Revolution." Chicago. 10 Dec. 1967.

————. "Sleeping through a Revolution." Washington, D.C. 31 March 1968. KC A.

————. "Standing by the Best in an Evil Time." Atlanta. 6 Aug. 1967. KC A.

————. "Statement: Death of Julia P. Borders." 24 Oct. 1965. KC A.

————. *Strength to Love.* New York: Harper & Row, 1963.

————. *Stride Toward Freedom: The Montgomery Story.* New York: Harper, 1958.

————. "Suffering and Faith." *Christian Century* 77 (1960): 510.

————. *Testament of Hope: The Essential Writings of Martin Luther King, Jr.* Ed. James Washington. New York: Harper, 1986.

————. "Three Dimensions of a Complete Life." *Strength to Love.* 67–77.

————. "A Time to Break Silence." *Testament of Hope.* 231–244.

————. "To Serve the Present Age." Los Angeles. 25 June 1967. KC A.

————. "A Tough Mind and a Tender Heart." *Pulpit.* 33 (1963) 1–3.

————. "A Tough Mind and a Tender Heart." *Strength to Love.* 1–7.

————. "Transformed Nonconformist." *Strength to Love."* 8–15.

————. "Transforming a Neighborhood into a Brotherhood." San Francisco. 10 Aug. 1967. KC A.

————. *Trumpet of Conscience.* New York: Harper, 1968.

————. "What Is Man?" Chicago. 12 Jan. 1958. KC A.

————. "What Is Man?" *Strength to Love.* 87–92.

————. *Where Do We Go From Here: Chaos or Community?* 1967. Boston: Beacon, 1968.

————. "Who Are We?" 5 Feb. 1966. Atlanta. KC A.

————. *Why We Can't Wait.* New York: Harper, 1963.

KING, MARTIN LUTHER, SR. (WITH CLAYTON RILEY). *Daddy King: An Autobiography.* New York: William Morrow, 1980.

KING, MARY. *Freedom Song.* New York: Morrow, 1987.

LAMBERTSON, JOHN. *Theory of Sermon Illustration as Revealed in Text Books and Other Pertinent Writings on Preaching, 1880–1955.* Diss. University of Pittsburgh, 1959.

LANDAU, GEORGE. *Victorian Types, Victorian Shadows.* Boston: Routledge and Kegan Paul, 1980.

LAUBACH, FRANK. *Wake Up or Blow Up.* New York: Revell, 1951.

LEVINE, LAWRENCE W. *Black Culture and Black Consciousness.* New York: Oxford University Press, 1977.

LEWIS, ANTHONY, et al. *Portrait of a Decade.* New York: Random, 1964.

LEWIS, DAVID. *King.* New York: Praeger, 1970.

LIEBMAN, JOSHUA. *Peace of Mind.* New York: Simon & Schuster, 1946.

LINCOLN, C. ERIC. Foreword, Mitchell, *Black Preaching.* New York: Lippincott, 1970.

————, ed. *Martin Luther King, Jr.: A Profile.* New York: Hill and Wang, 1984.

LOGAN, RAYFORD. *Howard University: The First Hundred Years.* New York: New York University Press, 1969.

LOMAX, LOUIS. *The Negro Revolt.* New York: Harper, 1962.

LOUTITT, H.I. "What Is Man?" Butler, *Best Sermons: 1949–1950.* 209–214.

LOVELL, JOHN. *Black Song.* New York: Macmillan, 1972.

LUCCOCK, HALFORD. *Christian Faith and Economic Change.* New York: Abingdon, 1936. BR115.S6 L75

———. *East Window.* New York: Abingdon, 1925.

———. *Haunted House.* New York: Abingdon, 1923.

———. *In the Minister's Workshop.* New York: Abingdon, 1944.

———. *Marching off the Map.* New York: Harper, 1952.

———. *Preaching Values in New Translations of the New Testament.* New York: Abingdon-Cokesbury, 1928.

———. "Sleeping Through a Revolution." *Marching off the Map,* 129–137.

LUNGER, HAROLD. *Finding Holy Ground.* St. Louis: Bethany, 1957.

LYELL, CHARLES. "A Negro Church in Savannah." *The Negro American: A Documentary History.* Ed. Leslie Fishel and Benjamin Quarles. Glenview, IL: Scott, 1967. 135–136.

MACCARTNEY, CLARENCE. *Facing Life and Getting the Best of It.* New York: Abingdon, 1940.

———. *MacCartney's Illustrations.* New York: Abingdon-Cokesbury, 1945.

MAKECHNIE, GEORGE. *Howard Thurman: His Enduring Dream.* Boston University Press, 1988.

MARTIN LUTHER KING, JR., Papers Project. "Martin Luther King, Jr.'s Student Papers." *Journal of American History.* Forthcoming.

MARTY, MARTIN. *Pilgrims in Their Own Land.* New York: Little, 1984.

MAYS, BENJAMIN. *Born to Rebel.* New York: Scribner's, 1971.

———. "Christian Youth and Race." *Crisis* 46 (1939): 364–365, 370. M-S C.

———. *The Christian in Race Relations: One of the Henry Wright Lectures Given at Yale University Divinity School.* West Haven, CT: Promoting Enduring Peace, n.d. [c. 1952]. BEM M-S.

———. "Eulogy for Mordecai Johnson." MJC M-S.

———. *Fifty Years of Progress in the Negro Church.* Pittsburgh: *Pittsburgh Courier* 1950: 4–5. BEM M-S.

———. "The Inescapable Christ." Butler, *Best Sermons: 1946 Edition.* 26–32.

———. *Lord, the People Have Driven Me On.* New York: Vantage, 1981.

———. *Seeking To Be Christian in Race Relations.* New York: Friendship, 1957.

———. "World Churchmen Score Prejudice." *Crisis* 44 (1937): 340–344.

MAYS, BENJAMIN, AND JOSEPH NICHOLSON. *The Negro's Church.* 1933. NY: Russell and Russell, 1969.

MCCRACKEN, ROBERT. "Discrimination—The Shame of Sunday Morning." *Pulpit* 26 (1955): 4–6.

———. *The Making of the Sermon.* New York: Harper, 1956.

———. "The Peril of Conformity." Butler, *Best Sermons: 1951–1952 Edition.* 19–25.

———. *Questions People Ask.* New York: Harper & Brothers, 1951.

———. "What Should Be the Christian Attitude Toward Communism." *Questions People Ask.* 163–172.

———. "What to Do with Our Fears?" *Questions People Ask.* 122–129.

MCGEE, MICHAEL. "Thematic Reduplication in Christian Rhetoric." *Quarterly Journal of Speech* 56 (1970): 196–204.

MCKINNEY, B. B. "Never Alone." *The Broadman Hymnal.* Nashville, TN: Broadman, 1940. N.p. Hymn No. 400.

MEIER, AUGUST. "Conservative Militant." Lincoln, *Martin Luther King, Jr.: A Profile.* 144–156.

MEIER, AUGUST, AND ELLIOT RUDWICK. *CORE.* New York: Oxford University Press, 1973.

MILLER, BASIL. "Our God Is Able." *American Pulpit Series.* Vol. 1. New York: Abingdon-Cokesbury, 1945. 37–49.

MILLER, KEITH D. "Composing Martin Luther King, Jr." *PMLA* 105 (1990): 70–82.

———. "Epistemology of a Drum Major: Martin Luther King, Jr. and the Black Folk Pulpit." *Rhetoric Society Quarterly* 18 (1988): 225–238.

———. "Influence of a Liberal Homiletic Tradition on *Strength to Love* by Martin Luther King, Jr." Diss. Texas Christian University, 1984.

———. "Martin Luther King, Jr. Borrows a Revolution." *College English* 48 (1986): 249–265.

———. "Voice Merging and Self-Making: The Epistemology of 'I Have a Dream.'" *Rhetoric Society Quarterly* 19 (1989): 23–32.

MILLER, ROBERT. *Harry Emerson Fosdick: Preacher, Pastor, Prophet.* New York: Oxford University Press, 1985.

MILLER, WILLIAM. *Martin Luther King, Jr.: His Life, Martyrdom, and Meaning for the World.* New York: Avon, 1969.

MITCHELL, HENRY. *Black Preaching.* New York: Lippincott, 1970.

———. *The Recovery of Preaching.* New York: Harper, 1977.

MOFFATT, JAMES, trans. *Holy Bible.* New York: Doran, 1922.

MOODY, ANNE. *Coming of Age in Mississippi.* 1968. New York: Dell, 1983.

MORRIS, ALDON. *The Origins of the Civil Rights Movement.* New York: Free Press, 1984.

MORRISON, C. C. "About Preachers and a Preacher." *Christian Century.* 76 (1959): 903–905.

MOTTER, ALTON. Foreword. *Sunday Evening Sermons.* 13–17.

——, ed. *Great Preaching Today.* New York: Harper, 1955.

——, ed. *Sunday Evening Sermons.* New York: Harper, 1952.

MUSTE, A.J. "Overcoming Fear." *Pulpit* 22 (1951): 14–16.

MYRDAL, GUNNAR. *An American Dilemma.* New York: Harper, 1944.

NELSON, WILLIAM STUART. *Bases of World Understanding.* Calcutta: Calcutta University Press, 1949. M-S C.

——, ed. *The Christian Way in Race Relations.* New York: Harper, 1948.

——. "Our Racial Situation in Light of the Judeo-Christian Tradition." *Religious Education* (March-April 1944): 74–77. M-S C.

——. "Satyagraha: Gandhian Principles of Non-Violent Non-Cooperation." *Journal of Religious Thought* (Autumn-Winter 1957–58): 15–24.

New York Journal American. 31 Aug. 1940. MJC M-S.

NEWTON, JOSEPH FORT, ed. *Best Sermons: 1924.* New York: Harcourt, 1924.

——, ed. *Best Sermons: 1926.* New York: Harcourt, 1926.

NIEBUHR, REINHOLD. *Beyond Tragedy.* London: Nisbet, 1938.

——. *Children of Light and Children of Darkness.* New York: 1944.

——. *Discerning the Signs of the Times.* New York: Scribner's, 1946.

——. *The Essential Reinhold Niebuhr: Selected Essays and Addresses.* Ed. Robert McAfee Brown. New Haven, CT: Yale University Press, 1986.

——. *Irony of American History.* New York: Scribner's, 1952.

——. *Moral Man and Immoral Society.* New York: Scribner's, 1932.

——. *The Nature and Destiny of Man: A Christian Interpretation: Volume I. Human Nature.* 1941. New York: Scribner's, 1964.

——. "Why the Christian Church Is Not Pacifist." 1940. *The Essential Reinhold Niebuhr.* 102–119.

NILES, D. T. "Summons at Midnight." *Christian Century* 71 (1954): 1037–1039. Rpt. in *The Preacher's Calling To Be Servant.* New York: Harper, 1959. 127–139.

NORRELL, ROBERT. *Reaping the Whirlwind.* New York: Vintage, 1985.

NYGREN, ANDERS. *Agape and Eros.* Trans. Philip Watson. Philadelphia: Westminster, 1953.

OATES, STEPHEN. *Let the Trumpet Sound: The Life of Martin Luther King, Jr.* New York: Harper & Row, 1982.

ONG, WALTER. *Interfaces of the Word.* Ithaca, NY: Cornell University Press, 1977.

——. *Orality and Literacy.* New York: Methuen, 1982.

O'REILLY, KENNETH. *"Racial Matters".* New York: Free Press, 1989.

PALMER, BEN. "De Progicul Son." *Quickened by De Spurit: Ten Negro Sermons.* Ed. John Henry Falk. Master's thesis. University of Texas, 1940. AFC LC.

PEABODY, STEPHEN. "Managing Our Fears and Anxieties" *Pulpit* 23 (1952): 1–14.

PERELMAN, CHAIM AND LUCIE OLBRECHTS-TYTECA. *The New Rhetoric: A Treatise on Argumentation.* Notre Dame, IN: Notre Dame Press, 1969.

PHILIPS, HAROLD. "An Angel in the Sun." *American Pulpit Series* Vol. 1. New York: Abingdon-Cokesbury, 1945. 9–24.

PIKE, JAMES. "Where Do We Go from Here?" *Pulpit Digest* 30 (1950): 31–37.

PIKE, JAMES. "Fear." *Beyond Anxiety.* New York: Scribner's, 1953. 9–19.

PIPES, WILLIAM. *Say Amen Brother! Old Time Negro Preaching.* Westport, CT: Negro Universities Press, 1951.

POPE, LISTON. *The Kingdom Beyond Caste.* New York: Friendship 1957.

"President's Annual Address [to the National Baptist Convention of 1898]." *Sermons, Addresses and Reminiscences and Important Correspondence.* Ed. E.C. Morris. Nashville: National Baptist Publishing Board, 1901. 78–87.

"Protestantism on Justice and Integration." *Christian Century* 75 (1958): 164–166.

RABOTEAU, ALBERT. *Slave Religion.* New York: Oxford University Press, 1978.

RAINES, HOWELL, ed. *My Soul Is Rested.* New York: Putnam, 1977.

RAMSEY, PAUL. *Basic Christian Ethics.* New York: Scribner's, 1950.

RAUSCHENBUSCH, WALTER. *Christianity and the Social Crisis.* New York: Macmillan, 1907.

———. *Christianizing the Social Order.* New York: Macmillan, 1912.

———. *A Rauschenbusch Reader.* Ed. Benson Landis. New York: Harper, 1957.

REAGON, BERNICE. *Voices of the Civil Rights Movement.* Booklet with recording. Washington, DC: Smithsonian, 1980.

———. "Songs of the Civil Rights Movement: 1955–1965." Diss. Howard University, 1975.

REDDICK, DAVID. *The Parables He Told.* Westwood, NJ: Revell, 1962.

REDDICK, L.D. *Crusader Without Violence.* New York: Harper, 1959.

RICHARDSON, HARRY. "What Can the Church Do?" Nelson, *Christian Way.* 111–127.

ROBINSON, JO ANN. *The Montgomery Bus Boycott and the Women Who Started It.* Ed. David Garrow. Knoxville: University of Tennessee Press, 1987.

ROBINSON, PAUL. "I Have a Glory." Butler, *Best Sermons: 1946.* 179–185.

ROSENBERG, BRUCE. *The Art of the American Folk Preacher.* New York: Oxford University Press, 1970.

———. *Can These Bones Live? The Art of the American Folk Preacher.* Urbana: University of Illinois Press, 1988.

RUOPP, HAROLD. "You Can Master Fear." *Pulpit* 19 (1948): 11–12.

RUSTIN, BAYARD. "The Watts 'Manifesto' and the McCone Report." *Commentary*

(March 1966). Rpt. in Rustin, *Down the Line.* Chicago: Quadrangle, 1971. 140–153.

SANGSTER, WILLIAM. *Craft of Sermon Construction.* Philadelphia: Westminster, 1951.

———. *He Is Able.* Nashville: Cokesbury, 1937.

———. "When Fears Transcend." *He Is Able.* 30–40.

SCHERER, PAUL. *Facts That Undergird Life.* New York: Harper, 1938.

SHEEN, FULTON. "Fears and Anxieties." *Life Is Worth Living.* New York: McGraw-Hill, 1953. 117–125.

SILVER, THEODORE. "Rev. M.L. King: Alabama Moses." *American Negro* 1 (1956): 13–17. KC BU.

SITKOFF, HARVARD. *The Struggle for Black Equality.* New York: Hill and Wang, 1981.

SITTLER, JOSEPH. "George Buttrick: A Tribute and a Reflection." *Christian Century* 16 (April 1980): 429–30.

SMITH, DONALD. "Martin Luther King, Jr.: Rhetorician of Revolt." Diss. University of Wisconsin, 1964.

SMITH, KELLY MILLER. *Social Crisis Preaching.* Macon, GA: Mercer University Press, 1984.

SMITH, KENNETH, AND IRA ZEPP. *Search for the Beloved Community.* Valley Forge: Judson, 1974.

SMYLIE, JAMES. "On Jesus, Pharaohs, and the Chosen People." *Interpretation* 24 (Jan. 1970): 74–91.

SNOW, MALINDA. "Martin Luther King's 'Letter from Birmingham Jail' as Pauline Epistle." *Quarterly Journal of Speech* 71 (1985): 318–334.

SOCKMAN, RALPH. *Date with Destiny.* New York: Abingdon-Cokesbury, 1944.

———. "Fears May Be Liars," *Now to Live!* 104–111.

———. *Highway of God.* New York: Macmillan, 1942.

———. *Live for Tomorrow.* New York: Macmillan, 1939.

———. *Man's First Love: The Great Commandment.* Garden City, NY: Doubleday, 1958.

———. *Now to Live!* New York: Abingdon-Cokesbury, 1946.

———. "Our Ultimate Rulers." Butler, *Best Sermons: Vol. 8 1962.* 211–219.

———. *The Paradoxes of Jesus.* New York: Abingdon, 1936.

———. "The Salt of the Earth." Newton, *Best Sermons: 1924,* 65–80.

———. *The Unemployed Carpenter.* New York: Harper, 1933.

SOPER, EDMUND. "The Negro in American Life." *Race: A World Issue.* New York: Abingdon-Cokesbury, 1947. 220–246.

SPILLERS, HORTENSE. "Martin Luther King and the Style of the Black Sermon." *The Black Scholar* 3 (1971): 14–27.

STAMM, FREDERICK. "Getting Things into Their True Perspective," *Pulpit Digest* 54.190 (1954): 55–60.

STEWART, JAMES. *A Faith to Proclaim.* New York: Scribner's, 1953.

------. *Heralds of God.* New York: Scribner's, 1946.

------. *Preaching.* London: Hodder, 1955.

------. *The Strong Name.* New York: Scribner's, 1941.

"Still the Trumpet Sounds." *Parish Visitor* 9 (June 1970): 1. Author's files.

STONE, RONALD. *Paul Tillich's Radical Social Thought.* Atlanta: John Knox Press, 1980.

STROUP, R.C. "The Two Tentmakers." Butler, *Best Sermons: 1951–1952.* 52–57.

STROUT, CUSHING. *The New Heavens and New Earth.* New York: Harper, 1974.

STUCKEY, STERLING. *Slave Culture.* New York: Oxford University Press, 1987.

SWEAZEY, GEORGE. *Preaching the Good News.* Englewood Cliffs, NJ: Prentice-Hall, 1976.

TAYLOR, GARDNER. "Some Comments on Race Hate." *The Pulpit Speaks on Race.* Ed. Alfred Davies. New York: Abingdon, 1965. 184–191.

------. "They Shall Ask the Way." *Pulpit* 23 (1952): 15–16.

THOMSON, J.A. *What Is Man?* New York: Putnam's, 1924.

THURMAN, HOWARD. *Deep River.* New York: Harper, 1955.

------. *Disciplines of the Spirit.* New York: Harper, 1963.

------. *The Inward Journey.* New York: Harper, 1961.

------. *Jesus and the Disinherited.* 1949. Richmond, IN: Friends United Press, 1981.

------. *The Luminous Darkness.* New York: Harper, 1965.

------. *Meditations of the Heart.* New York: Harper, 1953.

------. *With Head and Heart.* New York: Harcourt, 1979.

TILLICH, PAUL. *The Courage To Be.* 1952. New York: Yale University Press, 1971.

------. *The Eternal Now.* New York: Scribner's, 1963.

------. *The Shaking of the Foundations.* New York: Scribner's, 1948.

------. *Systematic Theology.* Vol. 1. Chicago: University of Chicago Press, 1951.

TINDLEY, CHARLES ALBERT. *A Book of Sermons.* Philadelphia: Duncan, 1932.

TITTLE, E.F. *A Mighty Fortress.* New York: Harper, 1949.

------. "Overcoming Fear." *Jesus after Nineteen Centuries.* New York: Abingdon, 1932. 147–169.

------. *The Religion of the Spirit.* New York: Abingdon, 1928.

------. "What Is Man?" *Religion of the Spirit,* 153–167.

------. *What Must the Church Do to Be Saved? And Other Discussions.* New York: Abingdon, 1921.

------. *A World That Cannot Be Shaken.* New York: Harper, 1933.

TRUETT, GEORGE W. "The Conquest of Fear." *"Follow Thou Me."* New York: Long and Smith, 1932. 103–115.

------. *The Prophet's Mantle.* Grand Rapids, MI: Eerdman's, 1948.

TUTU, DESMOND. *Hope and Suffering.* Grand Rapids, MI: Eerdman's, 1985.

Voices of the Civil Rights Movement. Smithsonian Collection, Smithsonian Institution R023, 1980.

WALKER, ALAN. "A Christian under Communism." *Pulpit* 31 (July 1960), 14–16.

WALKER, DAVID. *One Continual Cry: David Walker's Appeal to the Colored Citizens of the World.* New York: Humanities Press, 1965.

WALKER, WYATT. *Somebody's Calling My Name.* Valley Forge: Judson, 1979.

WALLIS, CHARLES. *A Treasury of Sermon Illustrations.* New York: Abingdon-Cokesbury, 1950.

WARREN, MERVYN. "A Rhetorical Study of the Preaching of Doctor Martin Luther King, Jr., Pastor and Pulpit Orator." Diss. Michigan State University, 1966.

WATLEY, WILLIAM. *Roots of Resistance: The Nonviolent Ethic of Martin Luther King, Jr.* Valley Forge: Judson, 1985.

WEATHERHEAD, LESLIE D. "Can A Christian Be A Communist?" *When the Lamp Flickers.* New York: Abingdon-Cokesbury, 1948. 96–103.

———. *In Quest of a Kingdom.* New York: Abingdon, 1944.

———. *Key Next Door.* New York: Abingdon, 1959.

———. *Prescription for Anxiety: How You Can Overcome Fear and Despair.* New York: Abingdon, 1956.

———. *That Immortal Sea.* New York: Abingdon, 1953.

———. *Thinking Aloud in War-Time.* New York: Abingdon-Cokesbury, 1940.

———. *Why Do Men Suffer?* New York: Abingdon-Cokesbury, 1936.

WEBBER, GEORGE. *God's Colony in Man's World.* New York: Abingdon, 1960.

WESLEY, JOHN. "What Is Man?" *The Works of John Wesley: Sermons III 71–114.* Vol. 3. Ed. Albert Outler. Nashville: Abingdon, 1986. 454–463.

———. "What Is Man?" *The Works of John Wesley: Sermons IV: 115–151.* Vol. 4. Ed. Albert Outler. Nashville: Abingdon, 1987. 19–27.

WHITE, NEWMAN. *American Negro Folk Songs.* Cambridge: Harvard University Press, 1928.

WILDER, AMOS. *Early Christian Rhetoric.* Cambridge: Harvard University Press, 1971.

WILKINS, ROY (WITH TOM MATHEWS). *Standing Fast: The Autobiography of Roy Wilkins.* New York: Viking, 1982.

WILLS, GARRY. *The Kennedy Imprisonment.* Boston: Little, Brown, 1981.

WILMORE, GAYRAUD. *Black Religion and Black Radicalism.* Garden City, NJ: Doubleday, 1972.

WOFFORD, HARRIS. *Of Kennedys and Kings.* New York: Farrar, 1980.

———. "The Law and Civil Disobedience." 20 Nov. 1959. KC BU.

———. "Non-Violence and the Law: The Law Needs Help." *Journal of Religious Thought* 15 (Autumn-Winter 1957–1958): 25–36. Rpt. in *Civil Disobedience: Theory and Practice.* Ed. Hugo Bedau. New York: Pegasus, 1969. 59–71.

WOLFF, RICHARD. "Mastering Our Fears." *Pulpit* 21 (1950): 271–272.

YOUNG, ANDREW. Introduction. King, Sr., *Daddy King*. 9–10.

YOUNG, HENRY J. *Major Black Religious Leaders: 1755–1940*. Nashville: Abingdon, 1977.

ZEPP, IRA. "The Intellectual Sources of Ethical Thought of Martin Luther King, Jr." Diss. St. Mary's University, 1971.

INDEX